Marcus Mosiah Garvey

=====================================

The Father of Black Lives Matter

A Contemporary Perspective on His Life & Legacy

Paul W. Ivey, PhD

Marcus Mosiah Garvey
The Father of Black Lives Matter
A Contemporary Perspective on His Life & Legacy

****~#~****

Other Books by Paul W. Ivey

================================

JAMAICA: Paradise and Paradox, Volume 1
(Published August 2018)

JAMAICA: Paradise and Paradox, Volume 2
(Published April 2021)

JAMAICA: Paradise and Paradox, Volume 3
(Published July 2022)

It All Began With The May Rains: An Introvert's Remarkable
Journey
(His autobiography, Published August 2015)

My Daughter and Me: Parenting a Polymath
(Published 2016)

Silent River
(Published August 2017)

The Matriarch
(Published January 2018)

The Golden Boy
(Published December 2016)

Toxic Masculinity: Disordered Models of Manhood in Jamaica
(Published February 2020)

My Life Has Gone To the Dogs
(Published July 2018)

Active Citizenship: Overcoming Political Apathy in Jamaica
(Published February 2020)

Marcus Mosiah Garvey

Fostering a Culture of Lawfulness: Fixing Jamaica's Normalised Abnormalities
(Published May 2021)

Jamaica: Likkle But Tallawah, Cultural Superpowers & Other Successes
(Published November 2021)

'The Case for Reparations for Chattel Slavery: An Overdue Debt for The Worst Crime in The History of The World.'
(Published May 2022)

****

"I do not speak carelessly or recklessly but with a definite object of helping the people, especially those of my race, to know, to understand, and to realize themselves." ~ Marcus Garvey, Halifax, Nova Scotia, 1937

*****

Marcus Garvey was unique in that he "sold the idea of the Black man to himself with the same zeal and enthusiasm that white Americans, Englishmen, and Frenchmen used preserving their racial identities." ~ S. A. Haynes

*****

   Although Garvey failed to realize all his objectives, his movement still represents liberation of Black People from the psychological bondage of racial inferiority.

*****

The more I read about Marcus Garvey, the more I admire his audacity in attacking racism and subjugation of Black People head-on at a time in history when they were the norm. He is truly a remarkable man!

******

"The only way to deal with an unfree world is to become so absolutely free that your very existence is an act of rebellion." ~ Albert Camus.

Contents

Other Books by Paul W. Ivey 3

Prologue: Father of Black Lives Matter 10

Putting Garvey in Context...22

    Garvey's Early Life..23

    National Hero & World-Class Philosopher.....................................24

    Who was Marcus Garvey? 31

    Chattel Slavery's Afterlife & Psychic Wounds...............................32

    Chattel Slavery & Europeans' Barbarity..33

    Colonialism: A Cannibalistic, Murderous Beast 39

    Emancipation & Concepts of Freedom 44

    Precarious Freedom..48

    Perverse Compensation to Enslavers 49

    Jamaica: Britain's Most Valuable Colony 54

    Reparations: An Overdue Debt...55

    Injustice in Post-Emancipation Jamaica..63

    Garvey's Arrival on the Scene..66

    Garvey: Stirred into Action! 71

Garvey's Vision & Mission 75

    Black Liberation & Empowerment...75

    Pan-Africanism & the UNIA 77

    UNIA's Declaration of Rights...79

    UNIA: Largest Mass Movement of Blacks.....................................90

    The 'Boule' & NAACP vs. The UNIA...93

Garvey The Psychologist...107

    Psychological Reprogramming 107

    Emancipation from Mental Slavery 108

    Consciousness-raising...111

    Trauma-informed Therapy 115

    Garvey: Profile in Courage 120

    Tough Love 122

Garvey: Intellectual & Adult Educator 129

The Responsibility of Intellectuals 129

Never Stop Learning 129

Andragogy 142

Oratory 144

ExL: A Pillar for Self-Reliance 145

Weaponisation of Psychology 148

Garvey The Social Engineer 150

Land Reform 150

History Matters 151

Globalization 159

The PJPCACA 160

The Africa & Caribbean Summit 163

Development Financing 171

'Crowd-Sourcing' of Financing 171

Garvey The Newspaperman 174

The Power of Media 174

Role of the Free Press 175

Garvey The Politician 177

Garvey's People's Political Party (PPP) 177

The PPP's Manifesto 177

Garvey: KSAC Councillor 178

Jamaica Imprisoned Garvey 178

Garvey The Entrepreneur 181

The Black Star Line 181

Other Businesses 181

Banishing the Psychology of Dependence 182

Garvey and God 185

Teaching Garveyism 253

Marcus Garvey Technical High School 267

Marcus Garvey's Courage 276

Marcus Garvey's Travails 281

    The 'Empire Strikes Back' 281

    'Marked' & Imprisoned 294

    Betrayed 295

    'Garvey Must Go!' 297

    Marcus Garvey's Letter from Prison 304

    Should Garvey Be Exonerated? 307

    Other Notable Black Martyrs 325

    Garvey and the KKK 355

Marcus Garvey's Two Wives 360

    Amy Ashwood Garvey 360

    Amy Jacques Garvey 361

'Interviewing' Garvey 371

Marcus Garvey's Death 380

Marcus Garvey's Enduring Relevance 382

    Persistent Hunger for Positivity 409

    Garvey Public Sector Graduate Scholarship 412

    Potent Cognitive Gems from Marcus Garvey 414

About the Author 428

Selected Bibliography 435

Prologue: Father of Black Lives Matter
===============####=============

I will begin by setting the record straight. African American Alicia Garza coined the phrase 'Black Lives Matter' in July 2013, after the acquittal of the racist George Zimmerman of murder in the shooting death of teenager Trayvon Martin, but the incontrovertible truth is that Marcus Mosiah Garvey (1887-1940), Jamaica's first national hero, launched the first international 'Black Lives Matter' Movement (BLMM) in history! He is the father of the Black Lives Matter Movement.

According to Jelani Cobb of The New Yorker, "The phrase 'Black Lives Matter' was born in July of 2013 in a Facebook post by Alicia Garza called "a love letter to black people." The post was intended as an affirmation for a community distraught over George Zimmerman's acquittal in the shooting death of (Black) seventeen-year-old Trayvon Martin, in Sanford, Florida" [Source: Jelani Cobb, The Matter of Black Lives, The New Yorker, March 7, 2016].

I am positing that Marcus Mosiah Garvey is the undisputed father of the Black Lives Matter Movement notwithstanding what is stated above by Jelani Cobb!

Marcus Garvey is the father of Black Nationalism and Pan Africanism.

He was one of the most renowned revolutionary minds and activists of the 20th century.

Surveying the state of Black People, Garvey asked the following piercing questions:

"Where is the Black man's government?"

"Where are his King and his kingdom?"

"Where is his President, his ambassador, his country, his men of big affairs?"

Garvey said "I could not find them. And then I declared, I will help to make them.'"

And Garvey resolved and dedicated his life to changing the condition of his race!

And he declared: "If you believe that the Negro has a soul, if you believe that the Negro is a man, if you believe the Negro was endowed with the senses commonly given to other men by the Creator, then you must acknowledge that what other men have done, Negroes can do. We want to build up cities, nations, governments, industries of our own in Africa, so that we will be able to have a chance to rise from the lowest to the highest position in the African Commonwealth." [Source: The Marcus Garvey and the UNIA Papers Project at the University of California, Los Angeles. Recording courtesy of Michigan State University, G. Robert Vincent Voice Library]

The establishment by Marcus Mosiah Garvey of the Universal Negro Improvement Association (UNIA) and the African Community League (ACL) in 1914, in Jamaica, was a critical vehicle for achieving his mission.

Marcus Garvey has earned international acclaim and adulation as a world-class philosopher and symbol of self-empowerment for formerly enslaved persons of African descent and Africans everywhere in the Diaspora. He grasped that all African-descended people were united by melanin.

He has also been subjected to opprobrium, vilification, scorn, and imprisonment.

I was 'called' to write this book after participating in several social media debates with friends who said things like:

- "Garvey was a segregationist wanting Blacks by themselves and whites by themselves. The country rejected that and embraced the Martin Luther King, Jr's approach of racial equality and racial integration. That's how we end up with our motto "Out of many, one people.""

- "Garvey was totally against mixed race as he pushed his pure "African breed" and so did not allow people like Barack Obama to become officers of his United Negro Improvement Association (UNIA). Most of Jamaica today is of mixed race. Will you (in reference to yours truly) be brave enough to say that? The problem is if you were to write that, then he would not appear to be such a visionary after all."

- "Garvey's central theme was Africa for Africans. Very few if any Jamaicans today bought into that philosophy. Young Jamaicans have selected to live all over the world, but not Africa."

- "There is also a lot about Garvey that is not widely known which opens the need for the publication of those. Let me see if you (in reference to me) are bold enough to do that critical analysis of Garvey and his relevance today."

- "What did Marcus Garvey do for him to be honoured as a national hero? That being the case, Bob Marley should have been made a national hero, the very day he died... He contributed 100 times more to the upliftment of Jamaica and the Jamaican people than Garvey could have ever done."

- "When you look at it carefully, Marcus Garvey's teachings made no sense for Jamaicans because no one followed them. We see young people taking loans to purchase expensive motor vehicles while living in rented houses. Could it be that we all need a course in Marcus Garvey's philosophies or a course in personal finance?"

I've observed that Garvey's detractors have one thing in common – they highlight his mistakes and missteps while his monumental achievements are minimized, given short shrift, or ignored. Garvey's detractors are blissfully ignorant, willfully obtuse, or blatantly intellectually dishonest. They will condemn no matter what.

On the other hand, supporters of Garvey ('Garveyites') also have one thing in common – they exhibit a near-universal propensity to be blinded to Garvey's mistakes and missteps, seeing only his monumental achievements in their hagiographic adulation of his life, legacy, and relevance. Garveyites are either engaged in one-dimensional romanticism or blatantly intellectually dishonest. They will defend Garvey no matter what.

From the above perspectives, one sees that Garvey and his philosophy of Garveyism exist on a continuum between ridicule and reverence.

Judged objectively, then, which one of the aforementioned personas and perspectives is the definitive Marcus Garvey? Has the passage of time allowed for a dispassionate and critical contemporary analysis of his life, legacy, impact, and relevance? Undertaking this analysis is the task I've set myself in writing this book.

Another one of my friends threw down the gauntlet when he said to me: "Make the findings and perspective worthwhile, to answer the real questions which bring doubt when his name comes up, and to establish beyond a shadow of a doubt what his influence means and his authenticity. If I had your time, interest, or skills, I would call the book: Garvey, National Hero or National Clown?"

This must be said: many Blacks seem to want perfect heroes, not realizing that other races simply "rally around their chosen champions".

Take Donald Trump, for example; his supporters don't care one bit whether he grabs women by their genitals or not. According to James Poniewozik in his book **'Audience of One: Donald Trump, Television, and the Fracturing of America,'** "While Trump is manifestly incapable of governing, he always knows how to entertain: He drums up conflict, foments chaos, barks insults, and concocts boogeymen. Trump learned that you can keep the audience on the side of the antihero by convincing them that his enemies were even worse, becoming a master of gambits that seem idiotic and even self-destructive but that work."

"What I struggle with understanding," laments an American Historian, "is how Trump, who is so self-evidently incompetent, morally repulsive, and biased in favor of the rich, holds onto his support among white-working and religious voters who attend his rallies and cheer hysterically for their hero."

In an article in Slate Magazine on July 9, 2021, titled **'Haters Gonna Hate and Vote'** Jason Johnson noted that "Donald Trump's path to the White House bewildered much of the political establishment. He was unqualified, dishonest, and nasty, running to lead a party that had prided itself on so-called traditional family values. Through the lens of the pre-Trump era, the venom he spewed about immigrants, Black folks, and women should have sunk his candidacy dozens of times. But it never did. And slowly it dawned on many observers that Trump didn't succeed despite his viciousness, but because of it."

Trump's 'genius,' notes Jason Johnson, "is his ability to get an audience full of white people of all classes and levels to see themselves as victims, and to convince them that their cruelty was so essential to preventing them from being victims when most of them have never experienced victimhood in their lives!"

Trump's supporters have found their champion, whom George F. Will, the Pulitzer Prize-winning Washington Post newspaper Columnist, described as a "sad, embarrassing wreck of a man, running a 'gangster regime'".

I've often wondered how America could have elected a man like Donald Trump to be its President. But America has been here before with a scoundrel as President.

History helps us to understand the present. The seeds of the present are sown in the garden of the past.

Here is an excerpt about Andrew Jackson, 7th US President, from 1829 to 1837: "In a conversation with Daniel Webster in 1824, Thomas Jefferson described [Andrew] Jackson as "one of the most unfit men I know of" to become president of the United States, "a dangerous man" who cannot speak in a civilized manner because he "choke[s] with rage," a man whose "passions are terrible." Jefferson feared that the slightest insult from a foreign leader could impel Jackson to declare war. Even Jackson's friends and admiring colleagues feared his volcanic temper. Jackson fought at least 14 duels in his life, leaving him with bullet fragments lodged throughout his body. On the last day of his presidency, he admitted to only two regrets: that he was never able to shoot Henry Clay or hang John C. Calhoun." [Source: Dan P. McAdams, The Atlantic, June 2016]

Other individuals have labelled Trump a "reckless buffoon"; a "racist moron"; and a "bizarre cosmic joke", who is "fundamentally unfit (intellectually, morally, temperamentally, and psychologically) for the office of President."

The writer Paul Auster described the election of Donald Trump as "the most appalling thing I've seen in politics in my life."

And former CIA Director John Brennan described Trump (who made the negation of Obama's legacy the foundation of his own, and with his cabal of conspiracy theorists forced Barack Obama to present his birth certificate to prove he was born in the USA and thus eligible to hold the office of President) in these terms: "When the full extent of your venality, moral turpitude, and political corruption becomes known, you will take your rightful place as a disgraced demagogue in the dustbin of history."

And when Michelle Obama spoke on August 17, 2020, at the Democratic Party National Convention, she was blunt: "Whenever we look to this White House for some leadership or consolation or any semblance of steadiness, what we get instead is chaos, division, and a total and utter lack of empathy. Let me be as honest and clear as I can. Donald Trump is the wrong president for our country. He has had more than enough time to prove that he can do the job, but he is clearly in over his head. He cannot meet this moment. He simply cannot be who we need him to be for us. It is what it is. If you take one thing from my words tonight, it is this: if you think things cannot possibly get worse, trust me, they can; and they will if we don't make a change in this election. If we have any hope of ending this chaos, we have got to vote for Joe Biden like our lives depend on it."

Even the magazine Christianity Today, founded by the late Rev. Billy Graham and revered by white evangelicals, its editor, on December 20, 2019, called for President Trump's removal from office and denounced him as "a near-perfect example of a human being who is morally lost and confused."

And when Donald Trump lost the November 3, 2020, presidential election to Joe Biden, the Economist Magazine described his loss as the "end of the embarrassment."

And when the graceless, twice impeached Trump left Washington DC on the morning of January 20, 2021, without attending the inauguration of Joe Biden, it was the end of an error.

Trump is jarring intrusion. His very presence destabilizes the existing political, economic, and social order.

But Trump's supporters have found their champion! And they are sticking to him despite his defilement of the highest office in America and taking a wrecking ball to that country's democratic ideals and institutions! The number of American voting for Trump in the 2020 presidential election was 74,216,154 - more than 10,000,000 than in 2016!

Black people can learn a lot from the modus operandus of Donald Trump's supporters – they are all in despite his "venality, moral turpitude, and political corruption" and whose Presidency, according to the New Yorker's Susan B. Glasser and Peter Baker, was "characterized by a fantastical degree of instability: fits of rage, late-night Twitter storms, abrupt dismissals" (or staff not showing fealty or obsequiousness to him).

But no, Black people choose instead to vilify leaders from Marcus Garvey to Martin Luther King Jr., to Robert Mugabe, to Malcolm X, and Louis Farrakhan for their human failings – real or fabricated - without a nuanced appreciation of the larger context of their activism and achievements.

While acknowledging that he was human and was by no means perfect, I must make clear here and now that I have no apology – none whatsoever - for my intellectual admiration of Marcus Garvey and his philosophy and opinions, and activism.

Whatever may be said about Marcus Garvey, it cannot be denied that his influence was impactful and history-shaping. He was sui generis (Sui generis is a Latin phrase that means "of its/his/her/their own kind", "in a class by itself", therefore "unique").

Fate is a remarkable thing. About two weeks before I decided to write this book, I was in a meeting with, and introduced to, Dr. Julius Garvey, son of Marcus Mosiah Garvey!

Another remarkable twist of fate is that I'm writing this book on Marcus Garvey, one of my former students is the Principal at the Marcus Garvey Technical High School in St. Ann, Jamaica.

I will say a few things now about my writing.

I employ the deep intellectual work of the scholarship of integration, which is the scholarly method that involves acquiring, selecting, distilling, melding, synthesizing, transmuting, connecting, and contextualizing existing ideas and information to create new and better vistas of understandings for readers. In employing the scholarship of integration, I found it necessary and valuable to take a panoramic (i.e., a 'big-picture') and gestalt view of my writing project and intended end-product; this wide aperture approach invariably resulted in necessary digressions, detours, and meaningful and relevant meanderings.

My writing is Black.

I write my mind. I write with brio. Therefore, in terms of cadence, tone, and resonance, I do not write apologetically. There's no badinage in my writing. My writing is brave, brazen, and bracing. My writing is lacerating, stinging, and fierce. My writing is forthright. My writing is impassioned. My writing is militant. My writing is radical. My writing is unrepentant. My writing is bristly. And urgent. I do not use ambiguity as a shield. Portions of my writing amount to fighting (i.e., cognitive combat) - I'm in full-on attack mode fiercely wielding my mind as a weapon! My writing is critical truth-telling! My writing is literary drum-banging and Abeng-blowing! My writing is an act of resistance that aims to subvert the status quo that supports anti-Blackness. My writing is literary flame-throwing to incinerate and lay waste to embedded oppressive structures and systems. W. E. B. Du Bois' in his 1925 essay 'Criteria of Negro Art' asserted that the Black artist must always write with the liberation of Black people in mind.

I take personal umbrage to historical and extant anti-Black-ness/anti-Melanin-ness and I've joined forces with the intellectual resistance in writing to oppose and counter it. I am pro-Melaninness! I am a Melaninaire!

I felt called to write. I care zero about being regarded as a polemic rhetor when I am writing truth! Those who are discomfited by my writing, so be it ... too bad for them. I refuse to join in the conspiracy of sepulchral silence; or in futile sophistry; or paralysing fear. An advocate and cerebral warrior cannot be seduced by moderation and political correctness; doing so means capitulating to the oppressor!

What is more, in the application of my mind as a tool in writing this book, I courageously embraced my academic freedom and constitutional right to freedom of expression (as antidotes against any possible viewpoint discrimination) and wrote from my cognitive positionality, perspective, lens, register, and frame as a cis Black African-Jamaican Academician and Griot (socio-cultural historian, observer, and commentator).

Right up front let me state that, while others may find this book informative and enlightening, my primary audience is my people – **my fellow Jamaicans and other Africa-descended people, who are universally united by melanin wherever they are domiciled.**

****

Putting Garvey in Context
=============####=============

There is Garvey the man, and there is the philosophy that he articulated and the movement that was scaffolded upon it. Garvey the man died on June 10, 1940. But Garveyism – his philosophy and the conjoined movement that the founded - lives on!

Nothing that exists may be properly understood divorced from its context, for it is a context that confers meaning to the things we think about and act on. Just as how 'setting' is important in writing a great novel, 'context' is important in understanding people, places, and events.

(Context: [Noun] - According to Wikipedia, context is "a frame that surrounds an event and provides resources for its appropriate interpretation." In simpler terms, context means "the circumstances that form the setting for an event, statement, or idea, and in terms of which it can be fully understood.")

Garvey and his significance are often misunderstood by people who delink him from the context in which he arose and launched his mission of empowerment of African people in Africa and the diaspora. This is a huge mistake that invariably leads to inaccurate conclusions about him.

Therefore, I will use context-informed and context-sensitive historical analysis, complemented by critical theory, in this contemporary evaluation of the life, legacy, and relevance of Marcus Mosiah Garvey, a remarkable man who was a champion for Black people.

Garvey's Early Life

Marcus Mosiah Garvey was born on August 17, 1887, in St. Ann's Bay, Jamaica, to Sarah Jane Richards and Marcus Garvey, Snr, 53 years after the abolition of chattel slavery in Jamaica.

Lewis, 2018, tells us that "Marcus Garvey, Snr. was an avid reader and collector of books, which he kept in an outhouse to which he would frequently retreat. He was influential in his community and used to select articles in the newspapers for public reading to make listeners aware of the significance of political occurrences ... a love for reading was a habit that was passed from father to son, who later was reputed to have had a large collection of books in his New York and Kingston homes in the 1920s and 1930s. Garvey testified that from his father's books he gathered inspiration and "what inspiration I gathered, changed my outlook from the ambition of wanting to be a wharf-man or a cow-boy, and made me look forward to being a personality in the world." Here we see how a parent's habit can profoundly influence a child's perspective and outlook on life.

(In my case, I regard as one of my greatest achievements deliberately raising my daughter in a cultural and psycho-cognitive space that led to her being comfortable in her skin - accepting and embracing her beautiful Blackness with palpable pride, as a born melaninaire! I also deliberately engaged in myth-free parenting of my daughter, to spare her mind from being polluted with cognitive garbage and detritus. She was mainly home-schooled. I had my own curriculum, so to speak. The formal education system was just a kind of complementary 'add-on.' I'm entreating all Black parents to do likewise because doing so is to engage in responsible Black parenting! Blackology!)

Lewis, 2018, continued: Marcus Garvey "Left elementary school at age fourteen. But already he was interested in world affairs; his boyhood friend from St. Ann's Bay, Isaac Rose, reported, "All the time when I meet him he wear a jacket and every time, his two jacket pockets full of paper, reading and telling us things that happen all over the world ... public speaking was one of Garvey's strengths, and he used every available opportunity he had to hone his talent. In 1910, he competed in a national elocution contest as the representative of St. Ann. It is therefore not surprising that elocution, contests, debates, recitations, and dramatic performances would later become an important part of the cultural productions of the Garvey movement."

National Hero & World-Class Philosopher

Marcus Mosiah Garvey was named Jamaica's first national hero in 1969, in keeping with the second schedule of the National Honours and Awards Act. According to the Jamaica Information Service (JIS), concerning National Honours, "The Order of National Hero is the most senior order. The honour of the Order of National Hero may be conferred upon any person who was born in Jamaica or is, or at the time of his or her death was, a citizen of Jamaica and rendered to Jamaica service of a most distinguished nature. A member of the

Order is entitled to be styled "The Rt. Excellent" and the motto of the Order is "He built a city which hath foundations."

Garvey has earned international acclaim as a world-class philosopher and symbol of self-empowerment for formerly enslaved persons of African descent, as well as Africans everywhere in the Diaspora.

"Molefi Kete Asante, professor and chair of the Africology and African American studies department at Temple University in Philadelphia, describes Marcus Garvey as probably "The most significant African political genius that has ever lived. "He infused the idea of Black self-sufficiency in all of the societies and communities in the Black world —the idea of 'you can organize and create institutions that fight for your own liberation,'" Asante says. [Source: Jordan Friedman, 'From Jamaica's Marcus Garvey came an African vision of freedom,' USA Today, February 14, 2018]

I think the establishment of HBCUs in the USA is an example of Black people creating institutions for their empowerment when spurned and excluded by white society.

Racism is the dark side of American exceptionalism.

"Historically Black Colleges and Universities (HBCUs) are institutions of higher education in the United States that were established before the Civil Rights Act of 1964 to primarily serve the African-American community. Most of these institutions were founded in the years after the American Civil War and are concentrated in the Southern United States. During the period of segregation in the

United States before the Civil Rights Act, the overwhelming majority of higher education institutions were predominantly white and completely disqualified or limited African-American enrollment. For a century after the end of slavery in the United States in 1865, most colleges and universities in the Southern United States prohibited all African Americans from attending, while institutions in other parts of the country regularly employed quotas to limit admissions of Black people. HBCUs were established to give opportunities to African Americans, especially in the South." [Source: Wikipedia]

(Between January to June 2021, Nikole Hannah-Jones - who is Black, is most known for her work on The New York Times Magazine's "1619 Project," which re-examines the role of race in the USA's founding - and the University of North Carolina (UNC), Chapel Hill, USA, waged a bruising battle over the grant of tenure to Hannah-Jones after initially offering her employment with tenure. But in the end, when the UNC Trustees grudgingly voted on June 30, 2021, to grant Nikole Hannah-Jones tenure, she told them to get lost, and instead accepted a position, with tenure, at Howard University. In announcing her decision to reject UNC's belated offer, Hannah-Jones declared: "And so to be denied it, and to only have that vote occur on the last possible day, at the last possible moment, after the threat of legal action, after weeks of protest, after it became a national scandal – it's just not something that I want anymore," Hannah-Jones told the hosts of the CBS 'This Morning' television show. "I've spent my entire life proving that I belong in elite white spaces that were not built for Black people," she told CBS. "I decided I didn't want to do that anymore. That Black professionals should feel free, and actually perhaps an obligation, to go to our own institutions and bring our talents and resources to our own institutions and help to build them up as well." Howard University is a prestigious historically Black university in Washington, D.C.)

Professor Asante also says Marcus Garvey is also responsible for symbols such as the red, green, and black Pan-African flag. Asante says Garvey took inspiration from such figures as Booker T. Washington, founder of the Tuskegee Institute, who sought to improve education for African Americans; the leaders of the Haitian Revolution, including Toussaint L'Ouverture and Henri Christophe; and the maroons, escaped slaves who established free communities in Jamaica." [Source: Jordan Friedman, 'From Jamaica's Marcus Garvey came an African vision of Freedom,' USA Today, February 14, 2018]

I need to dilate on why Garvey so earnestly wanted to meet Booker T. Washington. Garvey had great respect for education as a vehicle for the development of Africa-descended people in Jamaica. Indeed, he advocated for the setting up of a university! And, as further evidence he was an intuitive genius, Garvey recognized the value of communal solidarity and strategic partnerships. So, he wanted to meet Booker T. Washington, who, at the time, was President of Tuskegee Institute (now University) in Alabama, USA.

"Booker T. Washington was born into slavery in Virginia in 1856. By the time he died in 1915, he was the most powerful Black man in the United States, in part due to the establishment of Tuskegee Institute (now University). In the September 1896 issue of The Atlantic Magazine, he wrote: "My work began at Tuskegee, Alabama, in 1881, in a small shanty and church, with one teacher and thirty students, without a dollar's worth of property. The spirit of work and of industrial thrift, with aid from the State and generosity from the North, has enabled us to develop an institution of eight hundred students gathered from nineteen States, with seventy-nine instructors, fourteen hundred acres of land, and thirty buildings, including large and small. Washington believed that economic development was essential to African Americans claiming a stake in the nation. One of the objections sometimes urged against industrial education for the Negro is that it aims merely to teach him to work on the same plan that he was made to follow when in slavery. This is far from being the object at Tuskegee. At the head of each of the twenty-five industrial departments, we have an intelligent and competent instructor, just as we have in our history classes, so that the student is taught not only practical brick-masonry, for example, but also the underlying principles of that industry, the mathematics and the mechanical and architectural drawing. Or he is taught how to become master of the forces of nature so that, instead of cultivating corn in the old way, he can use a corn cultivator, that lays off the furrows, drops the corn into them, and covers it, and in this way, he can do more work than three men by the old process of corn-planting; at the same time much of the toil is eliminated and labor is dignified. In a word, the constant aim is to show the student how to put brains into every process of labor; how to bring his knowledge of mathematics and the sciences into farming, carpentry, forging, foundry work; how to dispense as soon as possible with the old form of antebellum labor.

By detailing how Tuskegee was a self-sustaining institution, built on both labor and knowledge, he provided context for what might have been seen as an incendiary critique of the economic domination experienced by Black southerners." [Source: Imani Perry, 'Reconsidering Booker T. Washington', The Atlantic, November 16, 2021]

In **'Self-Reliance,'** an essay that Booker T. Washington published in September 1896, he encouraged African Americans to emulate the kind of life he promoted at the Tuskegee Institute, an industrial college for Blacks in Alabama. To achieve equality, Washington suggested that African Americans must lift themselves out of poverty:

"When a mere boy, I saw a young colored man, who had spent several years in school, sitting in a common cabin in the South, studying a French grammar. I noted the poverty, the untidiness, the want of system and thrift that existed about the cabin, notwithstanding his knowledge of French and other academic subjects. Another time, when riding on the outer edges of a town in the South, I heard the sound of a piano coming from a cabin of the same kind. Contriving some excuse, I entered, and began a conversation with the young colored woman who was playing, and who had recently returned from a boarding-school, where she had been studying instrumental music among other things. Despite the fact that her parents were living in a rented cabin, eating poorly cooked food, surrounded with poverty, and having almost none of the conveniences of life, she had persuaded them to rent a piano for four or five dollars per month. Many such instances as these, in connection with my own struggles, impressed upon me the importance of making a study of our needs as a race, and applying the remedy accordingly......One of the objections sometimes urged against industrial education for the negro is that it aims merely to teach him to work on the same plan that he was made to follow when in slavery. This is far from being the object at Tuskegee... In a word, the constant aim is to show the student how to put brains into every process of labor; how to bring his knowledge of mathematics and the sciences into farming, carpentry, forging, foundry work; how to dispense as soon as possible with the old form of ante-bellum labor."

Interestingly, many graduates of the Jamaica School of Agriculture (now College of Agriculture, Science & Education [CASE] have attended Tuskegee University and have empowered themselves by pursuing graduate degrees in agricultural science and allied fields).

Garvey has achieved intellectual immortality!

He has been elevated to an earned place among the pantheon of great philosophers and thinkers!

In 2003, Ian Adams, honorary fellow of the University of Durham, and his co-author R. W. Dyson, director of the Centre for the History of Political Thought, jointly published **'50 Major Political Thinkers.'** This publication, in recognition of the colossal intellectual legacy (**'Garveyism'**) Garvey bequeathed to the world, listed him among giant thinkers and well-known philosophers over 2,000 years - beginning with Plato, Aristotle, and others such as St. Thomas Aquinas, Niccolò Machiavelli, and Karl Marx.

Greatness is measured by influence, which is defined as the capacity to impactfully affect people and situations. The British Broadcasting Corporation (BBC) credited Marcus Garvey as an inspirational figure for later civil rights activists. And Martin Luther King Jr called Marcus Garvey the first man "To give millions of Negroes a sense of dignity and destiny." King added these words at the shrine of Marcus Garvey on his visit to Jamaica in June 1965: "You (Jamaica) gave Marcus Garvey to the United States of America, and he gave the millions of Negroes in the United States a sense of manhood, and sense of somebodiness. As we stand here, let us pledge ourselves to continue the struggle in the same spirit of somebodiness."

Who was Marcus Garvey?

Additionally, in an article titled **'Who was Marcus Garvey?'** by Edward Seaga that was published in The Gleaner on August 25, 2017, it was noted that: "Garvey's stage was not Jamaica; it was the continents of coloured peoples. Yet he is a National Hero of Jamaica and his works carried a message that helped to shape and structure the whole character of the people of his own country, among millions of the other people throughout the world."

Seaga continued: "Men shape, build and extend the boundaries of nations; some are the economic giants or ideologists who chart the relationship of man to man; others immortalise themselves in their contribution to art, science, and technology; still others are heroes because they battle nature and extend the frontiers of knowledge; and then there are the national heroes, those who belong to no category because they are all. They shape the character of a nation and so build and unleash the spirit of the people that the germ of their works and thoughts affect all aspects of a nation's life. Of such was the man Marcus Mosiah Garvey."

(Sidebar: It was Lloyd E. Campbell and the Jamaican associations in Brixton, England, who arranged for Marcus Garvey's body to return to Jamaica; Edward Seaga only arranged for their landing in Jamaica.)

In an article titled **'We Need Garvey's Vision to Build Jamaica'** that was published in The Sunday Gleaner of August 16, 2020, our own Dr. Orville Taylor, Head, Department of the Department of Sociology at The University of the West Indies, a radio talk-show host, and author of **'Broken Promises, Hearts and Pockets,'** lauded Marcus Garvey as "the second greatest black man who walked the Earth (Jesus being the first)."

Jesus Christ gave Christianity to the world.

Garvey gave Garveyism to Black people and the world.

Chattel Slavery's Afterlife & Psychic Wounds

To better understand the contextual background against which Garvey emerged and was stirred into action, a brief recounting of aspects of the institution of chattel slavery and its aftermath (afterlife) in early post-emancipation Jamaican society is absolutely necessary.

I think this 'point of departure' is appropriate because it effectively reveals the depth of Garvey's radical genius, showing as it does, his intuitive recognition that psychological tourniquets needed to be applied to the abused psychitecture of his people, to arrest the hemorrhaging of their self-esteem inflicted by the indignities of centuries of colonialism-inspired enslavement - and its afterlife - that was manifested in the psychic burden and emotional disfigurement under which Black People still laboured.

Demonstrating remarkable perception, Garvey grasped the etiology of post-slavery traumatic syndrome that was afflicting Black People and the necessity for mental emancipation, emotional hygiene, collective catharsis, and emotional reshaping and reprogramming.

Emotional hygiene is being conscious of the state of one's psychological health and developing habits to monitor and address psychological wounds (Dr. Guy Winch, Psychology Today).

In her Pulitzer Prize-winning novel **'Beloved,'** Nobel Prize laureate Toni Morrison tells the story of Sethe, a formerly enslaved woman who escaped the wretched Southern USA State of Ohio in the 1870s, but despite her freedom, still found herself haunted and menaced by the trauma of her past.

According to Wikipedia "Etiology (pronounced; alternatively: aetiology or ætiology) is the study of causation or origination. The word is derived from the Greek 'aitiología' ("giving a reason for") and 'aitía' ("cause"). More completely, etiology is the study of the causes, origins, or reasons behind the way that things are, or the way they function, or it can refer to the causes themselves. The word is commonly used in medicine (pertaining to causes of disease) and in philosophy, but also in physics, psychology, government, geography, spatial analysis, theology, and biology, in reference to the causes or origins of various phenomena."

Chattel Slavery & Europeans' Barbarity

According to Sherlock and Bennett (1998), from 1500 to 1800 AD, 10-11 million Africans were kidnapped, torn from their gods, their land, their habits, their life, and taken by force to the Americas in European slave ships, among them many from the UK, to serve for life a strange owner of another race and to endure a life of utter terrorism on plantations (veritable prisons and torture sites of assault, brutality, terror, rape) and other enterprises owned and operated by UK citizens, who built an entire system of oppression and barbarity.

Having survived the horrific voyage across the Atlantic Ocean, even greater indignities awaited the enslaved Africans. They were then to spend the next 300 years as chattel (property) and subjected to unspeakable cruelty, dehumanization, and open exploitation in a society characterized by physical and psychological terrorism.

Enslaved Africans were reduced to mere 'property' ... machines, really ... to create wealth for the enslavers, their heirs, and successors. This scale of human trafficking – perpetrated by Europeans - is unprecedented in the history of humanity.

As chattel, enslaved Africans were denied full moral status, which refers to deserving the same rights and same moral consideration as any other human. Full moral status is also called 'personhood'.

Concerning the fate of Africans, and also to get an insight into the level and mélange of cruelty routinely perpetrated upon the enslaved Africans by 'civilized' Europeans, one only has to read, for example, the horrific and revolting entries – more than 10,000 pages - in the diaries of the despicable Thomas Thistlewood [see **'In Miserable Slavery'** by Prof. Douglas Hall] to get

Thistlewood's own accounts, written in his own hand, of the dreadful orgy of unimaginable and monstrous violence, brutality, and the dark, dank, and dastardly depth of degradation to which our kidnapped Africans ancestors were routinely subjected.

Thistlewood said this about his 'slave wife,' Phibba: "I pity her, she is in miserable slavery." Thistlewood recorded 3,852 acts of sexual exploitation (rape/violence) with 136 enslaved women in his 37 years in Jamaica.

(This is apt: "A devaluation of Black womanhood occurred as a result of the sexual exploitation of Black women during slavery that has not altered in the course of hundreds of years." ~ bell hooks)

The loathsome Thistlewood was also otherwise wicked and inhumane. He was a subhuman monster. In his 23 July 1756 entry, he described punishing a slave in the following manner: 'Gave him a moderate whipping, pickled him well, made Hector shit in his mouth, immediately put a gag in it whilst his mouth was full and made him wear it 4 or 5 hours.'" This is conduct from an alleged 'civilized' Englishman, whom we are told is superior to the 'barbaric negro.' The unvarnished truth is that it is the European colonizers who were spectacularly and phenomenally murderous and barbaric! History is the incontrovertible witness to their bottomless barbarity.

As a thing, "the diary," the scholar Irina Paperno writes, "represents a lasting trace of one's being." Thistlewood, through his lurid diaries, certainly ensured a lasting trace of his putrescent and despicable being.

"The history of contact between the white and black races for the last three hundred years or more, records only a series of pillages, wholesale murders, atrocious brutalities, industrial exploitation, disfranchisement of the one on the other; the strong against the weak." [Source: The Philosophy and Opinions of Marcus Garvey, Centennial Edition, 1887-1987]

"There was no Nazi atrocity – concentration camps, wholesale maiming and murder, defilement of women, or ghastly blasphemy of childhood – which Christian civilization or Europe had not long been practising against colored folks in all parts of the world in the name of and for the defense of a 'Superior Race' born to rule the world" [Source: W.E.B Dubois, The World and Africa, 1947].

Furthermore, Sherlock and Bennett (1998) noted that "Wherever the European colonizers went they pressed ahead with great cruelty in their relentless search for labour. How was it that they were so insensitive to human suffering and killed other human beings so easily?" (p. 60).

The European colonizers were spectacularly and phenomenally murderous and barbaric.

Let's be clear: the enslavement of Africans was a consciously merciless enterprise, implemented by consciously merciless Europeans.

Besides, some of America's revered 'Founding Fathers' owned enslaved persons of African descent. No less than 12 American Presidents were owners of enslaved persons: George Washington, Thomas Jefferson, James Madison,

James Monroe, Andrew Jackson, Martin Ban Buren, William Henry Harrison, John Tyler, James K. Polk, Zachary Taylor, Andrew Johnson, and Ulysses S. Grant. George Washington also had in his dentures no less than nine teeth from enslaved persons he owned.

Trinidadian-Canadian writer Dionne Brand in her book **'At the Full and Change of the Moon'** (1999) says, with justifiably palpable anger: "Anything you can grotesquely imagine has been perpetrated against the Black self." This is by no means an exaggeration. Some of the instruments of torture used by the 'civilized' enslavers to inflict unbelievable harm and extract humanity from Black people, and reveal the inhumanity of the brutish and murderous British, are on display at the Institute of Jamaica, in Kingston, and other museums.

The colonizers were liars, thieves, deceivers, murderers, rapists, treaty breakers, and other kinds of grotesque evil. This planet has not seen a more evil set of people!

What is amazing is that these cruel, heartless enslavers are the people who set themselves up as models of civility. And what is more, they dispensed unimaginable misery and cruelty with the Bible in their hand. For example, the despicable Thomas Thistlewood thanked God he wasn't killed by Congo Sam when, in my mind, "natural justice" would have been served were the vile bastard killed.

The enslavement of at least 12 million Africans is "the sum of all villainies, the cause of all sorrow ... the root of all prejudice." ~ W.E.B Du Bois

The character Killmonger delivered this memorable line in the movie Black Panther: "Bury me in the ocean with my ancestors, who jumped from ships because they knew death was better than bondage."

"The transatlantic slave trade was one of the most notorious historical epochs of barbarism, human suffering, and degradation of human dignity that the world has ever known. Even though slavery existed before in other civilizations like among the Greeks and the Romans, the transatlantic slave trade is peculiar with scholars like Thomas Sowell and Robert L. Harris terming it as western hemisphere Chattel slavery. This is because Africans were sold as movable commodities and stacked in slave ships to be transported to the new world in the western hemisphere where they would work on sugar, cotton, cocoa plantations, and gold, silver mines in very dehumanizing conditions." [Source: The African Exponent, June 2, 2020]

Because its occurrence is removed in time and history is distorted or not properly taught, many people – including and especially many Black People - are unaware of the ineffable horribleness and plentitude of incarnadine cruelty that were the essential and defining features of chattel slavery. But make no mistake about it, "The Trans-Atlantic Trade in Enslaved Africans is "The single-most heinous crime perpetuated against humans by humans in the history of the world." ~ Justice Patrick Robinson

Enslaved Africans were reduced to mere 'property' ... machines, really ... to create wealth for the enslavers, their heirs, and successors. This scale of human trafficking – perpetrated by Europeans - is unprecedented in the history of humanity.

It is estimated that during the Trans-Atlantic Trade in Enslaved Africans (mass human trafficking), about two million Africans lost their lives directly from the trip to North America and the Caribbean, with the mortality rate at times being as high as 30 per cent. This does not include the thousands of deaths while on the plantations (forced-labour camps and torture sites), and subsequently, brought about by the inhumane treatment and injustices meted out to the enslaved and their descendants.

And, of course, many chose death over bondage: As noted above, the character Killmonger delivered this memorable line in the movie Black Panther: "Bury me in the ocean with my ancestors, who jumped from ships because they knew death was better than bondage."

Colonialism: A Cannibalistic, Murderous Beast

Colonialism is like a cannibalistic beast that, by its elemental nature, sows destruction and barbarity and spills blood. "The instruments of colonial power are barbaric, brutal violence, and intimidation, Colonisation dehumanizes even the most civilized man; that the colonial enterprise, colonial conquest, which is based on contempt for the native and justified by that contempt, inevitably tends to change him who undertakes it; that the colonizer, who, to ease his conscience, gets into the habit of seeing the other man as an animal, accustoms himself to treating him like an animal, and tends objectively to transform himself into an animal. It is this result, the boomerang effect of colonisation."- Aime Cesaire.

"In 1954, when France normalized massacre and torture in its Algerian colony, Frantz Fanon was working as a psychiatrist in a hospital in Algiers. Confronted in his day job with both French police torturers and their Algerian victims, he became convinced that psychiatric treatment could not work without the destruction of colonialism, which he described as an "absolute evil" and "a machine of naked violence" that "only gives in when confronted with greater violence." Influenced by Fanon, Nelson Mandela, who was initially a disciple of Gandhi, led the African National Congress into an armed struggle in response to a massacre of Black South Africans in Sharpeville. "Government violence can do only one thing and that is to breed counter violence," Mandela said. Fanon presented counter violence as a kind of therapy for dehumanized natives: "As you and your fellow men are cut down like dogs," he wrote, "there is no other solution but to use every means available to reestablish your weight as a human being." [Source: Pankaj Mishra, **'Frantz Fanon's Enduring Legacy,'** The Atlantic Magazine, November 29, 2021]

For 183 years - from when they wrested Jamaica from the Spanish Government in 1655 to 1838 when enslavement was abolished - the brutal British presided over systematic cruelty and dehumanization of enslaved Africans in Jamaica.

In 2019, when he refused to be named an MBE (Member of the British Empire), George Mpanga, a British-born Spoken Word Poet of Ugandan descent, gave this pointed reason: "Your forefathers grabbed my motherland, pinned her down, and took turns. They did that every day for a couple of hundred years and then left her to treat her own burns. Now all of her children are born with a set of unique concerns and gaps in the information that we really do need to learn and none of us know why, why we got absorbed by a 'higher entity', why I have to fight for my identity." [Source: The UK Guardian, November 25, 2019]

This bears repeating: "There was no Nazi atrocity – concentration camps, wholesale maiming and murder, defilement of women or ghastly blasphemy of childhood – which Christian civilization or Europe had not long been practising against colored folks in all parts of the world in the name of and for the defense of a 'Superior Race' born to rule the world." [Source: W.E.B Dubois, The World and Africa, 1947]

"Racial and cultural dominance is a collectivist effort by wave after wave of Europeans who agreed, before leaving their continent, to work in concert for control of land and wealth. This includes mass murder and genocide, chattel slavery, religious inculcation and persecution, sexual violence and rape, and the commoditizing of Black indigenous people of colour bodies for profit, experimentation, and seizure -- all of which trickled down through history to the disparities (seen today). European imperialism hoards wealth and power in modern society and believes no other entity is as valuable as itself." [David G. Martínez, 'Blaming the Victim, Inside Higher Ed, September 4, 2020]

Consider this anguished testimony from the **'Narrative of the Life of Frederick Douglass, An American Slave'** in which he described how enslavement crushed his spirit and drained the humanity from his being, and also laid bare the utter and complete inhumanity of white, Christian enslavers ('devils,' as Malcolm X called them): "If at any time of my life more than another, I was made to drink the bitterest dregs of slavery (enslavement), that time was during the first six months of my stay with Mr. Covey. We were worked in all weathers. It was never too hot or too cold; it could never rain, blow, hail, or snow, or too hard for us to work in the field. Work, work, work was scarcely more the order of the day than of the night. The longest days were too short for him, and the shortest nights were too long for him. I was somewhat unmanageable when I first went there, but a few months of this discipline tamed me. Mr. Covey succeeded in breaking me. I was broken in body, soul, and spirit. My natural elasticity was crushed, my intellect languished, the disposition to read departed, and the cheerful spark that lingered about my eye died; the dark night of slavery (enslavement) closed in upon me, and, behold a man transformed into a brute."

Douglass continued: "Sunday was my only leisure time. I spent this in a sort of beast-like stupor, between sleep and wake, under some large tree. At times I would rise up, and a flash of energetic freedom would dart through my soul, accompanied by a faint beam of hope that flickered for a moment, and then vanished. I sank down again, mourning over my wretched condition. I was sometimes prompted to take my life, and that of Mr. Covey, but was prevented by a combination of hope and fear."

And Booker T. Washington wrote this: "I cannot remember a single instance during my childhood or early boyhood when our entire family sat down to the table together, and God's blessing was asked, and the family ate a meal in a civilized manner. On the plantation in Virginia, and even later, meals were gotten to the children very much as dumb animals get theirs. It was a piece of bread here and a scrap of meat there. It was a cup of milk at one time and some potatoes at another."

Is it possible for the human mind to conceive of a more horrible state of society than chattel slavery?

After Frederick Douglass tasted freedom, in September 1848, on the tenth anniversary of his escape, he published an open letter addressed to his former master, Thomas Auld, berating him for his conduct, and enquiring after members of his family who were still held by Auld. "In the course of the letter, Douglass adeptly transitions from formal and restrained to familiar and then to impassioned. At one point he is the proud parent, describing his improved circumstances and the progress of his own four young children. But then he dramatically shifts tone: Oh! sir, a slaveholder never appears to me so completely an agent of hell, as when I think of and look upon my dear children. It is then that my feelings rise above my control. ... The grim horrors of slavery rise in all their ghastly terror before me, the wails of millions pierce my heart and chill my blood. I remember the chain, the gag, the bloody whip, the deathlike gloom overshadowing the broken spirit of the fettered bondman, the appalling liability of his being torn away from their wife and children, and sold like a beast in the market. Your wickedness and cruelty committed in this respect on your fellow creatures are greater than all the stripes you have laid upon my back or theirs. It is an outrage upon the soul, a war upon the immortal spirit, and one for which you must give account at the bar of our common Father and Creator. In a graphic passage, Douglass asked Auld how he would feel if Douglass had come to take away his daughter Amanda as a slave, treating her the way he and members of his family had been treated by Auld." [Source: Wikipedia]

When Malcolm X referred to white people as devils, he was criticised, but having regard to the diabolical and ineffable nature of chattel slavery that was devised by them, was he wrong? Did he lie?

Some of the instruments of torture used by the alleged 'civilised' enslavers to inflict unbelievable harm and extract humanity from Black people, and reveal the inhumanity of the brutish and murderous British, are on display at the Institute of Jamaica, in Kingston, and other museums in other countries. Many Jamaicans 'admire' the so-called 'Royal Family' in the UK, but for me, they are the heirs and successors of the most heinous crimes ever committed on this planet.

How can anyone with even a passing knowledge, let alone detailed knowledge of the enslavement of Black People, oppose reparations?

Emancipation & Concepts of Freedom

After severe hardships, indescribable brutality, open rebellion on the sugarcane plantations (torture sites!) by the enslaved Africans fuelled by an insuppressible desire to be masters of their own destiny, and the agitation of so-called "people of conscience," the British parliament was forced to pass the Act of Emancipation of 1833.

The law came into force in 1834 and stated: "From and after the first day of August 1834, all persons who have been registered as slaves in this island, shall be, by force and virtue of the Act (the Law of 1834), become apprenticed labourers. And be it further enacted that all and every person who, on the said day of August 1834 shall be holden in slavery within the island, and from the first day of August 1834, to all intents and purposes shall be free and discharged from all manner of slavery and shall, absolutely and forever, be manumitted and the children to be born to any such persons, shall be set free from their birth ..."

We must think of freedom in at least two ways: freedom from domination and freedom to dominate. "In 'White Freedom: The Racial History of an Idea,' Tyler Stovall shows how both notions of freedom are tied up in the history of race and racial thinking. In societies like those of the United States and republican France, he writes, "belief in freedom, specifically one's entitlement to freedom, was a key component of white supremacy." The more white one was, he continues, "the more free one was." This "white freedom" is not named as such because it is somehow intrinsic to people of European descent, but because it took its shape under conditions of explicit racial hierarchy, where colonialism and chattel slavery made clear who was free and who was not. As an ideology, Stovall writes, white freedom meant both "control of one's destiny" and the freedom to dominate and exclude. What makes Stovall's work so valuable at this moment is that his study of "white freedom" helps illuminate the stakes of the present .... and the ongoing struggle, for some, to be free (or at least more free) of domination and hierarchy, and a fight, for others, to be free to (continue) to dominate." [Source: Jamelle Bouie,

45

'What Does 'White Freedom' Really Mean?' The New York Times, December 17, 2021]

Concerning the 'taste' of freedom, from the perspective of being previously dominated, Frederick Douglass wrote of his freedom and later arrival in New York City in these terms: "I have often been asked, how I felt when first I found myself on free soil. And my readers may share the same curiosity. There is scarcely anything in my experience about which I could not give a more satisfactory answer. A new world had opened upon me. If life is more than breath, and the "quick round of blood," I lived more in one day than in a year of my slave life. It was a time of joyous excitement which words can but tamely describe. In a letter written to a friend soon after reaching New York, I said: "I felt as one might feel upon escape from a den of hungry lions." Anguish and grief, like darkness and rain, may be depicted; but gladness and joy, like the rainbow, defy the skill of pen or pencil." [Source: 'Narrative of the Life of Frederick Douglas, An American Slave', 1845]

And this is how Booker T. Washington recalled the pregnant anticipation that met Emancipation in the USA, in 1865: "As the great day drew nearer, there was more singing in the slave quarters than usual. It was bolder, had more ring, and lasted later into the night. Most of the verses of the plantation songs had some reference to freedom... [S]ome man who seemed to be a stranger (a United States officer, I presume) made a little speech and then read a rather long paper—the Emancipation Proclamation, I think. After the reading, we were told that we were all free, and could go when and where we pleased. My mother, who was standing by my side, leaned over and kissed her children, while tears of joy ran down her cheeks. She explained to us what it all meant, that this was the day for which she had been so long praying, but fearing that she would never live to see." [Source: Wikipedia]

For her part, Toni Morrison examined the question of what freedom means for a human being in her 1987 novel **'Beloved'** which was inspired by the true story of a woman's escape from slavery and the unfathomable cost she had to pay for her freedom. Painting the state of being unlatched in her protagonist after escaping from enslavement, Morrison considers the deepest meaning of freedom, writing: "Listening to the doves in Alfred, Georgia, and having neither the right nor the permission to enjoy it because, in that place mist, doves, sunlight, copper dirt, moon — everything belonged to the men who had the guns. Little men, some of them, big men too, each one of whom he could snap like a twig if he wanted to. Men who knew their manhood lay in their guns and were not even embarrassed by the knowledge that without gunshot fox would laugh at them. And these "men" who made even vixen laugh could, if you let them, stop you from hearing doves or loving moonlight. So you protected yourself and loved small. Picked the tiniest stars out of the sky to own; lay down with head twisted to see the loved one over the rim of the trench before you slept. Stole shy glances at her between the trees at chain-up. Grass blades, salamanders, spiders, woodpeckers, beetles, and a kingdom of ants. Anything bigger wouldn't do. A woman, a child, a brother — a big love like that would split you wide open in Alfred, Georgia. He knew exactly what she meant: to get to a place where you could love anything you chose — not to need permission for desire — well now, that was freedom."

The Jamaican and American Emancipation Laws were admissions that, before their passage, Jamaica and the USA were prisons and spaces for the ineffable brutalisation and dehumanisation of enslaved Africans who were violently uprooted from their country, family, and culture and forcibly brought to these countries. It is also to be remembered that although the enslaved Africans in the British West Indies were ostensibly free after August 1, 1834, they were compelled to work as apprentices until 1838 (an additional four years of free labour was wrung out of them) - hence the term "full free" being used to refer to 1834.

Precarious Freedom

Though nominally free, the formerly enslaved Africans in Jamaica continued to face precarity after emancipation. There was no change in institutions or the culture of the planter class. On August 5, 2021, The Daily Observer, in an editorial, noted that the newly-freed African Jamaicans "Were advised that they would have to pay rent for the houses in which they lived and the lands they farmed from the day of Emancipation. The rent provision was contained in the Proclamation of Emancipation issued by Governor Sir Lionel Smith on July 9, 1838, which became effective August 1 that year. Without an ounce of shame, the governor described the proclamation as a "great blessing" and told the freed slaves: "Where you can agree and continue happy with your own masters, I strongly recommend you to remain on those properties on which you have been born, and where your parents are buried. But you must not mistake in supposing that your present houses, gardens, or provision grounds are your own property. They belong to the proprietors of the estates, and you will have to pay rent for them in money or labour, according as you and your employers may agree together." As if that were not despicable enough, he advised that people who decided not to work, but went wandering about the island would be "taken up as vagrants and punished in the same manner as they are in England". Sir Lionel then instructed our ancestors to listen to their pastors who, he said, would keep them out of trouble. He also told the freed slaves to recollect what was expected of them from the people of England, who have "paid a large price" for their liberty. In sharp contrast, indentured workers were given property and money, a move that historians have long argued contributed to the high level of poverty and landlessness among blacks in the former colonies."

Perverse Compensation to Enslavers

In a perverse act, owners of enslaved Africans in Jamaica were compensated by the British Government for the inconvenience and loss they were expected to endure when they no longer had access to free labour that had supported their affluent living. The estimate for the "inconvenience and loss of their property" experienced by the wicked enslavers when they no longer had access to the free labour of the enslaved African-Jamaicans that supported their affluent living was £47 million. And the British Government paid out £20 million, with an arrangement for a further period of 'apprenticeship' (a ruse to squeeze further free labour from the African-Jamaicans) to offset the balance of £27 million.

"The argument for slave-owner compensation relied on perverse logic. Under English law, it was difficult to claim compensation for the loss of chattel property, since rights to movable things – such as household possessions, tools, or livestock – were considered inherently unstable, expendable, and ambiguous. So, the West India interest in parliament, led by the likes of Patrick Maxwell Stewart, a rich London merchant who owned slaves in Tobago, made fanciful arguments to align the enslaved more with land or buildings, or even with body parts, than with human beings. According to one line of argument, because the government paid money to landowners when it took over fields for public works such as docks, roads, bridges, and railways, so too it had to pay slave owners for taking over their slaves. According to another argument, because the government paid soldiers for the injury to organs or the loss of limbs during war, so too it had to provide slave owners aid for cutting them off from their slaves, which maimed slave owners' economic interests. In September 1835, less than a month after the government received its loan (to compensate slave owners), slave owners began their feeding frenzy as they obtained compensation cheques at the National Debt

Office. Payment amounts were determined based on application forms that asked claimants to itemise the number and kinds of enslaved people in their possession and to provide certificates from the slave registrar. There were some 47,000 recipients of compensation in total." [Source: Kris Manapara, The UK Guardian, May 29, 2018]

"In addition to money, slave owners received another form of compensation: the guaranteed free labour of blacks on plantations for a period of years after emancipation. The enslaved were thus forced to pay reverse reparations to their oppressors. At the stroke of midnight on 1 August 1834, the enslaved were freed from the legal category of slavery – and instantly plunged into a new institution, called "apprenticeship". The arrangement was initially to last for 12 years but was ultimately shortened to four. During this period of apprenticeship, Britain declared it would teach African Jamaicans how to use their freedom responsibly and would train them out of their natural state of savagery. But this training involved continued unpaid labour for the same masters on the very same plantations on which they had worked the day before. In some ways, the "apprenticeship" years were arguably even more brutal than what had preceded them. With the Slavery Abolition Act, the duty to punish former slaves now shifted from individual slave owners to officers of the state. A state-funded, 100-person corps of police, jailers, and enforcers were hired in Britain and sent to the plantation colonies. They were called the "stipendiary magistrates". If apprentices were too slow in drawing water, or in cutting cane, or in washing linens, or if they took Saturdays off, their masters could have them punished by these magistrates. Punishments were doled out according to a standardised formula, and often involved the most "modern" punishment device of those times: the treadmill. This torture device, which was supposed to inculcate a work ethic, was a huge turning wheel with thick, splintering wooden slats. Apprentices accused of laziness – what slave owners called the "negro disease" – were hung by their hands from a plank and forced to "dance" the treadmill barefoot, often for hours. If they fell or lost their step, they would be battered on their chest, feet, and shins by the wooden planks. The punishment was often combined with whippings. The treadmill was used more during the apprenticeship period than it ever was under slavery, precisely because it was said to be a scientific, measurable, and modern form of disciplinary re-education, in line with bureaucratic oversight. One apprentice, James Williams, in an account of his life published in 1837, recalled he was punished much more after 1834 than before. Indeed, it is likely that slave-owners sweated their labour under apprenticeship, to squeeze out the last ounces of unpaid labour before full emancipation finally came in 1838." [Source: Kris Manapara, The UK Guardian, May 29, 2018]

On the other hand, the freed formerly enslaved Africans were not compensated (Sherlock & Bennett, 1998). There was no compensation at emancipation for the formerly enslaved. The perverse act of compensating the enslavers but not the enslaved was akin to rubbing salt into the psychological and physical wounds of the enslaved and has provided relentless motivation for the persons persistently agitating for reparations for the enslavement of Africans.

It is also to be remembered that the Government of Great Britain openly condoned the crime of slavery by passing laws that encouraged it — a blatant example is the preamble to the Act of Parliament 23 Geo. 11 Cap.31: "Whereas the trade to and from Africa is very advantageous to Great Britain, and necessary for the supplying the plantations (torture sites), and colonies thereunto belonging, with a sufficient number of Negroes, at reasonable rates."

And of course, there were bankers and insurance companies which, as co-conspirators in the nefarious activities, provided financing or gave risk cover to the diabolical venture.

And staunch defenders.

In a letter penned by Horatio Nelson (a British naval commander celebrated for his victories against the French during the Napoleonic Wars period) to his friend, Simon Taylor — a British plantation owner living in Jamaica — about slavery, he remarked: "I have ever been and shall die a firm friend to our present colonial system...neither in the field or in the Senate shall their interest be infringed whilst I have an arm to fight in their defence, or a tongue to launch my voice against the damnable and cursed doctrine of William Wilberforce and his hypocritical allies."

Jamaica: Britain's Most Valuable Colony

Besides, in a public lecture delivered at the Mona Campus of The University of the West Indies in July 2019, Justice Patrick Robinson (a Jamaica Jurist who also sits on the International Court of Justice, in the Hague, Netherlands) noted that: "In 1753 Jamaica was Britain's most valuable colony, with the average white person in Jamaica being 52.3 times wealthier than the average white person in England and Wales."

I will now directly say here that I unapologetically support the just demand for reparations (the Latin word for 'repair') for the barbarities, brutality, dehumanization, and indignities inflicted upon my ancestors, as well as for their centuries of uncompensated labour.

Enslavers stole even the children's milk! Harriet Ann Jacobs, a girl who was enslaved in the Southern USA, in her autobiography, **'Incidents in the Life of a Slave Girl,'** wrote: "My mother's mistress was the daughter of my grandmother's mistress. She was the foster sister of my mother; they were both nourished at my grandmother's breast. In fact, my mother had been weaned at three months old, so that the baby of the mistress might obtain sufficient food (milk)."

The foregoing makes clear that the children of the enslavers were leeches and parasites on enslaved women. This was a practice common also in Jamaica and other British colonies. I mean, can you just imagine this degree of untrammelled exploitation!

For centuries!

And I have folks, Black People included, telling me to "forget about slavery and move on." To them I say I am not going to add any fuel to the forgetting machine.

I am my ancestors!

And I have an obligation, nay, a duty, to them.

On June 28, 2022, CNN reported that a 101-year-old former Nazi camp guard was sentenced to five years in prison for Holocaust atrocities. But Black people have been told to 'move on' and forget about the chattel slavery of their ancestors.

The thing is, due to ignorance (willful or otherwise), or stunning poverty of imagination, some people are unable to fathom the indescribable horrors of enslavement. Willful ignorance is an egregious sin.

Reparations: An Overdue Debt

So, the demand for the payment of reparations is not begging for a handout. Rather, it is a demand for a legitimate unsettled debt – retroactive pay and payment for damages (the indemnity given by law, to be recovered from a wrongdoer by the person who has sustained an injury, either in his person, property, or relative rights, in consequence of the acts of another) - for the most atrocious crime ever committed against humanity in the history of humankind.

"In 2005, a group of British scholars and financial experts were asked to answer the question: "If the British were to pay the two million enslaved Blacks in the Caribbean a retroactive wage, fixed at the lowest level of an English field worker for 200 years, plus a sum for their lost assets in Africa and trauma inflicted, what would be the sum of the settlement?" The figure suggested by the team came to 7.5 trillion pounds, more than three times the 2005 current GDP of Britain. The figure reflected the value of slave labour to British economic growth, and illustrates how a small island economy on the outskirts of Western Europe was able to emerge as the major global economic force in the nineteenth century." [Source: 'Bars to Recovery: The Caribbean Claim to Reparations for Slavery in International Law.' A 2014 LLB Dissertation by Katarina Schwarz, University of Otago, N.Z.].

Concerning intergenerational benefits of enslavement, Harriet Ann Jacobs, an enslaved girl in the southern USA, in her autobiography, **'Incidents in the Life of a Slave Girl,'** mentions how her grandmother, from money saved from baking and selling pastries, loaned her mistress $300 but the mistress never repaid it. On the death of the mistress and with her son-in-law as executor of her will, Harriet's grandmother sought repayment from her mistress' estate but was denied when the dishonest son-in-law declared it was insolvent and so the law prohibited payment.

The insightful Harriet remarked: "It (the alleged insolvency) did not, however, prohibit him from retaining the silver candelabra, which had been purchased with that money. I presume that it will be handed down in the family, from generation to generation." This incident makes abundantly clear that descendants of enslavers enjoy the benefits of the proceeds of the crime of slavery!

Brutish Britain's development was built on the proceeds of slavery. "What claim have West Indians on

Britain? Briefly this: "It is the British who by their action in the past centuries are responsible for the presence in these islands of the majority of their inhabitants, whose ancestors as slaves contributed millions to the wealth of Great Britain, a debt which the British have yet to repay." [Source: Sir Arthur Lewis, **'Labour in the West Indies'**]. The descendants of enslavers continue to benefit from the proceeds of the crime of slavery, but to date, the descendants of the enslaved have not been paid a dollar in compensation.

"The British owners of enslaved Africans got the vastest compensation anywhere in history, and they built their castles and their stately homes and invested their money, and, therefore, there was a huge financial spin-off for them. However, for Jamaica, the enslaved population got nothing. Instead, they are left with the burdens of poor diet, underdevelopment, and broken homes. When you look at slavery in Jamaica, there was not only the physical torture that was exacted on the enslaved people but the destruction of these families. In chattel slavery, a man and a woman who produced a child could not stay together because one would be sold into another plantation, etc. The result is that children grew up without families, and I think that when they talk about transgenerational and intergenerational damage, that is an example. We see the manifestations today in the anger, the violence, and the difficulty in taking responsibility for our children." [Source: Anthony Gifford, The Gleaner, September 26, 2021]

"In law and in morality, righting a wrong always involves restitution, compensation, reparation, for the wrong committed. In our case, restitution was paid to the guilty party, the perpetrators, and not to the victims. This travesty cries out for justice. The descendants of the former plantocracy owe the descendants of the former slaves billions of dollars in reparation for the holocaust that was Jamaican chattel slavery, and its aftermath with which we currently live." - Peter Espeut

There are numerous other examples of beneficiaries of the proceeds of the crime of slavery. Harvard University was established in 1636 from the proceeds of the sale of enslaved persons by its first benefactor, clergyman John Harvard, whose death-bed bequest to the University "ensured its permanence." Modern-day criminals are not allowed by the Courts to retain the proceeds of their crime; on the same principle, present-day descendants of historical criminals who were involved in the crime of slavery should pay reparations.

As noted by prominent Attorney-at-Law Frank Phipps in an article in The Jamaica Observer newspaper on June 17, 2020 ('One Small act for Reparation Contributes to a Giant Leap for Mankind') all the ingredients of the crime have been established: the offence, the offenders, and the victims.

"Reparation is a straight-up financial debt. The case is unequivocal. The African American Intellectual W.E.B Du Bois was right when he described the enslavement of at least 12 million Africans as "the sum of all villainies, the cause of all sorrow, the root of all prejudice". In the

Caribbean, Britain received, in the words of Nobel prize-winning economist Arthur Lewis, "200 years of free labour – from over 15 million black people, and those who were indentured from India. The proceeds from this enslavement, and the heavily exploitative years of 'apprenticed' labour that followed it, provided the profits with which Britain modernised its economy. The systemic poverty that remains in the Caribbean can be directly traced to the era of enslavement and colonialism, at the end of which Britain walked away leaving 60% of the region's black inhabitants functionally illiterate."

By the way, let me declare here that no one, and I mean no one, can get me to subscribe to the very same religion under whose imprimatur my ancestors were subjected to unspeakable trauma by being oppressed, brutalized, subjugated, dehumanized, and murdered!

"As my ancestors are free from slavery, I am free from the slavery of religion. If we had put the energy on earth and on people that we put on mythology and Jesus Christ, we wouldn't have any hunger or homelessness." ~ Butterfly McQueen

On the matter of reparations, "Enough done be enough already!"

"It is for them (our ancestors) that we demand reparation from the complicit [and evil] European states that conceptualised, capitalised, legislated, and operationalised the system and co-opted others into their criminal enterprise. Our ancestors endured unspeakable trauma from capture, sale, and march to the coast, through confinement in coastal holding cells/barracoons, to the Middle Passage journey and enslavement in the Americas.

They never accepted their condition! This is why they fought relentlessly for their freedom. They were tortured and murdered for their activism - like the 77 burned alive in 1736 in Antigua; the 400 executed for joining Tacky and other Gold Coast Chiefs who led a war in St. Mary, starting in 1760; the 50 who died in battle; the 70 executed in the field; the 300 taken to Bridgetown for trial, of which 144 were executed and 132 sent away to another island after the war of 1816 in Barbados.

After the 1823 war in Guyana, hundreds of rebels were hunted down and killed, including 200 who were beheaded as a warning to other enslaved people. Quamina, who had argued against the violent protest, was tracked down by dogs and some indigenous people and killed. In the 1831-32 war in Jamaica, 200 were killed in battle and about 344 executed after "trials". [Source: Prof. Verene Shepherd, 'Honour is a must – reparation now Honour is a must – reparation now,' The Sunday Gleaner, July 26, 2020].

In his speech delivered at the Accra International Convention Centre, Ghana, in 2018, 'Prince Charles' said: "The appalling atrocity of the slave trade, and the unimaginable suffering it caused, left an indelible stain on the history of our world." Yet, the dense and obtuse 'Prince Charles' did not offer an apology. So much for being 'civilized.'

Therefore, I fully endorse the establishment of a National Council on Reparation by the Government of

Jamaica, the creation of the Centre for Reparation Research at the University of the West Indies, and the founding of the CARICOM Reparations Commission. And what of reparations to the Jews for the suffering they endured during the other Holocaust? In addition to the millions Germany has already paid to them in the past, as recently as December 13, 2019, the Associated Press reported that one of Germany's prominent families was giving millions of euros "to support Holocaust survivors as it seeks to atone for its use of forced labourers (slaves?) during the Nazi era and its enthusiastic support of Adolf Hitler."

"In the US, the Confederates who lost the civil war received compensation for the loss of their property. France had no issue extorting huge sums from Haiti for generations, as reparations for that nation's audacity in overthrowing slavery in 1804. This arrangement, euphemistically designed to "indemnify" French colonialists, persisted until 1947." [Source: Afua Hirsch, 'The Case for British Slavery Reparations Can no Longer be Brushed Aside, The UK Guardian, July 9, 2020].

In an article published in **Slate Magazine** on July 28, 2020, titled **'Throne of Blood,'** Brooke Newman, with copious evidence, clinically laid out the case "for the British royal family to make amends for centuries of profiting from slavery." Here is an excerpt from the compelling evidence Newman compiled: "As English planters in the Atlantic colonies clamored for more enslaved Africans, English enslavers profited and the African slave trade expanded. **"The Royal African**

Company of England," notes historian William Pettigrew, "shipped more enslaved African women, men, and children to the Americas than any other single institution during the entire period of the transatlantic slave trade." The company's seal captures how English enslavers, with Crown encouragement, eagerly harnessed the lives and bodies of Africans to generate commercial wealth and build an overseas empire. The seal shows an elephant bearing a castle, flanked by two enslaved African men. Surrounding the figures is the company's motto: Regio floret patrocinio commercium, commercioque regnum ("By royal patronage commerce flourishes, by commerce the realm")."

Newman also adduced this further evidence: "From its founding in 1672 to 1688, James, the Duke of York (the future King James II), served as the governor of the Royal African Company and its largest shareholder. James also held the position of Lord High Admiral, which enabled him to exercise punitive power over anyone who challenged the company's monopoly in West Africa or the English colonies. So intimately intertwined was the English monarchy with the slave trade that the company left a permanent mark of royal ownership on the bodies of the enslaved: Before they were shipped to the Americas, African captives were branded on the right shoulder or breast with the letters D.Y., for the Duke of York, or R.A.C.E., for the Royal African Company of England." The last sentence from the excerpt above is remarkable in its import. To wit: Africans were branded as property – inventory - just like how any other type of property of a company would be marked for identification and ownership.

Here's more evidence from Newman: "During the peak years of the Atlantic slave trade, between 1690 and 1807, European enslavers carried approximately 6 million enslaved Africans to the Americas; almost half of these captives arrived in British or Anglo-American ships. Protected by the Crown and Parliament, the slave trade became one of Britain's most profitable industries. The production of popular, labor-intensive agricultural products such as sugar, tobacco, cotton, and coffee in the Atlantic colonies hinged on the regular supply of African captives. The vast majority of enslaved African men, women, and children were destined for the sugar fields of Brazil and the Caribbean islands."

Newman concluded her article this way: "Officially acknowledging that the royal family both fostered and profited from the enslavement of millions, and affirming a commitment to reparatory justice as the Caribbean Community has urged the governments of Britain and Europe to do, is the very least the present-day British monarchy owes to the descendants of enslaved people. The Crown's act of willful forgetting demonstrates how easy it was to overlook—then and now—the pivotal role played by the royal family in accelerating England's involvement in the Trans-Atlantic slave trade and the development of an Atlantic empire built on the backs and blood of African and Indigenous people."

Injustice in Post-Emancipation Jamaica

After emancipation, Jamaican society was characterized by a socio--political order that saw the planter class conspiring to retain power over the freed African Jamaicans at all cost. African-Jamaicans had no input in the decision-making process as they were bereft of political power and representation or the economic means to make a decent livelihood. The rights and dignity of African-Jamaicans were held hostage to the self-interests of the plantocracy.

Peter Espeut, a Sociologist & Development Scientist asserts that "Emancipation did not change the social and economic relations within Jamaica, only the legal framework within which exploitation took place. Those who were exploited by slavery received no compensation for their oppression, while the exploiters received compensation for the "loss of their property". The Act of Emancipation was violence against those emancipated. No effort was made by public authorities to create a society which worked for the human development of those who lived here; the planters were still the politicians, judges, juries, prosecutors, and lawyers."

Another potent example of injustice after emancipation was this: enslavers used to hire out their property – as enslaved persons were then regarded – for four 'bitts,' or 1s 6d per day, but after emancipation, as 'free' people, the African-Jamaicans were being offered only two 'bitts' per day to continue working on the plantations (torture sites). Here we see that, although the Blacks were nominally free, the plantocracy still held economic power. And still does, even after 182 years!

James Mursell Phillippo in his 1843 book '**Jamaica: Its Past and Present State'** wrote, "...previous to the year 1823 there were not more than one or two schools in the whole island expressly for the instruction of the black population. Hence they were generally ignorant of the art of reading; while their improvement was universally opposed by the planters as inimical to the future peace and prosperity of the island...".

The pervasive, pernicious, and unbearable injustice that marked early post-emancipation Jamaica precipitated the Paul Bogle-led Morant Bay Protest in October 1865. As Nelson Mandela (1994) unapologetically averred, "To overthrow oppression has been sanctioned by humanity and is the highest aspiration of every free man" (p. 162). The Morant Bay Rebellion of 1865 further underscored the incessant and determined struggle of the Black Africans-turned-Jamaicans against continued oppression, indignities, suffering, and dehumanization. The rebellion demonstrated the dangerous anger of the Jamaican people when they are fed up.

In the aftermath of the Paul Bogle-led Morant Bay Protest against injustice and oppression, in St Thomas, calculated and vicious violence was unleashed by the Brutal British on the people who had the 'temerity' to demand better treatment and to live as dignified human beings. Punishment was swift and savage and left a trail of blood that soaked the soil and psychitecture of the land because "leniency would only operate as an indirect encouragement to the disaffected to persevere in their lawless design." And who was the principal perpetrator and violence producer? None other than the then Governor, Edward John Eyre - a monstrous, rabid, and sadistic pretense of a human being. A terroristic shred of human debris! A human-shaped monster! An Englishman. Let this sink in.

Eyre declared martial law, and ordered close to 500 persons (some sources say the number was higher), including pregnant women - yes, my fellow Jamaican, pregnant women! - executed or shot, hundreds more flogged, and more than 1,000 dwellings destroyed! This was raw terrorism unleashed on the people! Oh yes, make no mistake about it, casual cruelty has been a feature in Jamaica where life, in particular that of Black people, has long been devalued.

Paul Bogle and George William Gordon, now National Heroes of Jamaica since 1969, were among the casualties of Eyre's fetish and orgy of violence – both were executed, by hanging; Gordon on October 23, 1865, and Bogle the following day. I think it is reasonable to infer that it was the institution of chattel slavery that nourished Eyre's taste, appetite, and his torturer's cruel delight in the vicious punishment of Black African Jamaicans. Can Edward Eyre be truthfully described as being civilized?

Garvey's Arrival on the Scene

So, at the time of Garvey's birth in post-emancipation Jamaica, people of African descent in the country and indeed the world over were colonized, disenfranchised, and subjugated. They had the heavy baggage of the tragic legacy of chattel slavery on their shoulders as well as deeply embedded into their collective psychitecture. Thus, even after slavery was abolished, Blacks suffered from a persistent hangover from the despicable orgy of cruelty and denigration that were defining features of chattel slavery.

It must be remembered that African speech, religion, mannerisms, and other cultural norms were systematically denigrated as savagery and subhuman, to imbue Black people with a sense of collective worthlessness and inferiority (Sherlock & Bennett, 1998).

The ideology of racism used to legitimize African slavery was extended to the physical, genetic, and biological traits of Black people. The very colour of the African skin was deemed to be the first and lasting indicator of inferiority, together with the form of the mouth, nose, and hair texture. This need to extend the ideology of racism from cultural to physical traits was to guarantee that persons of African descent, however successful they were in internalizing and assimilating white culture, would be forever trapped in their status as just mere slaves who were permanently imprisoned in their Black skin (Girvan, 1988).

In his quest to restore Black people's dignity in a society that deliberately devised technologies to strip it away, Marcus Garvey countered with: "The Black skin is not a badge of shame, but rather a glorious symbol of national greatness." We must proudly wear our Blackness and reject the notion that our Black skin is a stigma of historical oppression. It is a manufactured ideology that

Black people are inferior and white people are superior – it is total fiction.

'Race' is not a biological reality; rather, it is a social construct. Born in Western Europe in the mid-1400s, racist ideas travelled to the rest of the world, infecting it.

"The construct of race has always been used to gain and keep power, to create dynamics that separate and silence. A racist idea is any idea that suggests something is wrong or right, superior or inferior, better or worse about a racial group. An antiracist idea is any idea that suggests that racial groups are equals." [Source: Jason Reynolds and Ibram X. Kendi, 'STAMPED: Racism, Antiracism, and You,' 2020, Little, Brown & Company]

Here's the thing. The 'psychological constitution,' the 'cognitive bandwidth' (i.e., the mind, intelligence, and IQ), and the physical features of Africans, and people of African descent, have long been prominent subjects of relentless denigrating colonial cultural and pseudo-scientific debates, designs, and racist ideologies [e.g., Joseph Conrad's **'Heart of Darkness'** (1899); Joyce Cary's **'Mister Johnson'** (1939); and Charles Murray's **'The Bell Curve'** (1994)]. The foregoing speaks to the weaponization of thought and the conscription of complicit and goitrous 'intellectuals' in service of a vile racist ideology that sought to enhance the value of whiteness, and the devaluing of blackness.

Indeed, one enslaver bragged of a desire to breed inferiority in Black people down to the 6th generation.

"Although Frantz Fanon understood the political and economic realities that reduced Black men to "crushing objecthood," his psychiatric training made him sensitive to the psychological power of the images imposed by enslavers on the enslaved. Fanon knew that Black men who internalized these images would find it impossible to escape their colonized selves in a world made by and for white men. White men had not merely conquered vast territories, radically reorganizing societies and exploiting populations. They also claimed to represent a humane civilization devoted to personal liberty and equipped with the superior tools of science, reason, and individual enterprise. "The Europeans wanted gold and slaves, like everybody else," the African narrator of V. S. Naipaul's novel "A Bend in the River" remarks. "But at the same time, they wanted statues put up to themselves as people who had done good things for the slaves." Naturally, "they got both the slaves and the statues. Fanon wrote about how the Black man, cowed by the colonists' unprecedented mixture of greed, righteousness, and military efficacy, tended to internalize the demoralizing judgment delivered on him by the white gaze. "I start suffering from not being a white man," Fanon wrote. "So I will try quite simply to make myself white." But mimicry could be a cure worse than the disease, since it reinforced the existing racial hierarchy, thereby further devastating the Black man's self-esteem." [Source: Pankaj Mishra, Frantz Fanon's Enduring Legacy, The Atlantic Magazine, November 29, 2021]

To be able to treat Black people in such utter disregard for their humanity, there had to first be a belief ... an ideology that they were unworthy. That ideology is white supremacy.

So, "The colonizers' sense of superiority, their sense of mission as the world's civilizers, depends on turning the Other into a barbarian. (Thus) the invention of the 'barbaric Negro' - and by extension, the fabrication of whiteness and all the racial boundary policing that came with it – required immense expenditures of psychic and intellectual energies of the West. An entire generation of 'enlightened' European scholars worked hard to wipe out the cultural and intellectual contributions of Egypt and Nubia from European history, to whiten the West to maintain the purity of the 'European' race. They also stripped all of Africa of any semblance of 'civilization,' using the printed page to eradicate their history and thus reduce a whole continent and its progeny to little more than beasts of burden or brutish heathens. The result is the fabrication of Europe as a discrete, racially pure entity, solely responsible for modernity, on the one hand, and the fabrication of the Negro on the other." [Source: Cedric Robinson, 'Black Marxism: The Making of the Black Radical Tradition, cited in Aime Cesaire's 'Discourse on Colonialism: A Poetics of Anticolonialism']

The foregoing is yet another example of the weaponization of thought and the conscription of complicit intellectuals in service of a vile racist ideology that is unable to resist bald facts: "To wit, the invention of arithmetic and geometry by the Egyptians. To wit, the discovery of astronomy by the Assyrians. To wit, the birth of chemistry among the Arabs. To wit, the appearance of rationalism in Islam at a time when Western thought had a furiously pre-logical cast to it [Source: Aime Cesaire, Discourse on Colonialism].

And so devastating has been the mental control of the mind of Africans and people of African descent that they have become both objects and architects of their own scare and denigration. Manifesting their psychic disfigurement, disarray, and disordedness, many try to run from themselves ... from their racial identity and features through, for example, skin bleaching. The renaming of enslaved persons, branding them as property (mere 'machines'), and other forms of systematic dehumanization were acts of 'identity-stripping' – early forms of identity theft! Erasure of humanity.

So, even after slavery was abolished in Jamaica, the formerly enslaved Blacks suffered from continued mental enslavement - a persistent hangover from the despicable orgy of cruelty and denigration that were defining attributes of chattel slavery.

Garvey: Stirred into Action!

Coming on the scene as he did in a post-emancipation Jamaica that was steeped in injustice and denigration of "Blackness," Garvey was stirred into action as if poked by a burr from a plant evolved to disseminate its seed inconspicuously.

Stirred into action! I like this construct because it elegantly encapsulates the idea that whenever one sees something that is not right, one must do something about it! He unmuted himself!

As a young boy, Garvey himself was exposed to racial prejudice: he used to play with the white daughter of the Methodist minister in the town of his birth, but this was discontinued by the child's mother simply because Garvey was Black (Sherlock & Bennett, 1998).

Garvey's early exposure to books from his father's and godfather's collections helped to arouse his curiosity and stimulated his interest in social issues. And he developed into an effective communicator of ideas largely through his determined efforts.

Further particularizing Garvey's keen intellect, Sherlock and Bennett (1998) noted that: "His richly stored mind linked the particular with the universal, the past with the present, the local or national with the global. To read even a few of his statements and reflections is to encounter a mind that illuminates the Jamaican historical experience; in his analysis of colonial society in the 1920s, for example, he demonstrates his methods of basing conclusions on observations and analysis (p. 293)."

The quote above reveals Sherlock & Bennett's recognition that Marcus Mosiah Garvey had a beautiful mind – that he was an intuitively radical genius!

And, reflecting the contemporary relevance and infinite afterlife of Garvey's philosophy, The Gleaner, in an editorial published on February 19, 2022, heaped praise and respect on him in these terms:

> "Marcus Garvey was born in Jamaica a mere 49 years after the end of slavery on the island. He, however, couldn't be contained by any system or philosophy that held that Africans and people of African descent were somehow intellectually inferior, or less than others. Indeed, by the

1920s, Marcus Garvey was not only espousing radical new thoughts about the place of black people in the world but had built a global organisation of millions of people in support of Back-to-Africa ideas. Marcus Garvey gave black people assuredness about their capacities, without the need for shorting-up or mentorship by other groups. In that sense, he was the forerunner to, and inspiration for, the leaders of the anti-colonial and imperial struggles in Africa and the Caribbean, many of whom acknowledged his influence."

Garvey was stirred and jolted into action by the contemporary realities facing Black African-Jamaicans after emancipation. This was the animating spark for his life's work - he weaponized his formidable intellect against the abominable status quo! Garvey decided to become an instrument.

Jamaicans of a certain age will remember when the regnant belief in the country was that Black Jamaicans were unsuitable for work as receptionists, bank tellers, or any work, except as gardeners and domestic helpers, that involved interaction with the middle- and upper-class people in that era.

An old advertisement for a job at the now-defunct Air Jamaica made the rounds on Facebook in June 2022 – it required applicants to be Jamaican citizens and have "good complexion and attractive hair."

This is the lamentation from one of my friends: "We reject our own language. We legislate against African religions and side-eye anything to do with our Africanness. We are the only people who have a God that looks like other races and a devil that looks like ours... We are the first to bleach and wear those hideous wigs, chemically straightened hair, and any tresses we can glue, sew, and attach to our head to look like another."

"As a Black woman, the decision to love yourself just as you are is a radical act. And I'm as radical as they come." ~Bethanee Epifani J. Bryant

****

Garvey's Vision & Mission
==============####=============

"Garvey's movement grew out of a burning passion to overcome the beliefs, prejudices, distortions, bigotry, half-truths, fears, conceits, and propaganda of vested interests, which had progressively threatened and denied the humanity of people of African descent in this region for some 400 years" - Edward Seaga

Black Liberation & Empowerment

Garvey had a vision of mental (psychological) liberation and economic empowerment for Africans (Black people) primarily through their own efforts. And he set out on a bold and audacious mission to achieve his vision. Using his mind as an instrument, Garvey devised a robust implementation plan.

Reflecting the depth of his intuitively radical genius, Marcus Garvey launched the first **'Black Lives Matter'** movement. About Garvey whom he revered, Dr. Martin Luther King, Jr. said, "He was the first man on a mass scale to give millions of Negroes a sense of dignity and destiny."

Garvey left Jamaica for Britain in 1912. There he attended Birbeck College where he studied law and philosophy for two years. In Britain, he was influenced and inspired by the Egyptian, Druse Mohammed Ali, in whose magazines, '**Africa Times and Orient Review'**, the appalling conditions under which Africans were living and ruled by colonial power were revealed. This exposure served to further motivate Garvey. In 1913, the African Times and Orient Review published his article, **'British**

West Indies in the Mirror of Civilization: History-Making by Colonial Negroes'. In 1914, The Tourist published another article by Garvey, **'The Evolution of Latter-Day Slaves: Jamaica, A Country of Black and White.'**

It was during his time in Britain that Garvey developed and crystallized his idea of one great international organization of Black people, educated, financially independent, having pride in their race; Black people who would take their place as equals on the world stage (Lewis, 1987). According to Hill (1987), Garvey committed himself to the implementation of the vision he articulated.

"Garvey arrived in America at the dawn of the "New Negro" era. Black discontent, punctuated by East St. Louis's bloody race riots in 1917 and intensified by postwar disillusionment, peaked in 1919's Red Summer. Shortly after arriving, Garvey embarked upon a period of travel and lecturing. When he settled in New York City, he organized a chapter of the UNIA, which he had earlier founded in Jamaica as a fraternal organization. Drawing on a gift for oratory, he melded Jamaican peasant aspirations for economic and cultural independence with the American gospel of success to create a new gospel of racial pride. "Garveyism" eventually evolved into a religion of success, inspiring millions of black people worldwide who sought relief from racism and colonialism." [Marcus Garvey: An Overview, UCLA, African Studies Center]

Pan-Africanism & the UNIA

Pan-Africanism - an idea that people of African descent around the world should work together for their liberation and empowerment. Garvey had a global Afro-centric agenda. That is, reflecting his revolutionary vision, Garvey had a pan-African vision of what African people could achieve on the continent and in the diaspora. He had a vision of united Black nations governed by conscious Black leaders.

Insightfully, Garvey recognised that Black people didn't have to be born in Africa to be Africans, because Africa was already born in them.

Garvey studied all of the literature he could find on African history and culture and decided to form the Universal Negro Improvement Association (UNIA) on July 15, 1914, to unify "All the Negro peoples of the world into one great body and to establish a country and government absolutely on their own."

A mission requires a message, methods, a vehicle, and means.

The UNIA was a machine.

An African-people-empowerment-machine!

On August 1, 1920, Marcus Garvey convened the first convention of the Universal Negro Improvement Association and African Communities League UNIA-ACL) in Harlem, New York.

Writing in The Sunday Gleaner on August 2, 2020, Professor Carolyn Cooper described the convention in these terms: "Emancipation Day in the West Indies was a most appropriate date for the inauguration. Fifty-five years after the abolition of slavery in the US, Garvey fully understood that the aftermath of this depraved institution was deadly. He knew that the liberation of black people from the shackles of racism was an ongoing battle that required collective action."

Professor Cooper continued: "Garvey conceived the assembly as "The First International Convention of the Negro Peoples of the World". Approximately two thousand delegates from twenty-two countries attended. The congress was a grand affair lasting for the entire month. On the opening day, there was a spectacular parade. Four mounted police led the procession. Next came the first vice-president of the Black Star Line Steamship Corporation and the secretary of the Negro Factories Corporation, also on horseback. A host of UNIA dignitaries followed in cars, chief among them Marcus Garvey and Gabriel Johnson, mayor of Monrovia, the capital of Liberia. Then came the foot soldiers. There was the Black Star Line Choir; the Philadelphia Legion; the Philadelphia UNIA band; the Black Cross nurses resplendent in their white uniforms; and UNIA representatives from countries such as Jamaica, The Virgin Islands, Panama, St Lucia, Barbados, Trinidad and Tobago, Guyana, Canada, and Nigeria. Approximately 500 cars followed – two mounted police brought up the rear. New York had never seen pageantry like this."

Professor Cooper continued: "The parade was not just about pomp and ceremony. The placards confirmed the militancy of the Garvey movement: **"Down With Lynching"**; **"Africa Must Be Free"**; **"The New Negro Has No Fear"**; **"Toussaint L'Ouverture Was an Abler Soldier Than Napoleon"**; **"What Will England Do In Africa"?** There was this declaration of universal freedom: "The New Negro Wants Liberty, 400,000,000 Black Men Shall Be Free". In 1920, only Liberia and Ethiopia were independent African countries. Haiti was the first Black-led republic. On the evening of August 1, there was a mass meeting at Madison Square Garden (MSG). More than 25,000 people attended Garvey's mass meeting. The choice of Madison Square Garden for the opening of the convention signified the broad scope of Garvey's vision. Last week, I invited MSG to consider acknowledging the historic event on their website. Garvey's mission for the liberation of Black People anticipated the Black Lives Matter movement (I say was the first BLM movement!). I also asked about the cost of renting the venue in 1920. I got a polite response, but no information. One of the major accomplishments of the 1920 convention was the adoption of "The Declaration of the Rights of the Negro Peoples of the World" which had 54 statements. The first was, "That nowhere in the world, with few exceptions, are black men accorded equal treatment with white men, although in the same situation and circumstances, but, on the contrary, are discriminated against and denied the common rights due to human beings for no other reason than their race and colour". The final statement was, "We want all men to know that we shall maintain and contend for the freedom and equality of every man, woman and child of our race, with our lives, our fortunes and our sacred honour."

UNIA's Declaration of Rights

The UNIA-ACL's "Declaration of the Rights of the Negro Peoples of the World" had 54 statements.

Preamble

Be It Resolved, That the Negro people of the world, through their chosen representatives in convention assembled in Liberty Hall, in the City of New York and United States of America, from August 1 to August 31, in the year of Our Lord one thousand nine hundred and twenty, protest against the wrongs and injustices they are suffering at the hands of their white brethren, and state what they deem their fair and just rights, as well as the treatment they propose to demand of all men in the future.

We complain:

1. That nowhere in the world, with few exceptions, are black men accorded equal treatment with white men,

although in the same situation and circumstances, but, on the contrary, are discriminated against and denied the common rights due to human beings for no other reason than their race and color.

We are not willingly accepted as guests in the public hotels and inns of the world for no other reason than our race and color.

2. In certain parts of the United States of America our race is denied the right of public trial accorded to other races when accused of crime, but are lynched and burned by mobs, and such brutal and inhuman treatment is even practiced upon our women.

3. That European nations have parcelled out among them and taken possession of nearly the entire continent of Africa, and the natives are compelled to surrender their lands to aliens and are treated in most instances like slaves.

4. In the southern portion of the United States of America, although citizens under the Federal Constitution, and in some States almost equal to the whites in population and are qualified land owners and taxpayers, we are, nevertheless, denied all voice in the making and administration of the laws and are taxed without representation by the State governments, and at the same time compelled to do military service in defense of the country.

5. On the public conveyances and common carriers in the southern portion of the United States we are Jim-crowed and compelled to accept separate and inferior accommodations and made to pay the same fare charged

for first-class accommodations, and our families are often humiliated and insulted by drunken white men who habitually pass through the Jim-crow cars going to the smoking car.

6. The physicians of our race are denied the right to attend their patients while in the public hospitals of the cities and States where they reside in certain parts of the United States.

Our children are forced to attend inferior separate schools for shorter terms than white children, and the public school funds are unequally divided between the white and colored schools.

7. We are discriminated against and denied an equal chance to earn wages for the support of our families, and in many instances are refused admission into labor unions and nearly everywhere are paid smaller wages than white men.

8. In the Civil Service and departmental offices we are everywhere discriminated against and made to feel that to be a black man in Europe, America and the West Indies is equivalent to being an outcast and a leper among the races of men, no matter what the character attainments of the black men may be.

9. In the British and other West Indian islands and colonies Negroes are secretly and cunningly discriminated against and denied those fuller rights of government to which white citizens are appointed, nominated and elected.

10. That our people in those parts are forced to work for lower wages than the average standard of white men

and are kept in conditions repugnant to good civilized tastes and customs.

11. That the many acts of injustices against members of our race before the courts of law in the respective islands and colonies are of such nature as to create disgust and disrespect for the white man's sense of justice.

12. Against all such inhuman, unchristian and uncivilized treatment we here and now emphatically protest, and invoke the condemnation of all mankind.

In order to encourage our race all over the world and to stimulate it to overcome the handicaps and difficulties surrounding it, and to push forward to a higher and grander destiny, we demand and insist on the following Declaration of Rights:

1. Be it known to all men that whereas all men are created equal and entitled to the rights of life, liberty and the pursuit of happiness, and because of this we, the duly elected representatives of the Negro peoples of the world, invoking the aid of the just and Almighty God, do declare all men, women and children of our blood throughout the world free denizens, and do claim them as free citizens of Africa, the Motherland of all Negroes.

2. That we believe in the supreme authority of our race in all things racial; that all things are created and given to man as a common possession; that there should be an equitable distribution and apportionment of all such things, and in consideration of the fact that as a race we are now deprived of those things that are morally and legally ours, we believed it right that all such things

should be acquired and held by whatsoever means possible.

3. That we believe the Negro, like any other race, should be governed by the ethics of civilization, and therefore should not be deprived of any of those rights or privileges common to other human beings.

4. We declare that Negroes, wheresoever they form a community among themselves should be given the right to elect their own representatives to represent them in Legislatures, courts of law, or such institutions as may exercise control over that particular community.

5. We assert that the Negro is entitled to even-handed justice before all courts of law and equity in whatever country he may be found, and when this is denied him on account of his race or color such denial is an insult to the race as a whole and should be resented by the entire body of Negroes.

6. We declare it unfair and prejudicial to the rights of Negroes in communities where they exist in considerable numbers to be tried by a judge and jury composed entirely of an alien race, but in all such cases members of our race are entitled to representation on the jury.

7. We believe that any law or practice that tends to deprive any African of his land or the privileges of free citizenship within his country is unjust and immoral, and no native should respect any such law or practice.

8. We declare taxation without representation unjust and tyrannous, and there should be no obligation on the part of the Negro to obey the levy of a tax by any law-

making body from which he is excluded and denied representation on account of his race and color.

9. We believe that any law especially directed against the Negro to his detriment and singling him out because of his race or color is unfair and immoral, and should not be respected.

10. We believe all men entitled to common human respect and that our race should in no way tolerate any insults that may be interpreted to mean disrespect to our race or color.

11. We deprecate the use of the term "nigger" as applied to Negroes, and demand that the word "Negro" be written with a capital "N."

12. We believe that the Negro should adopt every means to protect himself against barbarous practices inflicted upon him because of color.

13. We believe in the freedom of Africa for the Negro people of the world, and by the principle of Europe for the Europeans and Asia for the Asiatics, we also demand Africa for the Africans at home and abroad.

14. We believe in the inherent right of the Negro to possess himself of Africa and that his possession of same shall not be regarded as an infringement of any claim or purchase made by any race or nation.

15. We strongly condemn the cupidity of those nations of the world who, by open aggression or secret schemes, have seized the territories and inexhaustible natural wealth of Africa, and we place on record our most solemn determination to reclaim the treasures and possession of the vast continent of our forefathers.

16. We believe all men should live in peace one with the other, but when races and nations provoke the ire of other races and nations by attempting to infringe upon their rights, war becomes inevitable, and the attempt in any way to free one's self or protect one's rights or heritage becomes justifiable.

17. Whereas the lynching, by burning, hanging or any other means, of human beings is a barbarous practice and a shame and disgrace to civilization, we therefore declare any country guilty of such atrocities outside the pale of civilization.

18. We protest against the atrocious crime of whipping, flogging and overworking of the native tribes of Africa and Negroes everywhere. These are methods that should be abolished and all means should be taken to prevent a continuance of such brutal practices.

19. We protest against the atrocious practice of shaving the heads of Africans, especially of African women or individuals of Negro blood, when placed in prison as a punishment for crime by an alien race.

10. We protest against segregated districts, separate public conveyances, industrial discrimination, lynchings and limitations of political privileges of any Negro citizen in any part of the world on account of race, color or creed, and will exert our full influence and power against all such.

21. We protest against any punishment inflicted upon a Negro with severity, as against lighter punishment inflicted upon another of an alien race for like offense, as

an act of prejudice and injustice, and should be resented by the entire race.

22. We protest against the system of education in any country where Negroes are denied the same privileges and advantages as other races.

23. We declare it inhuman and unfair to boycott Negroes from industries and labor in any part of the world.

24. We believe in the doctrine of the freedom of the press, and we therefore emphatically protest against the suppression of Negro newspapers and periodicals in various parts of the world, and call upon Negroes everywhere to employ all available means to prevent such suppression.

25. We further demand free speech universally for all men.

26. We hereby protest against the publication of scandalous and inflammatory articles by an alien press tending to create racial strife and the exhibition of picture films showing the Negro as a cannibal.

27. We believe in the self-determination of all peoples.

28. We declare for the freedom of religious worship.

29. With the help of Almighty God we declare ourselves the sworn protectors of the honor and virtue of our women and children, and pledge our lives for their protection and defense everywhere and under all circumstances from wrongs and outrages.

30. We demand the right of an unlimited and unprejudiced education for ourselves and our posterity forever.

31. We declare that the teaching in any school by alien teachers to our boys and girls, that the alien race is superior to the Negro race, is an insult to the Negro people of the world.

32. Where Negroes form a part of the citizenry of any country, and pass the civil service examination of such country, we declare them entitled to the same consideration as other citizens as to appointments in such civil service.

33. We vigorously protest against the increasingly unfair and unjust treatment accorded Negro travelers on land and sea by the agents and employee of railroad and steamship companies, and insist that for equal fare we receive equal privileges with travelers of other races.

34. We declare it unjust for any country, State or nation to enact laws tending to hinder and obstruct the free immigration of Negroes on account of their race and color.

35. That the right of the Negro to travel unmolested throughout the world be not abridged by any person or persons, and all Negroes are called upon to give aid to a fellow Negro when thus molested.

36. We declare that all Negroes are entitled to the same right to travel over the world as other men.

37. We hereby demand that the governments of the world recognize our leader and his representatives chosen by the race to look after the welfare of our people under such governments.

38. We demand complete control of our social institutions without interference by any alien race or races.

39. That the colors, Red, Black and Green, be the colors of the Negro race.

40. Resolved, that the anthem "Ethiopia, Thou Land of Our Fathers etc.," shall be the anthem of the Negro race. . . .

41. We believe that any limited liberty which deprives one of the complete rights and prerogatives of full citizenship is but a modified form of slavery.

42. We declare it an injustice to our people and a serious Impediment to the health of the race to deny to competent licensed Negro physicians the right to practice in the public hospitals of the communities in which they reside, for no other reason than their race and color.

43. We call upon the various government[s] of the world to accept and acknowledge Negro representatives who shall be sent to the said governments to represent the general welfare of the Negro peoples of the world.

44. We deplore and protest against the practice of confining juvenile prisoners in prisons with adults, and we recommend that such youthful prisoners be taught gainful trades under human[e] supervision.

45. Be it further resolved, that we as a race of people declare the League of Nations null and void as far as the Negro is concerned, in that it seeks to deprive Negroes of their liberty.

46. We demand of all men to do unto us as we would do unto them, in the name of justice; and we cheerfully accord to all men all the rights we claim herein for ourselves.

47. We declare that no Negro shall engage himself in battle for an alien race without first obtaining the consent of the leader of the Negro people of the world, except in a matter of national self-defense.

48. We protest against the practice of drafting Negroes and sending them to war with alien forces without proper training, and demand in all cases that Negro soldiers be given the same training as the aliens.

49. We demand that instructions given Negro children in schools include the subject of "Negro History," to their benefit.

50. We demand a free and unfettered commercial intercourse with all the Negro people of the world.

51. We declare for the absolute freedom of the seas for all peoples.

52. We demand that our duly accredited representatives be given proper recognition in all leagues, conferences, conventions or courts of international arbitration wherever human rights are discussed.

53. We proclaim the 31st day of August of each year to be an international holiday to be observed by all Negroes.

54. We want all men to know that we shall maintain and contend for the freedom and equality of every man,

woman and child of our race, with our lives, our fortunes and our sacred honor.

These rights we believe to be justly ours and proper for the protection of the Negro race at large, and because of this belief we, on behalf of the four hundred million Negroes of the world, do pledge herein the sacred blood of the race in defense, and we hereby subscribe our names as a guarantee of the truthfulness and faithfulness hereof, in the presence of Almighty God, on this 13th day of August, in the year of our Lord one thousand nine hundred and twenty. [Source: UNIA Declaration of Rights of the Negro Peoples of the World, New York, August 13, 1920. Reprinted in Robert Hill, ed., The Marcus Garvey and Universal Negro Improvement Papers, Vol. 2 (Berkeley, University of California Press, 1983), 571–580].

UNIA: Largest Mass Movement of Blacks

The UNIA grew rapidly like a gormandizer.

By 1919 there were over 30 branches throughout the United States, the Caribbean, Latin America, and Africa. Garvey said over a million people had joined his organization in three years. In nine years, Garvey built the largest mass movement of people of African descent in the history of the USA - never before had one Blackman mobilised so many Black people!

"Marcus Garvey scholars generally agree on the global reach of his philosophy. Their consensus turns on the proliferation of branches of the Universal Negro Improvement Association (UNIA) across the world and its rhetoric of race uplift." [Source: Nicholas Patsides, 2005]

"At its height, the UNIA had an estimated four million members with more than 1,000 branches in more than 20 countries and is generally considered the largest mass movement in Afro-American history. Many major African political figures would recall being influenced by Garvey, including Ghana's Kwame Nkrumah, Kenya's Jomo Kenyatta, and Nigeria's Nnamdi Azikiwe. Much of the African National Congress leadership in 1920s South Africa belonged to the UNIA. So did Elijah Muhammad, who, to a large extent, patterned his Nation of Islam movement on the UNIA. Malcolm X's father was a UNIA organiser, and Vietnamese leader Ho Chi Min attended UNIA meetings." [Source: Kevin O'Brien Chang, 'Marcus Garvey: Black champion of vision and destiny,' The Gleaner, August 3, 2012]

"You could claim that Garvey is the father of African independence," Robert Hill, a research professor of history at UCLA and a Garvey expert, says. "I'd be willing to make that claim, and he's regarded as such by many, many people in Africa."

"Garvey established the ideological pillars of twentieth-century pan-Africanism in promoting self-determination and self-reliance for African's independence.

Garvey's success in the USA did not sit well with some rivals for Black leadership. Garvey was also described in uncomplimentary terms by the American civil rights protagonist W.E.B. DuBois, as "a little man, black and fat and ugly, but with intelligent eyes and a big head." Dubois and A. Phillip Randolph campaigned against Marcus Garvey and colluded with the vile and evil J.

Edgar Hoover and the Federal Bureau of Investigation (FBI) to have Garvey deported from the USA and the UNIA dismantled. The first Black FBI agent that was hired was employed to infiltrate Garvey's organization.

"So intent was he (J. Edgar Hoover) on bringing Garvey down (whom he described as 'the notorious Negro agitator') that he thought nothing of deploying black agents as undercover operatives to successfully and effectively infiltrate Garvey's Universal Negro Improvement Association (UNIA), and thus ensure the inevitable impairment of his organisation. The inefficient way in which the Black Star Line Steamship Company was ultimately run, can be largely attributed to undercover Black Bureau of Investigation (BOI) officers, as well as other notable traitors within Garvey's movement, such as Joshua Cockburn, the ship captain for the **Yarmouth** (the first ship purchased for the Black Star Line Steamship Company), and one of the few Black men at the time qualified to be a ship's captain. Cockburn advised Garvey to pay an inflated price of US$165,000 for the ship and then secretly received a kickback payment from the seller of the ship for making such a profitable deal for him. The Yarmouth was a fairly old vessel and actually way past its prime. Garvey, not having prior experience in purchasing ships, relied on and trusted Joshua Cockburn because of his many years of experience in captaining ships." [Source: Dr. Michael Barnett, 'Unfettering Marcus Garvey,' The Jamaica Observer, February 20, 2022]

This is also apt: "Hoover's FBI harassed three generations of Black activists, from Marcus Garvey's Black nationalists to Martin Luther King Jr's integrationists to Huey Newton's Black Panthers, including my father." ~

Ta-Nehisi Coates, The Atlantic, January/February Issue, 2017

The 'Boule' & NAACP vs. The UNIA

I will mention the 'Boule' now and its rivalry with Marcus Garvey. "The 'Boule' is a Black Greek secret society based on another secret society founded at Yale University called ...Skull & Bones. The Boule's primary founder was Dr. Henry McKee Minton along with Drs. Eugene T. Henson, Edwin Clarence Howard, Algernon Brashear Jackson, Robert Jones Abele, and Richard John Warrick; all of Philadelphia. They are the so-called "talented 10th" WEB DuBois is famous for speaking of. The founding member of the New York City chapter, W.E.B DuBois, said the Boule's major ambition was to steal the Black professional from the ranks of Marcus Garvey, who, at that time in 1918 was reaching over one million-plus Diasporic Africans mainly in North America without television or radio via his newspaper ...The Negro World. DuBois was one of the strongest opponents of Garvey and was an instrumental "tool" in stopping one of the strongest grassroots movements of the last century. What was Garvey's plan? His plan was to take as many Africans from the America's and start a settlement in the nation of Liberia and then help this new nation produce and control their own rubber crops and create other industries made of natural resources. It needs to be acknowledged that Firestone became the controlling entity of the rubber crops ruling Liberia with an iron hand. Garvey said: "If the oil of Africa is good for Rockefeller's interest, iron is good for Carnegie trust; the

Oppenheimer's raping and stripping Africa of her natural resources of gold, silver, diamonds...then these minerals are good for us. Why should we allow Wall Street and the capitalist group of America and other countries to exploit our country when they refuse to give us a fair chance in the countries of our adoption? Why should not Africa give to the world its Black Rockefeller, Rothschild, and Henry Ford? This would have potentially meant no Firestone, Goodyear, or U.S. Steel as we know it today because it would have set a precedent that would make all Africans aware of their land and mineral wealth it offers. This also would have shattered the financial arm of white supremacy right when it was getting started. DuBois, along with Alain Locke ...the first Black (Cecil) Rhodes' scholar...publicly defiled Garvey by calling him a gorilla and "a little, fat black man, ugly with a big head." Locke was quoted as saying: "We hope the white man delivers because we crushed a great Black thing, but we know he'll deliver or our people will attack and plague us forever more." Astonishingly these two house-negroes didn't believe in African self-reliance and deferred their allegiance to their overseer hoping they'd be given table scraps instead of making their own." [Source: H. Lewis Smith, Staff Writer, ThyBlackman.com]

DuBois stressed, according to futurologist Steve Cokely, "The importance to steal the Black professional away from Garvey because an Afrocentric organization that articulated and captured the Black professional would give whitey no safe haven in the black community, so the Boule' — the remaking of the house negro was necessary to build a group of negroes who had an investment in protecting the white system as produced by whitey having stolen this land...This is post-reconstruction. Taking away the articulate negro, now desiring to replace them with organized institutions to keep them away from self-improvement." [Source: Mildred Europa Taylor, Face2Face Africa, July 2, 2020]

The animus between Marcus Garvey and his United Negro Improvement Association (UNIA) and W.E.B. DuBois and the National Association for the Advancement of Colored People (NAACP) exemplifies how internecine conflict and disunity undermine the progress of Black people and dissipate the collective energy they should harness and deploy against their real, common enemy – white supremacists and the white establishment!

Other Black intellectuals such as C.L.R. James and George Padmore also mounted campaigns in London against Garvey. According to Colin Grant, these individuals, "instead of realizing that they shared a commonality of purpose, circled round each other in a narcissistic battle of minor differences. Theirs was a mirror of the many skirmishes Garvey had fought with other black leaders in Jamaica."

In Jamaica, Marcus Garvey, then a councillor in the Kingston and St. Andrew Corporation, and Norman Manley, at the time a barrister who was developing a reputation as one of the best in the region, would go head to head in 1934 at a KSAC meeting over a gas station dispute.

In a Letter to the Editor of The Gleaner on September 18, 2011, communications specialist Ken Jones (who also wrote a book **'Marcus Garvey Said'**) gave an account of the face-off between Garvey and Norman Manley:

"The fuss nearly 80 years ago was over what was then called the historic gas station at the corner of Old Hope and Oxford roads. The controversy that swirled around this building persisted for some six years before a settlement was reached. At one point, two of our now national heroes came close to fisticuffs after a heated debate in the meeting room of the Kingston and St Andrew Corporation. The complex, convoluted controversy began sometime in 1932 when George Penso, a businessman and landed proprietor, decided to build a gas station in what was then considered a quiet residential area. It would be a match and competitor to another gas station at the intersection of Half-Way Tree and Oxford roads; and also a convenience for ladies and gentlemen who were breaking style by driving their own cars instead of using chauffeurs. Mr. Penso had made an application to the KSAC building authorities, received permission and proceeded with construction. However, as the building neared completion, an influential resident across the road, Dr. Godfrey, raised a protest on grounds that a nuisance was being created - there would be the noise of car engines, bright lights late at night, and such activity as would tend to decrease the value of premises in the area. What followed caused an explosion of arguments. Some members of the council that had approved the building and supervised its construction persuaded the mayor that the meeting that granted approval was not properly constituted and that Mr. Penso should reapply for permission. Legal battle lines were drawn. Mr. Penso retained Mr. Leslie Ashenheim to argue that he had put up his building in good faith and should not reapply. The mayor engaged Manton & Hart, which firm retained Mr. Norman Manley to help sort out the tangled situation. Meanwhile, public discussion raged, and Marcus Garvey, then a KSAC councillor, held a public meeting on the matter at Old Wolmer's Yard, next door the parish church.

The gallery was packed tight on the day of the meeting called to consider the burning question. At once, it was stated by Mayor George Seymour that Garvey was not competent to sit or vote on the matter, as learned counsel had advised that he was disqualified. Garvey made a long statement in which he denied alleged conflict of interest because Mr. Penso had once stood surety for him. The mayor then said:

"It has been brought to my attention, and I am advised Councillor Garvey, that you are not competent to sit and vote on this occasion, not on account of any matter that you have explained, but on another matter entirely. And that matter is in connection with the meeting at Old Wolmer's and at which you invited a mandate from the people to say whether you were to vote for the keeping of the gas station at the corner of Oxford and Old Hope roads. I am advised by counsel that that disqualifies you as showing bias in the matter ... ."

Garvey responded: "Well, I know the legal mind and I know there are always subterfuges ... . I am going to bow to your ruling only, but I am going to differ from your counsel who does not seem to know that an elected representative always possesses the right to consult the people who elected him on any matter; and I am sorry for the legal intelligence, the political intelligence of counsel, if he does not know that that could not disqualify one dealing with a public matter representing the people. But I bow to your ruling." An annoyed Norman Manley rose to his feet, declaring, "Mr Chairman, I attended here at your request because of the difficulties the Corporation has been in, but I am not going to remain here to listen to Councillor Garvey making his offensive remarks. He knows nothing about law."

Garvey: I know as much as you about this matter.

Manley: I have not been invited here to listen to any impertinence from Mr Garvey

Garvey: Neither from you, too.

Manley: I have given my opinion and he has not the decency and intelligence ...

Garvey: You are most irresponsible.

Manley: And you are a positive disgrace.

Garvey: Look here, Manley, I don't care about you. You fellows seem to assume some right that is not justifiable.

When the chairman intervened, Garvey continued heatedly:

... How dare him call me impertinent, Sir, when I have only exercised my right to say what I understand about the matter. You must be one of the socially drunk people who think that.

Manley: Look here, you are a loud-voiced person and I am not going to answer you in any way. If you insist on being rude and impertinent ....

Garvey: You are not physically well enough to be loud-voiced.

Manley (visibly upset): Do you really think so? Then step outside.

Garvey: I would be sorry for what would happen to you.

Manley indicated a readiness to step outside but Garvey remained in his seat. The bitter argument continued and Mr. Ashenheim walked out of the meeting after saying that his client would not be reapplying and that the Corporation was running the risk of expensive litigation. At the end of the meeting, the Corporation voted "against the application" although there was no application other than the original, which had been approved. After that, advice was sought from the attorney general and the matter reached the Supreme Court, which ruled that the meeting that had approved the erection of the building was, in fact, not properly constituted. However, there was no ruling as to whether or not the Corporation should approve, as the decision was entirely its business.

The controversy dragged on and on. At a subsequent meeting, Mr. Garvey argued that the meeting at which he was not allowed to vote was, in fact, ultra vires because it had not been called at the request of any councillor, but just by the mayor. Furthermore, it had taken place sooner than the required six months after the previous meeting. He was also against the Corporation wasting money on litigation instead of fixing roads and bridges for the people. He was overruled.

The matter remained undecided for many months, leading into years. Meanwhile, the times were changing; and so were values and attitudes. Mr. Penso sold the gas station to Trinidad Leaseholds, a British company that had built the oil refinery in Trinidad and would soon operate as Regent and later Texaco. Also, Dr. Godfrey, the leading protester against the gas station, had applied for and got permission to erect a 'Chinese shop' on land he owned across the street. Still, the city fathers continued to argue.

In 1937, fully four years after the controversy began, Councillor Earnest Rae wanted the building torn down forthwith and an absorption pit that had been dug removed. None of this was done, as the Corporation continued to be wary of getting into deeper legal waters. Eventually, in 1939, the matter came to a head when the corporation ruled that Oxford Road was the northern boundary of the commercial district. After that, the station was legally opened for business.

As for that Manley-Garvey altercation in which Marcus declined Norman's invitation to "step outside", H.G. Delisser wrote, with tongue in cheek: "Possibly, Mr. Garvey was well aware that although ... Mr. Manley, in his opinion, does not look 'physically well enough to be loud-voiced'; although Mr. Manley is slim and even delicately looking - Mr. Garvey may have been aware ... that Mr. Manley is by way of being a lightweight pugilist ... really an athlete in good condition; he understands boxing and wrestling and would be an ugly customer to tackle."

On the other hand, there is no telling what might have happened had vexed members of the pro-Garvey gallery accompanied him and become part of the contest."

Concerning the difficulties he faced with other Blacks, here is Garvey in his own words: "Because of my attempt to lead my race into the only solution that I see would benefit both groups, I have been maliciously and wickedly maligned, and by members of our own race. I have been plotted against, framed up, indicted, and convicted."

Remarkably, while many of Garvey's antagonists are largely forgotten, he now occupies a place of honour as the 'Black Moses'.

Professor Rupert Lewis notes, "Self-denial, denigration, and defining one's identity according to colonial Britishness were hallmarks of brown and black West Indians' ambition to escape blackness and what they perceived as Africa's lack of civilization and its savagery. Black Jamaicans were a product of British commercial, military, and missionary incursions into Africa, but when Garvey proposed a redemptive mission for Africa – that is, a wresting of Africa from European control – the idea was met with hostility, particularly by educated West Indians." [Source: Rupert Lewis, 'Marcus Garvey' 2018, The University of the West Indies Press]

Wow!

"Educated West Indians!" Here we see the deliberate outcome that colonial education aimed to achieve – producing allegedly educated stooges and mimics to voluntarily maintain the status quo! Breaking this dense psychological hardpan is difficult.

I will dilate on this 'colonial education' thingy some more, below.

Education systems have been implicated in the maintenance of structures of domination by being vehicles for the reproduction of classism, racism, sexism, and hierarchical historical privilege. Colonial-inspired and implemented education, for example, is designed to produce an army of subordinate functionaries.

The question of the 'type' of education children are exposed to in a post-colonial society is not a trifling matter to be glossed over. Rather, it is of fundamental importance.

You see, education has long been a space of animated contestation in post-colonial discourse. In a sense, education is a type of 'programming,' hence a country's education system must be subjected to careful deliberation and consideration of its intent. And this cannot be left to chance.

The most critical issue that must be addressed is dismantling the 'colonialist intent' which was designed primarily to promote Eurocentric cultural, epistemic, and intellectual hegemony and homogenous ideas about development and change while ignoring post-colonial realities, talent, and worth.

And as to how the colonialist intent skillfully and insidiously engendered self-hate and self-loathing among Blacks, Chinua Achebe, in an essay called **'African Literature as Restoration of Celebration,'** wrote about his first exposure in a colonial-run boarding school to colonialist 'literature classics' such as **'Prester John,'** "I did not see myself as an African, to begin with ... The white man was good, reasonable, intelligent, and courageous. The savages arrayed against him were sinister and stupid or, at the most, cunning. I hated their guts."

At university, Achebe's eyes got clearer to the viciousness of the psychological terrorism against African embedded in colonial education: "At University College, Ibadan (where he initially planned to study medicine), Achebe encountered the novel **'Mister Johnson,'** by the Anglo-Irish writer Joyce Cary, who had spent time as a colonial officer in Nigeria. The book was lauded by Time Magazine as "The best novel ever written about Africa."

But Achebe was appalled by Joyce Cary's depiction of his homeland and its people. In Joyce Cary's portrait, the "Jealous savages . . . live like mice or rats in a palace floor;" dancers are "grinning, shrieking, scowling, or with faces which seemed entirely dislocated, senseless and unhuman, like twisted bags of lard." It was the image of blacks as "unhuman," a standard trope of colonial literature, that Achebe recognized as particularly dangerous. "It began to dawn on me that although fiction was undoubtedly fictitious it could also be true or false, not with the truth or falsehood of a news item but as to its disinterestedness, its intention, its integrity," he wrote later. This belief in fiction's moral power became integral to his vision for African literature." [Source: Ruth Franklin, 'Chinua Achebe and the Great African novel,' The New Yorker, May 19, 2008]

Chinua Achebe could not abide the awful, grotesque, and obscene travesty. So, like the courageous Marcus Garvey before him, Achebe was stirred into action. He actioned his anger! Achebe became a human instrument! A human weapon!

Achebe made the ugliness latent and embedded in various so-called 'classics' of English Literature impossible to ignore. And he redirected his intellectual prowess to writing – he had originally planned to study medicine - to contribute to remedying the disgusting intellectual violence. Things Fall Apart his first novel was released in 1958 when he was 28 years old. Achebe 'instrumentalised' his intellect through writing, to counter deliberate colonial-inspired unflattering distortions and depictions of Africa and Africans.

(Marley Dias is a 12-year-old Jamaican-American student living in the USA. In June 2022, she appeared on American television to promote her **'1000 Black Girl Books'** initiative. Dias said: "I started this campaign because I wanted to read more books where black girls are the main characters."

Here are some tips for fixing the love of reading in our children: "A love of reading is the most important legacy we can offer to our children and our students. Reading opens windows to new ideas, peoples, places, and experiences. Reading also provides mirrors for students to see themselves and their lives reflected in the characters they meet in books. Reading builds vocabulary and background knowledge, empowering children with the tools needed to express themselves and think about the world around them. Nurturing joyful reading in children primes their brains for lifelong learning and develops important social emotional skills like stamina, reflection, and empathy. As we build readers, we must make reading pleasurable and help children understand that reading is a skill that builds over time. Here are a few tips for parents and educators to create environments that invite children to confidently embrace and fall in love with stories and books.

Tips for parents:

- Model reading. Read, read, read to your child, with your child, or in front of your child every day.
- Immerse your child in books. Transform your entire home into a reading zone by placing books in every room.
- Affirm your child's culture, language, and race by choosing books and stories with characters, places, and experiences that reflect their background.
- Awaken your child to new ideas, places, people, or experiences in books and stories by asking them questions and always answering the question they have.
- Empower your child by allowing them to choose books to read, whether based on what interests them or on book covers and titles.
- Arm your child by always leaving home with books. When your child gets older ask them if they have a book before leaving for school, the doctor, or a long ride.
- Cultivate your child's use of language and words. Talk with your child about what is happening in their lives and the world around them.
- Build your child's ability to make connections. When you watch television or movies, make connections to characters or ideas in books you have read together.
- Expand your child's reading beyond fiction. Children have great curiosity about events taking place in the world, plants, animals, and people. It's never too early to expose them to historical fiction or non-fiction books.
- Advocate for curricula, partnerships, books, and resources for classrooms and schools that are culturally relevant and responsive.

Tips for educators:

- Model reading. Read, read, read to your students, with your students, or in front of your students every day.
- Immerse school culture in talks about books. Book talks over the intercom, book clubs, social media chats, and school-wide read alouds are a few ways to do this.
- Affirm your students' culture, language, and race by integrating books and stories with characters, places, and experiences that reflect their backgrounds into the curriculum.
- Awaken students as participants in their own learning by having them create reading goals for themselves, for example, minutes of reading, chapters read, and reading new genres.
- Empower students by allowing them to choose books based on what interests them or on book covers and titles.
- Arm your students with the power of their own language and stories by providing them with multiple ways to make personal connections to the texts they read.
- Cultivate independent reading by creating comfortable reading spaces throughout schools. Classrooms, cafeterias, libraries, and cozy nooks in hallways are all fair game.
- Build classroom libraries of interesting, appropriate, and relevant fiction and non-fiction texts.
- Expand your reading beyond fiction. Students have great curiosity about events taking place in the world, plants, animals, and people. Use historical fiction or non-fiction books as tools to capture this interest.
- Advocate for curricula, partnerships, books, and resources for classrooms and schools that are culturally relevant and responsive." [Source: GrassRoots Community Foundation dot. org, contributed by Dr. Lauren Wells, Chief Education Officer, City of Newark])

When 'educated' West Indians' hostility toward Garvey's ideas is considered against the background of the intent of colonial education, it is not surprising. The chapter on education in Michael Manley's magnum opus, **'The Politics of Change: A Jamaican Testament'**, is a 'must-read.'

Professor Rupert Lewis (2018) also mentioned the other 'minefields' through which Garvey had to trudge, to wit: "Throughout Garvey's life, controversy about his ideals and his leadership meant that he functioned in perpetual ideological, cultural, political, and economic minefields as he sought to challenge the racial subordination and economic exploitation being experienced by Africans. He was not always right on tactical issues, but the need for realignment of power in the interest of Africa and its peoples called for the fundamental restructuring of global power."

Garvey was up against tremendous countervailing forces - the all-powerful and ruthless colonial edifice and, sadly, a sizable number of his own people. Let us be clear, the cost of challenging the establishment can be high; it can be everything. But Garvey was undaunted. He was a profile in radical courage! And bravery! And audacity! He declared that "Real men laugh at opposition; real men smile when enemies appear." Fear is a reaction; courage is a decision.

"If there is no struggle, there is no progress. Those who want to profess to favour freedom, and yet deprecate agitation, are men who want crops without plowing up the ground. They want rain without thunder and lightning. They want the ocean without the awful roar of its many waters." [Frederick Douglass]

Garvey The Psychologist
===============####===========

The elegance of Garvey's radical and razor-sharp genius becomes even more obvious when one sees that he intuitively recognized that the starting point for his project of liberation, enlightenment, and empowerment of Black People had to be the application of a tourniquet to their abused psychitecture (their mental 'landscape') to arrest the hemorrhaging of their self-esteem that resulted from the indignities of chattel slavery and its aftermath.

Psychological Reprogramming

Garvey intuitively recognized that the 'condition' that would later be called post-traumatic stress disorder (PTSD) was at epidemic proportions among Black people living in post-colonial societies, including Jamaica. He started by providing supportive psychological first aid and realized, given the chronic and deep-seated nature of the malady, that a sustained regimen of psychological reprogramming was necessary as a sine qua non (an essential condition; a thing that is absolutely necessary) for psychical healing and empowerment of Black People!

Frantz Fanon stated that European imperialists had "Behaved like real war criminals in the underdeveloped world" for centuries, using "deportation, massacres, forced labor, and slavery" to accumulate wealth. Among their "most heinous" crimes was the rupturing of the

Black man's identity, the destruction of his culture and community, and the poisoning of his inner life with a sense of inferiority." [Source: Pankaj Mishra, Frantz Fanon's Enduring Legacy, The Atlantic, November 29, 2021]

Garvey intuitively knew the importance of self-identity, self-confidence, and self-reliance to the prospects of a people. He knew that the affirmation or consciousness of the value of Black or African history, culture, heritage, and identity – is a potent weapon to counter, overthrow, and vanquish the obscene ideology and contrived fiction of the 'barbaric Negro'. Marcus Mosiah Garvey understood this intuitively. Genius!

Sherlock and Bennett (1998) noted that "Garvey was one of the few of his time who understood how seriously the inner world [the psychitecture] of the African had been damaged, and in some instances destroyed, by the experience of enslavement combined with alienation" (p. 294).

(Sidebar: Charlotte Forten [1837-1914], a Black woman and an anti-slavery activist, poet, and educator, was one of the first persons to call the melancholic state of mind that she discovered among formerly enslaved Blacks in the Southern USA "the blues." I think Forten was observing symptoms of the yet unnamed disorder post-traumatic stress disorder (PTSD) and in particular post-traumatic slavery stress disorder (PTSSD)).

Emancipation from Mental Slavery

Marcus Garvey grasped that the 'colonial reach' persisted deep in the corridors of the minds of the Black

People within whom was housed the enduring legacy of the effects of dehumanisation. And because Garvey was intuitively aware that psychological murder and maiming were real phenomena and how seriously the psychologicalscape of Blacks was damaged, he proclaimed:

"We are going to emancipate ourselves from mental slavery because whilst others might free the body, none but ourselves can free the mind. Mind is your only ruler, sovereign. The man who is not able to develop and use his mind is bound to be the slave of the other man who uses his mind."

This is one of the most profound proclamations ever made by a Black Man! Ever! The installation of a new cognitive operating system is a prerequisite - a sine qua non (an essential condition; a thing that is absolutely necessary) - for true Black liberation and Black empowerment.

Marcus Garvey knew, intuitively (instinctively), that true freedom was an inside job.

So, because Marcus Mosiah Garvey understood the effects of the psychic maiming of Black People and the need for their psychical healing, he sought to install a new mindset among them. This is akin to installing a new operating system on a computer. He also sought to establish new expectations of themselves among Blacks.

That is why, for example, he emphatically stated: "Up, up ye mighty race ... without confidence, you are twice defeated in the race of life ... chance has never yet satisfied the hope of a suffering people ... action, self-reliance, the vision of self and the future have been the only means by which the oppressed have seen and realized the light of their own freedom."

And Garvey also said, "The time has come for the Black man to forget his hero worship of other races and to create and emulate heroes of his own."

I am positing that a part of the "hero worship of other races" to which Garvey referred, includes worshipping a God that looks like the oppressors of Black people!

In '**Redemption Song'** Jamaican reggae artist, icon, and Rastafarian, Bob Marley, popularized Marcus Mosiah Garvey's potent message to Black people to "emancipate yourselves from mental slavery." The idea of mental slavery [mental enslavement is capturing and holding people in psychological imprisonment]; Garvey meant it in the context of knowing one's history, specifically African history, and again, continuing the fight for equality, racial justice, and economic empowerment.

Despite their bottomless physical barbarity, colonialists have been most effective at the psychological level in the subjugation of Black people. And Marcus Garvey recognised this!

So, being fully cognizant of the colonial ideology that deliberately and systematically denigrated Blackness as inferior and whiteness as superior, Garvey started his mission first by attempting to raise the consciousness of Black People about themselves as a race by focusing on racial pride and self-esteem in an attempt to break their continued mental enslavement that manifested itself in self-contempt, self-doubt, and cynicism.

The evil colonisers knew that sustained subjugation of Black People rested on this: "Capture their minds, and their hearts and souls will follow. For once their minds are reached, they're defeated without bullets." ~ Anonymous

The evil colonisers knew that intergenerational subjugation of Black People could be scaffolded on this: "If you can control a man's thinking, you do not have to worry about his actions." ~ Carter G. Woodson

Psychological disfigurement is a real phenomenon. To become self-empowered, and self-determined, a revolution was needed - a consciousness revolution. Marcus Garvey thus clearly demonstrated his understanding that consciousness-raising is a precursor to significant learning. Still, further evidence of Garvey's radical genius is seen in his use of consciousness-raising not as the culmination of his project, but as the initial scaffolding upon which to build a more sustained programme of learning and action.

Consciousness-raising

The fact that 'consciousness-raising' was Garvey's starting point is hugely significant. Here is why. You see, 'dysconsciousness' is the antonym for consciousness. Dysconsciousness refers to "an uncritical habit of mind (including perceptions, attitudes, assumptions, and beliefs) that justifies inequity and exploitation by accepting the existing order of things as a given. This cognitively limited mode of thinking shapes one's identity and distorts one's consciousness - that is, one's awareness and sense of agency." [Source: Joyce E. King, 1991]

Change begins at the level of the cogito – the cognitivesphere. So, Marcus Mosiah Garvey had to first 'wake' his people up! Even if he had not done anything else, just this recognition by Marcus Mosiah Garvey was hugely insightful.

"It was not just a case," said Garvey, "of freedom, acceptance, tolerance or political rights, or of simple social justice. It was a case of having to flush out 100 years of misconceptions and errors. The total product was wrong because the initial formula, equation, or prescription were wrong; the conclusions were incorrect because the assumptions were faulty. There could be no compromise." The new world had been built on a belief in the second-class character of the people of Africa: that they were a cheaper model made by God, a second-rate product devised from inferior materials and therefore not expected to give a first-class performance, a less carefully designed instrument created specifically for menial work requiring little thought or skills. And because every agency of education and communication in the New World tended to be tainted by this belief in inequality, the people of African descent themselves received a distorted image of their own humanity, directly or implied, in books, pictures, lectures, sermons and on social occasions, whether in school, at home, at the workplace, or in places of recreation and worship. Being thus conditioned, there was a natural desire on the part of aspiring people of African descent to attempt to conform to the system of inequality. By adopting its mores, even when these were at odds with their own physical appearance, they hoped for some degree of acceptance. But Marcus Garvey would have none of that. Having a clear insight into this dilemma, Marcus Garvey focused his campaign, not only on the oppressive system and those who ran it but on the so-called victims as well: "You will be victims as long as you believe that you are less than others. No matter how respected the fount of information may be, if it tells you that you are less, it is lying to you. Cast it out; flush out every vestige, suggestion, or insinuation that your colour is a badge of inferiority," he counselled. "Don't seek acceptance at the expense of your self-respect, your soul. Why hammer at gates where you are not wanted? Build your own mansions, enterprises, nations, and governments. Build them so powerfully that the world will have no choice but to acknowledge them and take them seriously ... Create your own titles, symbols, uniforms, ceremonies and rituals, based on those things which uplift, ennoble, refresh and dignify your humanity and which glorify your achievements." This was Garvey's thinking, and he put his thoughts into action. Marcus Garvey saw clearly that if 95 percent of the people of Jamaica felt themselves to be inferior, the country was doomed. He began the process of flushing out the impurities and poisons from the collective consciousness, from the speech and beliefs, stories, and images of the society. [Source: Edward Seaga, 'Who was Marcus Garvey,' The Gleaner, August 25, 2017]

Marcus Mosiah Garvey sought to install a new mindset among Black people. This is akin to installing a new operating system or changing the settings on a computer.

Garvey recognised that without this new metanoia – this new imaginary - Africa-originated people would just be confirming, and living, the faux (false) reality others had created for them about themselves. Garvey sought to empower Blacks to redraw their psychological map of themselves and their possibilities.

Since Garvey, the field of Black psychology has developed with thought leaders such as **Prof. Amos N. Wilson** ('The Development Psychology of the Black Child'; Black on Black Violence: The Psychodynamics of Black Self-Annihilation in Service of White Domination', 'The Falsification of Afrikan Consciousness: Eurocentric History, Psychiatry and the Politics of White Supremacy', 'The Psychology of Self-Hatred and Self-Defeat: Towards a Reclamation of the Afrikan Mind', 'Afrikan-Centered Consciousness Versus the New World Order: Garveyism in the Age of Globalism'); **Dr. Frantz Fanon** ('Black Skin, White Masks'); **Dr. Frances Cress Welsing** ('The Isis Papers: The Keys to the Colours').

Marcus Garvey, the intuitive genius, also recognized the utility and tremendous value of deploying culture as a psycho-social balm to heal, define, and empower a people. People store trauma in their bodies. Trauma is also heritable epigenetically. In biology, epigenetics is the study of heritable phenotype (observable) changes that do not involve alterations in the DNA sequence of organisms.

One of the powerful ways to 'mop-up' trauma is through the expressive arts, which enable us to create, connect, engage in making meaning, express ourselves and communicate and imagine and synthesize new narratives and vistas of hope and possibilities. Trauma is an invisible force that shapes people's lives – it is at the root of their deepest wounds.

"Trauma is not what happens to people. Trauma is what happens inside of people, as a result of what happens to people." ~ Dr. Gabor Mate

Trauma-informed Therapy

Recognizing this, Marcus Garvey engaged in trauma-informed action. He established Edelweiss Park at 67 Slipe Road in Kingston as a Black Empowerment Centre, where, demonstrating his vast repertoire of adult education methods, used pageantry, role-playing, promenades, and concerts as psychological medicine (psychotherapy) - antidotes, balms, tourniquets, and energizers - to the thousands of people who flocked there to have the lesions present in their mentalscapes soothed, and their psychological operating system repaired and re-programmed. Persons also flocked Edelweiss Park simply to get a glimpse of the man – their Champion - who looked like them and carried the message of Black pride, inspiration, and anti-colonialism!

Edelweiss Park was an Empowerment Centre "for spiritual upliftment, self-improvement, political indoctrination, and purposeful recreation. Political and religious instruction formed part of the weekly programme, and was intended to 'combat ignorance and narrow-mindedness among the masses. Thousands thronged to hear Garvey speak on Sunday nights and young and old journeyed from far off rural places, just to get a glimpse of the man who carried the message of inspiration and anti-colonial solidarity." (Sherlock & Bennett 1998, page 311)

Concerning Garvey's impact on the Black race, it was once said: "He made them feel like somebody among white people who have said they were nobody."

Garvey intuitively understood the power of symbols and symbolism. Symbolism is thinking in images. Symbols are visual messages that can exert powerful effects at the level of the human sub-consciousness. Seeing images affects how people think. That is why, for example, colonial statues that still festoon Jamaica (and other formerly colonised countries) are not benign.

"Those who know the truth must teach." ~ African Wisdom. This is what Garvey was doing.

There are parallels between Marcus Garvey and Chinua Achebe, Nigerian novelist, academic, and activist. The latter with his masterpiece, '**Things Fall Apart'**, one of the first works of fiction to present African village life from an African perspective, Achebe began the literary reclamation of his country's history from generations of colonial writers who trafficked in vulgar lies, including the stereotype of the 'barbaric negro' - a "lesser creature" (to white Europeans) who, with patient guidance and being told what to think, will grow up one day and become civilized (by mimicking their 'European betters'). Achebe has always advocated for a socially and politically motivated literature. Since literature was complicit in colonialism, he says, let it also work to exorcise the ghosts of colonialism [Source: Ruth Franklin, 'Chinua Achebe and the Great African Novel,' The New Yorker, May 19, 2008].

"Before '**Things Fall Apart'** was published, most novels about Africa had been written by European authors, portraying Africans as savages who needed western enlightenment. Achebe broke from this outsider view, by portraying Igbo society in a sympathetic light. This allows the reader to examine the effects of European colonialism from a different perspective. He commented: "The popularity of '**Things Fall Apart'** in my own society can be explained simply ... this was the first time we were seeing ourselves, as autonomous individuals, rather than half-people, or as Conrad would say, 'rudimentary souls'." Nigerian Nobel laureate Wole Soyinka has described the work as "the first novel in English which spoke from the interior of the African character, rather than portraying the African as an exotic, as the white man would see him." [Source: Wikipedia]

("Garvey's birthplace [is] in shabby condition and not the fine national monument that it should be. Nothing like the Mandelas' home in Soweto, South Africa, a national heritage site and tourist must-see, which I have seen. One of the things about Marcus Garvey that we have failed to emulate is his understanding of the importance of impressive stateliness for the pride and dignity of a people. National monuments, where they exist at all, are generally in poor, run-down condition. And even Garvey's Liberty Hall had to be restored. Much of the National Heroes Park, in which his repatriated remains are interred, is a dust bowl and parking lot instead of being a beautiful, gracious, and significant space in the heart of the city, grand as green space for recreation as well as being a tribute to the national heroes. [Source: Martin Henry, The Gleaner, August 23, 2015)

Culture is a powerful thing. Culture is destiny. Both positives and negatives reside in a people's culture. Put simply, culture is the way a people think about and do things – all the ways and means a people expresses itself through the interplay of genetics and history. From a sociological perspective, culture is analyzed as the ways of thinking and describing, the ways of acting, and the material objects (artefacts) that together shape a people's way of life.

"A general definition of culture that can be applied to all cultures is patterns of behavior that are common within a particular population of people. One way to think about culture is to break down the concept into two distinct categories: The 'Big C' and the 'little c.' The 'Big C' is an overarching general concept that can be applied to all culture groups; it is the anthropological perspective. The 'little c' is the particulars of a specific culture group" [Source: Bohannan, Paul and Mark Glazer. 1988. High Points in Anthropology, 2nd edition. New York: McGraw-Hill, Inc]

The Center for Advanced Research on Language Acquisition defines culture as shared patterns of behaviours and interactions, cognitive constructs, and understanding that are learned by socialization. According to Cristina De Rossi, an anthropologist at Barnet and Southgate College in London, "Culture encompasses religion, food, what we wear, how we wear it, our language, marriage, music, what we believe is right or wrong, how we sit at the table, how we greet visitors, how we behave with loved ones, and a million other things" [Source: Glenville Ashby, 'Sex and the Death of Black Culture Why There Is an Urgent Need for Self-Reflection,' The Sunday Gleaner, September 8, 2019]

Some scholars posit the view that culture is the deepest and most determinative aspect of human life. Thus, culture matters bigly in the success, or otherwise, of different peoples. Is this cultural determinism?

The significant efforts of Marcus Mosiah Garvey to raise the consciousness of Africa-originated people were especially important as a counterfoil to the "colonial ideological policy that consistently debased Africa as well as people and things African. In the process of the formation of Jamaica as a nation, the negation of Africa and Blackness has been constant. And so, has the resistance [to this negation] by Black people." [Source: Rupert Lewis, 1987]

One sees here, when the contextual realities are accounted for, how daunting Marcus Mosiah Garvey's challenge was to raise the consciousness of Africa-originated people. But he had the fortitude, the cojones, the audacity, and courage to initiate his crusade as well as to pursue it with great perseverance.

"A civilization is not destroyed by wicked people; it is not necessary that people be wicked but only that they be spineless." ~ James Baldwin

A significant factor in determining the preparedness of individuals to adopt a dissident stance is fear of the consequences.

Marcus Mosiah Garvey was a profile in courage! He dared to imagine a better world for Black People. He declared that "Real men laugh at opposition; real men smile when enemies appear" and "men who are in earnest are not afraid of consequences." He added: "Fear is a state of nervousness fit for children and not men. When a man fears a creature like himself, he offends God, in whose image and likeness he is created. Man being created equal fears not man but God. To fear is to lose control of one's nerves, one's will – to flutter, like a dying fowl, losing consciousness, yet alive."

Garvey: Profile in Courage

Courage is the currency of change. Courage is what it takes to speak up. Courage is what it takes to convert talk into action. Revolutionaries and change agents must have courage. Courage is a 'foundation virtue.' As Maya Angelou [American poet, memoirist, and civil rights activist] notes "Courage is the most important of all the virtues because without courage you can't practice any other virtue consistently. You can practice any virtue erratically, but nothing consistently without courage."

Marcus Mosiah Garvey's fierce courage and tenacity

are best understood when one considers that the "empire always strikes back," and struck back it did.

According to Sherlock and Bennett (1998), Garvey was: "A man who through his life lived his message; and did so through triumph and disaster, in the face of derision, disdain, disapproval, and oppression, of imprisonment and of rejection. Those in the centers of white power and influence in Jamaica, in the United States, and Europe saw Garvey as a formidable threat and used all means in their power, the law included, to obstruct and vilify him; they projected the image of a black racist subversive, a rabble-rouser, a confidence man, and trickster (p. 293)."

Garvey found the going tough: "I never knew there was so much colour prejudice in Jamaica, my own native home until I started the work of the Universal Negro Improvement Association …. The daily papers wrote me up with big headlines and told of my movement. But nobody wanted to be a Negro. 'Garvey is crazy; he has lost his head.' 'Is that the use he is going to make of his experience and intelligence?' – such were the criticisms passed upon me. Men and women as Black as I, and even more so, had believed themselves white under the West Indian order of society. I was simply an impossible man to use openly the term 'Negro'; yet everyone beneath his breath was calling the Black man a nigger." [Source: The Philosophy and Opinions of Marcus Garvey]

Concerning the quote immediately above, Rupert Lewis, professor emeritus of political thought, The University of the West Indies, in his brilliant biography of Marcus Mosiah Garvey said: "Self-denial, denigration, defining one's identity according to colonial Britishness – these were the hallmarks of brown and black West Indians' ambition to escape blackness and what they perceived as Africa's lack of civilization and its savagery."

(Writing in The New Yorker on July 17, 2017, Hua Hsu said this about Jamaican scholar Stuart Hall: "His father, Herman, was the first nonwhite person to hold a senior position with the Jamaican office of United Fruit, an American farming and agricultural corporation; his mother, Jessie, was mixed-race. They considered themselves a class apart, Hall explains, indulging a "gross colonial simulacrum of upper-middle-class England." From an early age, he felt alienated by their cozy embrace of the island's racial hierarchy. As a child, his skin was darker than the rest of his family's, prompting his sister to tease, "Where did you get this coolie baby from?")

Tough Love

Martin Henry notes that Garvey dished out tough love to his people: "Perhaps the best known and most repeated Garvey quote, is "Up, you mighty race! You can accomplish what you will." The trouble is, this Garvey statement doesn't mean what most people think it means. It is not a note of triumphalist exuberance at all. It is a cry of despair and disillusionment. Ken Jones, in his book **'Marcus Garvey Said'** devotes a section of his book to what Marcus Garvey had to say about 'Negro Weaknesses'. "The Negro fights himself too much," Garvey complained. "His internal conflicts constitute the puzzle of our age .... Every other day he is smashing up what he has made, and so the process goes on. He never permanently constructs. We now realise that the system takes us nowhere." Later on, Garvey hit even harder. "The monumental disgrace of the Negro race is that wherever it finds itself, it is more occupied with fighting and destroying its own institutions than in seriously helping to build them." Much of this tendency, Garvey blamed on the bad education of the Negro. "Having had the wrong education as a start ... the Negro becomes his greatest enemy". He then declared, "Most of the trouble I have had in advancing the cause of the race has come from Negroes." "Those who know me as a Negro leader," Garvey said in 1936, only four years short of his early death at 53, a disillusioned man, "cannot say that I have ever flattered the race or tried to deceive it against its own interest. I have always been frank - and brutally so - even to my own disadvantage. I intend to be frank ... and to be brutally so for the purpose of drawing to the attention of the sleeping Negro the seriousness of his position in a material civilisation." It was the sleeping Negro who was shouted at in that famous Garvey quote. "Up [wake up], you mighty race! You can accomplish what you will." [Source: Martin Henry, The Gleaner, August 23, 2015]

This is another example of the demonisation of Marcus Garvey: When Dr. Robert Morton, who succeeded Booker T. Washington as President of Tuskegee Institute in Alabama, USA, visited Jamaica in 1916, the British colonial government in Jamaica, saw Garvey as a threat to the colonial order, and advised Dr. Morton not to contact

Garvey because he was a 'trouble-maker.'

"[In the USA], after World War I, the Federal Bureau of Investigations (FBI) closely followed Garvey. On its website, the FBI acknowledges seeking to "deport him as an undesirable alien." In 1922, Garvey was convicted of mail fraud in connection with a stock sold to keep his Black Star Line from bankruptcy. After serving three years of his sentence, Garvey was released and deported to Jamaica. Garvey's movement waned in the USA after his deportation, but his influence remains, historians say." [Jordan Friedman, 'From Jamaica's Marcus Garvey Came an African Vision of Freedom,' USA Today, February 14, 2018]

The 'empire' almost always exacts a steep social cost on change agents and revolutionaries. History is replete with examples of such agents paying a steep price, oftentimes with their liberty and even their life.

About enemies, Harriet Tubman [African-American abolitionist and political activist] noted, "Marcus Garvey had in his time. We just had a more vulnerable enemy." Tubman also expressed her only challenge with her own Africa-originated (Black) people, in these terms: "I freed thousands of slaves, and could have freed thousands more if they had known they were slaves."

Marcus Mosiah Garvey's valorous mission of positive identity-building and conscious-raising was meant to awaken and arouse the consciousness of African-Jamaicans and Africans everywhere in the diaspora (circa 400,000,000 of them at the time) to respond to his passionate entreaty of "Up, Up Ye Mighty Race, You Can

Accomplish What You Will" (Source Jacques-Garvey, 1969, p.18).

Channelling Marcus Garvey, Peter Tosh, included the track 'African' on his album 'Equal Rights' which was released in 1977:

"Don't care where you come from
As long as you're a Black man, you're an African
No mind your nationality
You have got the identity of an African"

That Garvey sought to unite all Africans was another dimension of his genius. He recognized that Africans everywhere were being discriminated against, and that unity was strength – coalesced power. So, he wanted to imbue in them a sense of common purpose – racial solidarity – as the scaffolding on which to reclaim and surpass the past glory of our race.

The existence or absence of communal solidarity is a huge factor in the success, or lack thereof, of a race! In the book **'Minorities and Power in a Black Society: The Jewish Community in Jamaica,'** Dr. Carol Holzberg lists several reasons why Jews have been successful in Jamaica, and she includes communal solidarity high on the list.

The case of Tidjane Thiam, originally from the Republic of Côte d'Ivoire, who, as CEO, made Credit Suisse Bank in Switzerland profitable again, but was rejected by the "mentality of the Swiss establishment' as an outsider, and ousted from his job in February 2020, highlights the relevance of Garvey's Pan-Africanism that Blacks (i.e., Africans) everywhere were subjects of racially-inspired racism, and hence needed to unite. Mr. Thiam's story, carried by the New York Times on October 3, 2020 ('**The Short Tenure and Abrupt Ouster of Banking's Sole Black C.E.O.**') makes for fascinating, if sad, reading. For Mr. Thiam's sister Yamousso, one question about the Swiss still lingers. "I would be curious to know," she said, "if today they'd finally have the honesty to recognize that seeing a Black man at the top of one of their most prestigious companies was unbearable."

In the case of Masterpiece Cakeshop Ltd., et. al. v. Colorado Civil Right Commission, the US Supreme Court on June 4, 2018, ruled for the proposition that "Our society has come to the recognition that gay persons and gay couples cannot be treated as social outcasts or as inferior in dignity and worth."

My question is this: Why this same proposition cannot be applied to Black People?

For historian Darryl Pinckney, Blackness is not an essential quality found in the blood, the spirit, or even the genes, but a social construct that sees Blackness as being synonymous with being at the bottom of the social hierarchy of society.

There is also a 'hierarchy of suffering and victimhood' among distinct groups in society.

In the last of his six Netflix specials as part of a $50-million deal, **The Closer**, aired in October 2021, irreverent observational comedian Dave Chappelle dilated on the hierarchy of suffering and immunity to criticism some groups (not Blacks) enjoy in America. "Chappelle has always been clear about the political argument he is making with this material: In a few short years, gay- and trans-rights activism has achieved the kind of cultural veto that Black Americans have failed to win through decades of struggle. In Chappelle's telling, no other movement has such power. In the United States, he says, you can shoot and kill a Black person, "but you better not hurt a gay person's feelings." And no other movement, Chappelle asserts, has been granted such immunity to criticism. "You think I hate gay people, and what you're really seeing is that I am jealous of gay people. Oh, I'm jealous. And I am not the only Black person who feels this way. We Blacks, we look at the gay community and we say: Goddamn it, look how well that movement is going. Look at how well you are doing, and we have been trapped in this predicament for hundreds of years. How the hell are you making that kind of progress?" The Closer is Dave Chappelle pushing all of our buttons, and inviting us to reflect on which ones provoke a reaction. [Sources: Helen Lewis, The Atlantic, October 13, 2021; Nicole Lewis, Slate Magazine, October 14, 2021].

Chappelle focussed on Black pain. Because Blacks are relegated to the bottom of everything - even when it comes to the hierarchy of victimhood and suffering. "Why is it easier for Bruce Jenner to change his gender than it is for Cassius Clay to change his name?" Chappelle pointedly asked. His emphasis on anti-Black discrimination is a dramatic device and a political choice. His pointed comedy is a corrective. Because race is more important to, and in, our daily lives than we think. Chapelle's comments animated many people. A furore ensued - an article in **The Economist** had more than 30,000 comments; a group of workers at Netflix walked off their job because, according to them, the company did not punish or condemn Chappelle; still others called for him to be 'cancelled.'

But did Chappelle lie? Of course not!

Chappelle had always understood the risk inherent in riffing on the racial realities of America to undermine them. So, what he did was to put a match subversively and courageously to institutionalised anti-Black racism. And the furore that ensued was another instance of attempts to deploy social silencing and lynching tools against another Black man who dared to speak the truth in America! Other Blacks are not as lucky as Dave Chapelle, who is famous and rich enough to tell his critics to go and perform self-coitus!

The thing is, Chappelle is insulated by the prerogatives that wealth purchases. His response to all the 'noise' was "I said what I said … I will not be bending to anyone's demands!" Chapelle is immune to 'cancel culture.'

According to Wikipedia, "Cancel culture or call-out culture is a modern form of ostracism in which someone is thrust out of social or professional circles – whether it be online, on social media, or in person. Persons subjected to this ostracism are said to have been 'cancelled.' The expression 'cancel culture' has mostly negative connotations and is used in debates on free speech and censorship."

Marcus Mosiah Garvey

******

Garvey: Intellectual & Adult Educator
======================####======================

The Responsibility of Intellectuals

"One of the responsibilities of intellectuals is to speak truth to the powerless and to make apparently powerless people aware that, together with others, they need not remain powerless. David Hume recognised this in his 1741 maxim that 'power is in the hands of the governed.' The first requirement, therefore, is to make such people aware of the true situation and hence of the possibility of their helping to bring about change." [Source: 'The Responsibility of Intellectuals: Reflections by Noam Chomsky and others after 50 years,' 2019, edited by Nicholas Allott, Chris Knight and Neil Smith].

Marcus Mosiah Garvey emphasized education and knowledge as the foundation of self-awareness, identity, empowerment, and productivity.

Never Stop Learning

Concerning Intelligence, Education, Universal Knowledge, and How to Get It, Marcus Garvey expressed issued these instructions/lessons to his fellow Blacks:

"You must never stop learning. The world's greatest men and women were people who educated themselves outside of the university with all the knowledge that the university gives, [and] you have the opportunity of doing the same thing the university student does---read and study.

One must never stop reading. Read everything that you can that is of standard knowledge. Don't waste time reading trashy literature. That is to say, don't pay any attention to the ten cents novels, Wild West stories and cheap sentimental books, but where there is a good plot and a good story in the form of a novel, read it. It is necessary to read it for the purpose of getting information on human nature. The idea is that personal experience is not enough for a human to get all the useful knowledge of life, because the individual life is too short, so we must feed on the experience of others. The literature we read should include the biography and autobiography of men and women who have accomplished greatness in their particular line. Whenever you can buy these books and own them and whilst you are reading them make pencil or pen notes of the striking sentences and paragraphs that you should like to remember, so that when you have to refer to the book for any thought that you would like to refresh your mind on, you will not have to read over the whole book.

You should also read the best poetry for inspiration. The standard poets have always been the most inspirational creators. From a good line of poetry, you may get the inspiration for the career of a life time. Many a great man and woman were first inspired by some attractive line or verse of poetry.

There are good poets and bad poets just like there are good novels and bad novels. Always select the best poets for your inspirational urge.

Read history incessantly until you master it. This means your own national history, the history of the world---social history, industrial history, and the history of the different sciences; but primarily the history of man. If you do not know what went on before you came here and what is happening at the time you live, but away from you, you will not know the world and will be ignorant of the world and mankind.

You can only make the best out of life by knowing and understanding it. To know, you must fall back on the intelligence of others who came before you and have left their records behind.

To be able to read intelligently, you must first be able to master the language of your country. To do this, you must be well acquainted with its grammar and the science of it. Every six months you should read over again the science of the language that you speak, so as not to forget its rules. People judge you by your writing and your speech. If you write badly and incorrectly they become prejudiced toward your intelligence, and if you speak badly and incorrectly those who hear you become disgusted and will not pay much attention to you but in their hearts laugh after you. A leader who is to teach men and present any fact of truth to man must first be learned in his subject.

Never write or speak on a subject you know nothing about, for there is always somebody who knows that particular subject to laugh at you or to ask you embarrassing questions that may make others laugh at you. You can know about any subject under the sun by reading about it. If you cannot buy the books outright and own them, go to your public libraries and read them there or borrow them, or join some circulating library in your district or town, so as to get the use of these books. You should do that as you may refer to them for information.

You should read at least four hours a day. The best time to read is in the evening after you have retired from your work and after you have rested and before sleeping hours but do so before morning, so that during your sleeping hours what you have read may become subconscious, that is to say, planted in your memory. Never go to bed without doing some reading.

Never keep the constant company of anybody who doesn't know as much as you or [isn't] as educated as you, and from whom you cannot learn something or reciprocate your learning, especially if that person is illiterate or ignorant because constant association with such a person will unconsciously cause you to drift into the peculiar culture or ignorance of that person. Always try to associate with people from whom you can learn something. Contact with cultured persons and with books is the best companionship you can have and keep.

By reading good books you keep the company of the authors of the book or the subjects of the book when otherwise you could not meet them in the social contact of life. NEVER GO DOWN IN INTELLIGENCE to those who are below you, but if possible help to lift them up to you and always try to ascend to those who are above you and be their equal with the hope of being their master.

Continue always in the application of the thing you desire educationally, culturally, or otherwise, and never give up until you reach the objective---and you can reach the objective if other[s] have done so before you, proving by their doing it that it is possible.

In your desire to accomplish greatness, you must first decide in your own mind in what direction you desire to seek that greatness, and when you have so decided in your own mind, work unceasingly toward it. The particular thing that you may want should be before you all the time, and whatsoever it takes to get it or make it possible should be undertaken. Use your faculties and persuasion to achieve all you set your mind on.

Try never to repeat yourself in any one discourse in saying the same thing over and over except [when] you are making new points, because repetition is tiresome and it annoys those who hear the repetition. Therefore, try to possess as much universal knowledge as possible through reading so as to be able to be free of repetition in trying to drive home a point.

No one is ever too old to learn. Therefore, you should take advantage of every educational facility. If you should hear of a great man or woman who is to lecture or speak in your town on any given subject and the person is an authority on the subject, always make time to go and hear him. This is what is meant by learning from others. You should learn the two sides to every story, so as to be able to properly debate a question and hold your grounds with the side that you support. If you only know one side of a story, you cannot argue intelligently or effectively. As for instance, to combat communism, you must know about it, otherwise people will take advantage of you and win a victory over your ignorance.

Anything that you are going to challenge, you must first know about it, so as to be able to defeat it. The moment you are ignorant about anything the person who has the intelligence of that thing will defeat you. Therefore, get knowledge, get it quickly, get it studiously, but get it anyway.

Knowledge is power. When you know a thing and can hold your ground on that thing and win over your opponents on that thing, those who hear you learn to have confidence in you and will trust your ability.

Never, therefore, attempt anything without being able to protect yourself on it, for every time you are defeated it takes away from your prestige and you are not as respected as before.

All the knowledge you want is in the world, and all that you have to do is to go seeking it and never stop until you have found it. You can find knowledge or the information about it in the public libraries, if it is not on your own bookshelf. Try to have a book and own it on every bit of knowledge you want. You may generally get these books at second hand book stores for sometimes one-fifth of the original value.

Always have a well-equipped shelf of books. Nearly all information about mankind is to be found in the Encyclopedia Britannica. This is an expensive set of books, but try to get them. Buy a complete edition for yourself, and keep it at your home, and whenever you are in doubt about anything, go to it and you will find it there.

The value of knowledge is to use it. It is not humanly possible that a person can retain all knowledge of the world, but if a person knows how to search for all the knowledge of the world, he will find it when he wants it.

A doctor or a lawyer although he passed his examination in college does not know all the laws and does not know all the techniques of medicine but he has the fundamental knowledge. When he wants a particular kind of knowledge, he goes to the medical books or law books and refers to the particular law or how to use the recipe of medicine. You must, therefore, know where to find your facts and use them as you want them. No one will know where you got them, but you will have the facts and by using the facts correctly they will think you a wonderful person, a great genius, and a trusted leader.

In reading it is not necessary or compulsory that you agree with everything you read. You must always use or apply your own reasoning to what you have read based upon what you already know as touching the facts on what you have read. Pass judgement on what you read based upon these facts. When I say facts I mean things that cannot be disputed. You may read thoughts that are old, and opinions that are old and have changed since they were written. You must always search to find out the latest facts on that particular subject and only when these facts are consistently maintained in what you read should you agree with them, otherwise you are entitled to your own opinion.

Always have up-to-date knowledge. You can gather this from the latest books and the latest periodicals, journals and newspapers. Read your daily newspaper every day. Read a standard monthly journal every month, a standard weekly magazine every week, a standard quarterly magazine every quarter and by this you will find the new knowledge of the whole year in addition to the books you read, whose facts have not altered in that year. Don't keep old ideas, bury them as new ones come.

How to Read

Use every spare minute you have in reading. If you are going on a journey that would take you an hour carry something with you to read for that hour until you have reached the place. If you are sitting down waiting for somebody, have something in your pocket to read until the person comes. Don't waste time. Any time you think you have to waste put it in reading something. Carry with you a small pocket dictionary and study words whilst waiting or travelling, or a small pocket volume on some particular subject. Read through at least one book every week separate and distinct from your newspapers and journals. It will mean that at the end of one year you will have read fifty-two different subjects. After five years you will have read over two hundred and fifty books. You may be considered then a well-read man or a well-read woman and there will be a great difference between you and the person who has not read one book. You will be considered intelligent and the other person be considered ignorant. You and that person therefore will be living in two different worlds; one the world of ignorance and the other the world of intelligence. Never forget that intelligence rules the world and ignorance carries the burden.

Therefore, remove yourself as far as possible from ignorance and seek as far as possible to be intelligent.

Your language being English you should study the English language thoroughly. To know the English language thoroughly you ought to be acquainted with Latin, because most of the English words are of Latin origin. It is also advisable that you know the French language because most of the books that you read in English carry Latin and French phrases and words. There is no use reading a page or paragraph of a book or even a sentence without understanding it.

If it has foreign words in it, before you pass over [them] you should go to the dictionary, if you don't know the meaning and find out the meaning. Never pass over a word without knowing its meaning. The dictionary and the books on word building which can be secured from book sellers will help you greatly.

I know a boy who was ambitious to learn. He hadn't the opportunity of an early school education because he had to work ten hours a day, but he determined that he would learn and so he took with him to his work place every day a simplified grammar and he would read and memorize passages and the rules of grammar whilst at work.

After one year he was almost an expert in the grammar of his language. He knew the different parts of speech, he could paraphrase, analyse and construct sentences. He also took with him a pocket dictionary and he would write out twenty-five new words with their meanings every day and study these words and their forms and their meaning. After one year he had a speaking vocabulary of more than three thousand words. He continued this for several years and when he became a man he had a vocabulary at his command of over fifteen thousand words. He became an author because he could write in his language by having command of words. What he wrote was his experiences and he recorded his experiences in the best words of his language. He was not able to write properly at the same age and so he took with him to work what is called in school a copying book and he practised the copying of letters until he was able to write a very good hand. He naturally became acquainted with literature and so he continued reading extensively. When he died he was one of the greatest scholars the world ever knew. Apply the story to yourself.

There is nothing in the world that you want that you cannot have so long as it is possible in nature and men have achieved it before. The greatest men and women in the world burn the midnight lamp. That is to say, when their neighbours and household are gone to bed, they are reading, studying and thinking. When they rise in the morning they are always ahead of their neighbours and their household in the thing that they were studying, reading, and thinking of. A daily repetition of that will carry them daily ahead and above their neighbours and household. Practise this rule. It is wise to study a couple of subjects at a time. As for instance---a little geography, a little psychology, a little ethics, a little theology, a little philosophy, a little mathematics, a little science on which a sound academic education is built. Doing this week after week, month after month, year after year will make you so learned in the liberal arts as to make you ready and fit for your place in the affairs of the world. If you know what others do not know, they will want to hear you. You will then become invaluable in your community and to your country, because men and women will want to hear you and see you everywhere.

As stated before, books are one's best companions. Try to get the[m] and keep them. A method of doing so is every time you have ten cents or twenty five cents or a dollar to spend foolishly[,] either on your friends or yourself [,] think how much more useful that ten or twenty five cents or dollar would be invested in a book and so invest it. It may be just the thing you have been looking for to give you a thought by which you may win the heart of the world. The ten cent, twenty five cent or a dollar, therefore, may turn out to be an investment of worth to the extent of a million dollars. Never lend anybody the book that you want. You will never get it back. Never allow anybody to go to your bookshelf in your absence because the very book that you may want most may be taken from the shelf and you may never be able to get one of the kind again.

If you have a library of your own, lock it when you are not at home. Spend most of your spare time in your library. If you have a radio, keep it in your own library and use it exhaustively to listen to lectures, recitals, speeches and good music. You can learn a lot from the radio. You can be inspired a lot by good music [lines repeated]. Good music carries the sentiment of harmony and you may think many a good thought out of listening to good music.

Read a chapter from the Bible every day, Old and New Testaments. The greatest wisdom of the age is to be found in the Scriptures. You can always quote from the Scriptures. It is the quickest way of winning approval.

Tragedy of White Injustice

1. Read and study thoroughly the poem "Tragedy of White Injustice" and apply its sentiment and statements in connection with the historic character and behaviour of the white man. Know it so well as always to be able to be on guard against any professions of the white man in his suggested friendship for the Negro.

The poem exposes the white man's behaviour in history and is intended to suggest distrust of him in every phase of life. Never allow it to get into the hands of a white man if possible.

2. You can improve your English as you go along by reading critically the books of the language; that is to say, you must pay close attention to the construction of sentences and paragraphs as you see them in the books you read. Imitate the style.

Read with observation. Never read carelessly and recklessly.

3. In reading books written by white authors of whatsoever kind, be aware of the fact that they are [not] written for your particular benefit or for the benefit of your race. They always write from their own point of view and only in the interest of their own race.

Never swallow wholly what the white man writes or says without first critically analyzing it and investigating it. The white man's trick is to deceive other people for his own benefit and profit.

Always be on your guard against him with whatsoever he does or says. Never take chances with him. His school books in the elementary schools, in the high schools, in the colleges and universities are all fixed up to suit his own purposes, to put him on top and keep him on top of other people. Don't trust him. Beware! Beware!

You should study carefully the subject of ethnology. It is the subject that causes races to know the difference between one race and another.

Ethnic relationship is important as it reveals the characteristic of one people as different from another. There is no doubt that each race has different habits and manners of behaviour. You must know them so as to be able to deal with them. There are books on this subject in the library. In your reading and searching for truth always try to get that which is particularly helpful to the Negro. Every thought that strikes you, see how it fits in with the Negro, and to what extent you can use it to his benefit or in his behalf. Your entire obsession must be to see things from the Negro's point of view, remembering always that you are a Negro striving for Negro supremacy in every department of life, so that any truth you see or any facts you gather must be twisted to suit the Negro psychology of things.

The educational system of today hides the truth as far as the Negro is concerned. Therefore, you must searchingly scan everything you read, particularly history, to see what you can pick out for the good of the race. As for instance, you will read that the Egyptians were a great people, the Carthagenians, the Libyans, etc., but you will not be told that they were black people or Negroes. You should, therefore, go beyond the mere statement of these events to discover the truth that will be creditable to your race. You would, therefore, in a case like that ask where did the Libyans get their civilization from or the Carthagenians or the Egyptians.

Following that kind of an investigation you will come upon the truth that it was all originally Negro and subsequently became Negroid. That is to say, subsequent people were mixed with other people's blood, who were no doubt conquered by the Negro. As a fact, the original Egyptians were black men and women, and so the Carthagenians and Libyans, but in the later centuries they became mixed in blood, just as how [now?] the blacks are being mixed in

America and the West Indies by the infusion of white blood through the domination of the white man.

Never yield to any statement in history or made by any individual, caring not how great, that the Negro was nobody in history. Even if you cannot prove it always claim that the Negro was great. Read everything you can get written by Negroes and their ancestry, going back six thousand years. There are statements in the Bible in the Old and New Testaments to show that black was always an important colour among the races of men. Abraham had company with a black woman, even though he had his wife Sarah, by whom he had Ishmael.

All the original Pharaohs were black. Tutankumen, whose bones and body were dug up not very long ago at Luxor in Egypt, was a black Pharaoh. The sphinx, in Egypt which has stood through the millenniums, has black features. It is evident that as art it was portrayed to teach us of the greatness of men. When you are dealing with Jews let them know that they were once your slaves in Egypt if you have to say so. There is good ground to say that civilization started in Africa and passed from and through Northern Africa into Southern Europe, from which the Greeks and Romans and the People of Asia Minor made good copies. The swarthy colour of the Asiatics and the brunette colour of the South Europeans were due to the fact that the cultured and civilized blacks of Africa mixed their blood with them. Search all history and all literature and the Bible and find facts to support this argument but hold to it with a grip that will never loosen. Things that may not be true can be made if you repeat them long and often enough, therefore, always repeat statements that will give your race a status and an advantage. That is how the white man has built up his system of superiority. He is always telling you he is superior and he has written history and literature to prove it. You must do the same. One of the great backgrounds for your argument which cannot be disputed is that you are older than any other man as a race because you are black. Your argument is that in nature everything by way of age darkens. That you are darker than the rest of men proves logically, that you are older than the rest of men. Another proof of that is that even among white people they grow darker in skin as they grow older in age in a lifetime.

If the one individual were to live for six thousand years he would surely be not white. If he were born white he would be as dark as the darkest man. Therefore, the old argument that the black man is black because as man he is older than the other man is good. Use it everywhere you go to defeat the white man in his belief that you sprung from something else. Use the argument that the white man is white because most of the time when the black man was great in Africa and had succeeded in running him across the Mediterranean into South Europe he had to hide himself in caves where there was very little light and air. He was almost covered up for most of the time in darkness. In natural creation the child in the womb of the mother is almost white even though it be a black child and it is almost born white and doesn't change colour until it comes in contact with light and air.

Living in caves for so many centuries the white man, therefore, became colourless and the length of time always made it so that he was born naturally white. You must interpret anthropology to suit yourself. The thing for you to do is to refute every pertinent statement of the white man which tends to degrade you and to elevate him. Turn the tables on him and search for all reasons in the world you can find to justify it. That is how new thoughts are given out by creation. Never yield to the statement of your inferiority.

In reading Christian literature and accepting the doctrine of Jesus Christ lay special claim to your association with Jesus and the Son of God. Show that whilst the white and yellow worlds, that is to say---the worlds of Europe and Asia Minor persecuted and crucified Jesus the Son of God, it was the black race through Simon the black Cyrenian who befriended the Son of God and took up the Cross and bore it alongside of Him up to the heights of Calvary. The Roman Catholics, therefore, have no rightful claim to the Cross nor is any other professing Christian before the Negro. The Cross is the property of the Negro in his religion, because it was he who bore it.

Never admit that Jesus Christ was a white man, otherwise he could not be the Son of God and God to redeem all mankind. Jesus Christ had the blood of all races in his veins, and tracing the Jewish race back to Abraham and to Moses, from which Jesus sprang through the line of Jesse, you will find Negro blood everywhere, so Jesus had much of Negro blood in him.

Read the genealogical tree of Jesus in the Bible and you will learn from where he sprang. It is a fact that the white man has borrowed his civilization from other peoples. The first civilization was the Negro's---black people. The second civilization was the brown people---Indians, the third civilization was the yellow people, Chinese or Mongols; the last civilization up to today is the white man and all civilization goes back to the black man in the Nile Valley of Africa. In your reading, therefore, search for all these facts. Never stop reading and never stop until you find the proof of them.

You must pay great attention to sociology. Get the best books on the subject that you can and read them thoroughly. Find out the social relationship among other races so [t]hat you may know how to advise your people in their social behaviour. Never admit that the Negro is more immoral than the white man but try to prove to the contrary. Socially the white man has debauched and debased all other races because of his dominant power. He is responsible for more illegitimacy among races than any other race. He has left bastard children everywhere he has been; therefore, he is not competent to say that he is socially and morally purer than any other race.

The mixed population among Negroes from slavery to the present in certain countries is due to [t]he white man's immorality. Therefore, if you should hear anyone talking about moral depravity of Negroes and the moral excellence of the whites, draw the above facts to their attention.

When through reading and research you have discovered any new fact helpful to the dignity and prestige, character and accomplishment of the Negro, always make a noise about it. You should keep always with you a note book and fountain pen or indelible pencil and make a note in that book of anything you hear or see that you would like to remember. Keep always at home a larger note book to which you must transfer the thought or experience, so that it will not be lost to your memory. Once at least every three months read over that book and as the book becomes more voluminous with facts, read it over at least once a year.

By the constant reading of these facts they will be planted on your subconscious mind and you will be able to use them without even knowing that you are doing so. By keeping your facts registered and your very important experiences, at the end of a full life you may have a volume of great value such as Elbert Hubbard's Scrap Book. Get a copy of this Scrap Book. Ask any publisher in your town to get it for you. It contains invaluable inspiration. Always have a thought. Make it always a beautiful thought. The world is attracted by beauty either in art or in expression. Therefore, try to read, think and speak beautiful things." [Source: The Marcus Garvey and UNIA Papers Project, UCLA]

Andragogy

It is little-recognized that, in the execution of his mission, Garvey deployed andragogical (i.e., adult education) methods. Yes, it was in implementing his vision that Garvey the adult educator, and his grasp and expert deployment of andragogical methods, become obvious.

Cookson (1998) defined the term adult education "as a comprehensive 'umbrella' term which includes all forms of training and education for adults" (p. 4). And Knowles (1998) alluded to two separate and dichotomous models of learning. They are pedagogy (from the Greek paid, meaning 'child,' and agogus, meaning 'leader), which refers to the teaching of children, and andragogy (from the Greek aner, meaning 'adult'), referring to the art of helping adults learn.

As models of learning, pedagogy and andragogy are predicated on a suite of different assumptions about children and adults as learners. Flowing from these different sets of assumptions, different methods of teaching children and helping adults learn have been developed.

In 2014, I wrote a paper titled **'Illuminating the Andragogical Dimension of Marcus Garvey's Legacy'** which was published in the Journal of Arts Science and Technology (Volume 7, 2014, pp. 1-11).

The paper's abstract reads: "Marcus Mosiah Garvey, Jamaica's first national hero, has earned international acclaim as a world-class philosopher and symbol of self-empowerment for formerly enslaved persons of African descent and Africans everywhere in the Diaspora. However, a little-known or recognized facet of the colossal intellectual legacy Garvey bequeathed to the world is that, in implementing his vision, he expertly deployed andragogical strategies. In this paper, historical analysis and evaluation are used to situate Garvey's legacy within an andragogical framework and illuminate it from a similar perspective. But, to facilitate a better understanding of what stirred Garvey into action, this paper starts by briefly recounting aspects of chattel slavery and the realities of early post-emancipation Jamaica. Illustrative narrative examples are used herein to show that, in implementing his vision of self-empowerment, Garvey's strategies and methods are rooted in the andragogical model of learning, which refers to the art of helping adults learn. This paper also posits Garvey's direct involvement in politics as the zenith of his effective andragogy, aimed at ensuring the sustainability of his efforts. It is concluded that 'Garvey's Andragogy' represents a template that may be adopted or adapted by an individual, a community or a nation aiming for transformation and empowerment."

I will now dilate on some of the andragogical methods – which I mentioned in my paper - that Garvey deployed expertly.

Oratory

Oratorical persuasion was another one of the tools in Garvey's andragogical toolkit. He was an avid reader as a young boy and, as mentioned earlier, always carried a pocket dictionary from which he built a good vocabulary. Perhaps he had sensed his calling as he later utilized his awesome vocabulary as a public speaker and orator. When Garvey moved from St. Ann to Kingston, he began to improve his oratorical skills by visiting churches and watching the ministers in full flight. He also rehearsed reading aloud, participated in and organized elocution competitions, and seized every opportunity to appear on public platforms.

Having honed his oratorical skills, Garvey then arranged numerous public meetings and gatherings wherever he went and used these skills to mesmerize and touch the heart and spirit of his audiences (Sherlock & Bennett, 1998).

A large part of Garvey's emotional power, and success, was linked to his oratorical prowess.

Consider being a member of the 25,000-strong crowd hearing Garvey in full flight, proclaiming at Madison Square Gardens: "We are the descendants of a suffering people; we are the descendants of a people determined to suffer no longer ... we shall raise the banner of democracy in Africa or 400,000,000 of us will report to God why ... we pledge our blood to the battlefield of

Africa where we will fight for true liberty, democracy and the brotherhood of man. It will be a terrible day when the blacks draw the sword to fight for their liberty; I call upon the 400,000,000 blacks to give the blood you have shed for the white man to make Africa a republic for the Negro (Sherlock & Bennett, 1998, p. 304)."

This is powerful oratory imbued with passion from a courageous adult educator. One sees here that passion for one's calling is a highly desirable attribute for success. Garvey had passion.

ExL: A Pillar for Self-Reliance

Garvey had an economic agenda and he deployed experiential learning (ExL) to execute this agenda. Garvey fervently thought that Black people should experientially learn self-reliance and focussed industriousness by creating their own economic institutions to embed the institutionalisation of learning to be self-reliant through intentional entrepreneurship! Here we see that Marcus Garvey was a proponent of entrepreneurship long before it became popularised!

What is experiential learning? Experiential learning involves learning from experience. It is, simply put, learning by doing - the process of making meaning from direct experiences (P.R. McCarthy & H. M. McCarthy, 'When Case Studies are not Enough: Integrating Experiential Learning into Business Curricula,' 2006).

"Experiential learning is a powerful way to help people identify changes required to their skills, attitudes, and behaviours, and then implement those changes for better performance." [Source: Experientiallearning.org]

Garvey, the intuitive genius that he was, recognized that experiential learning was one of the pillars needed for Black self-reliance.

Self-reliance taps into and leverages the energy, creativity, and ingenuity –the 'collective muscle' - of a people to architect their own well-being through entrepreneurship. But self-reliance begins with the mindset of a people. Garvey recognized that one of the crippling legacies of centuries of colonialism and enslavement was an acute affliction with 'dependency syndrome' – both physical and psychological.

Channelling Marcus Garvey, Malcolm X declared that "A race of people is like an individual man; until it uses its own talent, takes pride in its own history, expresses its own culture, affirms its own self-hood, it can never fulfill itself."

Over the years, I've interacted with the heads and senior staff members in several core public institutions in Jamaica. And I've discovered that whenever these technocrats develop policies and derived projects, their mindset, like that of their political bosses, is locked into "getting money from overseas" – whether in the form of grants or loans – to implement them!

But this reflexive and learned mendicancy is not just a Jamaica thing –it's also a Caribbean thing. I was at a conference that included delegates from several other Caribbean islands. The conference was convened by a Geneva-based United Nations-affiliated body and it sought to build the capacity of various Caribbean countries to become more innovative; the presenters were Europeans. In one of the sessions, the Caribbean delegates were invited to make presentations on the 'state of innovation' in their respective countries.

I sat there mortified as every one of them kept talking about "lack of resources" being "challenges" to them in making meaningful progress. When they were finished, I felt compelled to tell them I was disappointed with their presentations because what our people need to do was to deploy creative imagination and use the resources that each country is endowed with to orchestrate prosperity. Chastened, they agreed with me.

Marcus Garvey warned Black people: "Dependence upon the progress and achievements of others is like depending upon a broken stick, resting upon which eventually consigns one to the ground. Prayer alone is not going to improve our condition, nor is the policy of watchful waiting. We must strike out for ourselves in the course of material achievements and by our own effort and energy present to the world those forces by which the progress of man is judged."

Garvey wanted Black people to make mendicancy a fugitive and self-reliance their default mode of thinking and acting! Hence, he sought to install a new mindset among Black people. Therefore, Garvey had a vision of mental (psychological) and economic emancipation for Black people. In other words, Garvey believed that Blacks (African-Jamaicans and Africans everywhere) should learn self-reliance by creating their own social and economic institutions.

Weaponisation of Psychology

"Colonisation is based on [the weaponization of] psychology ... there are in this world groups of men who suffer from what must be called a dependency complex ... these groups are psychologically made for dependence, they need dependence, they crave it, ask for it, demand it – this is the case with most colonized peoples" [Source: Aime Cesaire, Discourse on Colonisation: A Poetics of Anticolonialism'].

Historian Nell Irvin Painter in her book **'The History of White People'** cites this story about the psychological sphere of enslaved persons in ancient Greece: "Herodotus relates an anecdote demonstrating the two sides of slave life: a chance for upward mobility and a circumscribed possibility for success. In roughly 512 BCE the Scythian army undertook a war against the Persian King Darius that continued for twenty-eight years. And the Scythians won. But twenty-eight years of absence had wrought changes at home. As Herodotus explains, "For the Scythian women, when they saw that time went on, and their husbands did not come back, had intermarried with their slaves." On the warriors' return, children of the slaves and the Scythian women put up stiff resistance so long as the warriors fought with spears and bows. But the warriors succeeded once they capitalized on the essentially servile nature of the half-slave children. "Take my advice," one Scythian warrior told his army, "Lay spear and bow aside, and let each man fetch his horse-whip, and go boldly up to them. So long as they see us with arms in our hands, they imagine themselves our equals in birth and bravery; but let them behold us with no other weapon but the whip, and they will feel that they are our slaves, and flee before us." Herodotus tells us that this tactic worked: the slaves' progeny "forgot to fight, and immediately ran away." A mere sight of the whip had returned the children of slaves to their innate, slavish character, an early example of the close association of status and temperament."

"Capture their minds, and their hearts and souls will follow. For once their minds are reached, they're defeated without bullets." ~ Anonymous

******

Garvey The Social Engineer
================####============

Garvey also advocated for lands to assist farmers and peasants and the building of roads and ports to transport their produce. Not many people appreciate the historical roots and implications of land-poverty in Jamaica. When the formerly enslaved African-Jamaicans were emancipated in 1834, they were landless!

Land Reform

Garvey was thus an early advocate for land reform in Jamaica! Sadly, landlessness still bedevils Jamaica society where, at last count, it was estimated that up to 900,000 Jamaicans are 'squatters' (that is, illegally occupying property they do not own or have legal right to occupy).

En passant, I will mention that in the parish in Jamaica where I grew up, St. Catherine, the Custos George McGrath had a "whole heap of land." From where my family and I lived, to "as far as the eyes could see," was owned by this man. It's difficult to imagine that he had actually purchased what amounted to many thousands of acres of land.

As youngsters, we were told that he got the land as some kind of "gift" from the colonial government for "service in the war" (presumably World War 2). Whatever the method by which he acquired the land, it was mightily disproportionate in quantity compared with that owned by the regular people in the neighboring communities. So, growing up, I saw close-up the historical imbalance in land ownership in Jamaica, which persists.

Interestingly, during the Michael Manley Government of 1972-1980, the George McGrath property was one of several large properties Island-wide made part of Project Land-Lease. This resulted in the property being sub-divided into 1–5-acre plots for hundreds of small farmers. This was another one of Prime Minister Manley's initiatives aimed at the "empowerment of the people." However, these property acquisitions weren't without a political price. They fed into the belief of many persons from the middle and ruling classes that such acquisitions confirmed one of their strongly held beliefs about communism: that it represented "taking from the rich" for redistribution to the poor.

I am compelled to mention here that my paternal grandmother Edith 'Pearl' Ivey [1905-1990], a higgler, used the modest proceeds from her 'market-basket' to purchase many acres of land, which she shared among her children, thus preventing my family from experiencing 'land-poverty'; the import of this achievement never fails to impress me. In fact, it motivated me to write a book **'The Matriarch: Life and Legacy of Edith 'Pearl' Ivey'** as a literary monument in her honour. My grandmother was a genius who was prescient and knew the intergenerational value of real property.

History Matters

The derisive characterization of landless Jamaicans as 'squatters' fails to take account of history.

History is an important academic discipline. But one of the problems in Jamaican society is that many people devalue history. The past incessantly animates the present. Therefore, as an unapologetic 'student of history,' like an archeologist, I excavate, autopsy, and mine insights from history because its true value is educational.

History also helps one to discern the 'crevices' where historical tricks lurk and the forms they may have evolved into now, or might in the future; in other words, history is a window that allows us to peer from whence we've travelled to be where we are now and are likely to go in the future.

Marcus Garvey intuitively recognized the value of history when he declared that "A people without knowledge of their history, origin, and culture are like a tree without roots." And he added: "History is the landmark by which we are directed into the true course of life. The history of a movement, the history of a nation, the history of a race is the guidepost of that movement's destiny, that nation's destiny, that race's destiny."

These views from Randall Robinson are also apt: "Far too many Americans of African descent [the same may be said of Jamaicans of African descent in Jamaica] believe their history starts in America with bondage and struggles forward from there toward today's second-class citizenship. The cost of this obstructed view of ourselves, of our history, is incalculable. How can we be collectively successful if we have no idea or, worse, the wrong idea of who we were and, therefore, are? We are history's amnesiacs fitted with the memory of others. Our minds can be trained for individual career success but our group morale, the very soul of us, has been devastated by the assumption that what has not been told to us about ourselves does not exist to be told." [Source Randall Robinson, The Debt: What America Owes to Blacks]

To know the past is to know the present. It is by knowing Jamaica's past that we will be able to fully understand Jamaica's present.

"Look back over the past, with its changing empires that rose and fell, and you can foresee the future, too." ~ Marcus Aurelius [26 April 121 – 17 March 180]

History enables us "to grasp more exactly the unique significance of what is present" posits Professor Elsa Goveia of The University of the West Indies.

History enables us "to make sense of the ambiguities of progress, the dynamics of social change, the complexities of human nature, and the tragedies, crimes, and struggles that shaped our world," says Prof. Steven Mintz of the University of Texas, USA.

History continues to ramify (branch out) into the present. So, for example, the contemporary consequences of Jamaica's post-colonial history include a society structured around class, race, colour, and deeply embedded inequities.

I remain undaunted and nonplussed by my friends who roll their eyes at me because I need no convincing that looking at things through the lens of history clarifies much about the present and helps to chart the future. History can be a useful psychological compass because historical antecedents have contributed to shaping the present.

It is important to appreciate that academic historians' understanding of history is not as a disconnected thing from the past, but as "a continuing dialogue between the present and the past." The history of a nation is the guidepost of that nation's destiny. The thing is that many Jamaicans, including some of my friends, fail to appreciate that the past is never really past, but it constantly shapes and informs the present because it is from seeds sown in the garden of the past that the fruits of the present originate.

"I cannot wrap my head around the notion that a person can be truly educated without knowledge of their history," says Verene Shepherd, Professor of Social History at The University of the West Indies. I agree with Professor Shepherd. Prof. Shepherd has been doing a sterling job educating Jamaicans about their history.

This is a part of Prof. Shepherd's profile that is posted on the website of The University of the West Indies: "Raised in the community of Hopewell in St. Mary, before completing her certification as a trained teacher at the Shortwood Teachers' College in Kingston, Jamaica, Professor Shepherd attended Huffstead Basic School, Rosebank Primary School, and St. Mary High School. In 1972, she gained entry to the Mona campus of the University of the West Indies, where she completed a BA in history and a M.Phil. both in History in 1976 and 1982, respectively. The award of a scholarship took her to the University of Cambridge to read for her PhD in History, which she completed in 1988. Her thesis, **'Pens and Pen-keepers in a Plantation Society: Aspects of Jamaican**

Social and Economic History, 1740–1845,' examined the economic history of colonial Jamaica. Her work has also contributed to the international human rights and justice agenda at the United Nations, where - from 2010 to 2014 - Professor Shepherd was been a member of the United Nations Working Group of Experts on People of African Descent (WGEPAD), serving as the Working Group's Chair from 2011-2014. It was while serving as Chair of the WGEPAD that her contributions assisted in shaping the Programme for The International Year for People of African Descent; which ultimately led to the declaration of the United Nations Decade for People of African Descent. She is currently the Director of The Centre for Reparation Research at The UWI."

And the **Daily Observer** commented in these terms on Prof. Shepherd's important work as an academic and public intellectual: "Today we gratefully and respectfully acknowledge and salute the contribution of Professor Verene Shepherd to educating the Jamaican people about their history through her writing and speaking, especially her Nationwide radio programme, **Talking History**. This is an invaluable contribution to nation-building. Among her numerous books (sole and co-authored) are Livestock, Sugar & Slavery: Contested Terrain in Colonial Jamaica (2009); I Want to Disturb My Neighbour (2007); Maharani's Misery: Narratives of a Passage from India to the Caribbean (2002), and Engendering History: Caribbean Women in Historical Perspectives (1998). She is a public intellectual who has put her knowledge to the service of the people by extending her teaching beyond the university classroom. Her persona personifies Jamaican culture and African heritage. Our most respected educators are revered with the title Teacher. We say "nuff" respect, Teacher Shepherd. Future Jamaicans will salute you."

But, to illustrate the cavernous depth of the challenge we face as a people, someone wrote these ignorant and corrosive comments under the Jamaica Observer's editorial about Prof. Shepherd's work: "Some people make a livelihood out of dredging up past racial atrocities that further stir hate, anger, and division. How is this ever a useful exercise? It surely guarantees that current opportunities will be missed by the constant reflection and agitation. Race-baiting has become a profession that can be financially rewarding and platform building. When we recall all those who use grievance and outrage within the black race for personal advancement...we can see these people are more popular, connected, and personally well off than the masses they seek to advocate for. The racial grievance industry is lucrative and more and more "elites" know how to position themselves. Sadly, nothing will ever change for the black race until the culture therein changes."

While we note them, we must not be detained by ignorant, vacuous, and spurious comments such as those immediately above. We must educate these sick people – this is the treatment they need.

Reflecting his perspicacity yet again, Marcus Mosiah Garvey tells us that "A people without the knowledge of their history, origin, and culture are like a tree without roots."

"Black people must know that their histories did not begin with enslavement. "Our history is taught that it begins at slavery. That's not where it began. Mali has the world's first university. Do we know about the history of many of the world's first developments and occurrences that began with people with melanin? The truth is that the Black consciousness train is out of control, and for many persons, it's hard to be what they cannot see. Black people must visualise images of greatness in their own people and the excellence of previous, current, and future endeavours. Images of derailment in the journey and deliberate attempts to keep excellence hidden must never become the dominant speak. We need more Jamaicans to know about Jamaicans in spaces of excellence. But the global increasing consciousness post George Floyd's murder shows what is possible and shows that we can call out what is not okay. People need to understand that they have more power than they are told." [Source: Ayana Samuels, The Sunday Gleaner, February 14, 2021]

The grave in which the past is interred is so shallow that it frequently pops out to place its claim on the present. Also, "When we attempt to answer the question, What is history? our answer, consciously or unconsciously, reflects our own position in time, and forms part of our answer to the broader question, what view we have of the society in which we live." [Source:

E.H. Carr, 'What is History?' New York: Vintage Books (1961)]

Malcolm X (whose father was a Garveyite) insisted that people of African descent (and continental Africans) should constantly seek to understand their history. He once said in a speech to Black People: "I don't think any of you will deny the fact that it is impossible to understand the present or prepare for the future unless we have some knowledge of the past. And the thing that has kept most of us- that is, the Afro-Americans- almost crippled in this society (USA) has been our complete lack of knowledge concerning the past. The number one thing that makes us different from other people is our lack of knowledge concerning the past. If we don't go into the past and find out how we got this way, we will think that we were always this way. And if you think that you were always in the condition that you're in right now, it's impossible for you to have too much confidence in yourself, you become worthless, almost nothing."

(The **Autobiography of Malcolm X** is one of the "most powerful" books I have read in terms of its impact on my mind. I came to read it almost by accident, but only due to my habit of being an avid reader. A friend of a friend left the book at the first friend's house after a visit. I happened by a few days later, saw it, and lent it to myself. I learned from this book how one could be bold, fearless, and uncompromising in defense of one's beliefs just by sheer force of will. Malcolm X was, for me, then, the first person I encountered, through his written words of course, who didn't give a damn who was offended by what he had to say. According to Pablo Neruda, "The books that help you most are those which make you think the most. The hardest way of learning is that of easy reading; but a great book that comes from a great thinker is a ship of thought, deep freighted with truth and beauty." Malcolm X impressed me immensely with his views on race and his badass attitude. I felt disappointed not to have read his book much earlier in my life. Interestingly, as a Jamaican, I read this book even before I was exposed to the magnificent Philosophy and Opinions of Marcus Mosiah Garvey.)

Globalization

Another plank of Marcus Mosiah Garvey's economic agenda was his advocacy for a shipping line that would be used by farmers to transport their products to the different available markets of the world. Garvey also called for the establishment of trade commissioners and marketing and advertising agencies in the principal countries to facilitate the marketing of Jamaican products. Here we see that Garvey's vision included globalization long before the term and concept entered mainstream thought! Genius! (Sources: Rupert Lewis, 1988; Sherlock & Bennett, 1998).

Globalization is a process that seeks to be agnostic of national geographic boundaries and other barriers in the movement of goods, services, capital, technology, and finances.

Garvey's vision of diaspora firms doing business with the motherland of Africa is doable. When she took over the chairmanship of CARICOM in December 2019,

Barbados' Prime Minister Mia Motley's committed to forging stronger links with Africa. She alluded to unleashing "people-to-people communication and cooperation, and the trade and investment opportunities such that our nations can prosper – relying on each other [Source: The Jamaica Observer, December 8, 2019].

The PJPCACA

Interestingly, the Percival James 'P.J.' Patterson Centre for Africa-Caribbean Advocacy (PJPCACA) was officially launched at The University of the West Indies (The UWI) on Friday, June 26, 2020. The new Centre's mandate is to coordinate public policy and advocacy in fostering development relations between the Caribbean and Africa.

I think the establishment of the PJCACA) is excellent use by former prime minister Patterson of his residual power.

In his remarks at the launch, Mr. Patterson, who is a Statesman in Residence at the UWI, referenced the COVID-19 pandemic and underscored the relevance of the Centre, saying, "The world we knew no longer exists. The world that emerges will be entirely different. The reconfiguration of global power and the restructuring of the global economy cannot be left to the market or the dictates of a few determined to continue to shape the future by unilateral decisions without international consultation. The interest of the less developed, less powerful, and most vulnerable can no longer be ignored. The peoples of African descent must forge through dialogue to a consensus agenda to articulate a vision of a reordered world in which our governments and regional organisations have a leadership role".

With that, the Statesman in Residence declared, "We propose a dialogue at the level of the Heads of Government to agree on a common agenda and to initiate a programme of international cooperation among countries in Africa and the global diaspora of people of African descent. There is a compelling need for the African Union and CARICOM to act in tandem with all the international organisations to which we belong, to ensure that our region's rights and interests of our peoples, especially women, children, and persons with disabilities are actively defended," he said.

According to Mr. Patterson, the new Centre "Will contribute to the intellectual dialogue which could help to formulate and assist in the technical analysis, without which, our just cause will never be accomplished. CARICOM and the African Union must marshal the political will, backed by compelling evidence, to combat global racism, wherever in the world this is manifested, and to promote a deeper understanding of the historical processes that have engendered poverty and social justice on our planet earth." The Centre, Patterson added, "Will do its part in building the bridges through academic exchanges and collaborations with institutions around economic and trade policy, cultural interaction and governance, climate change, and other critical areas.

Speaking at the launch at the Centre, Vice-Chancellor of The UWI, Professor Sir Hilary Beckles said that the Centre has the blessing of the entire UWI as well as that of the current Prime Minister of Jamaica, the Most Honourable Andrew Holness, who has offered his support. "No Centre in any university could have been more timely," said Vice-Chancellor Beckles. "The conversations taking place in the world today, point to a need for us as people in the modern world to remove the debilitating features of colonisation, slavery, and all the other extractive models that have demonstrated harm to this region over many centuries. The world is looking for justice. The world is looking for a new sensibility and certainly the people of the Caribbean are looking for a new relationship with ancestral Africa" Beckles asserted.

Vice-Chancellor Beckles added, "(Jamaica) invested heavily in the liberation of Africa starting with the late Marcus Garvey, laying the foundation for that vision. But, long before Garvey, Caribbean folks have been talking about liberation and the freedom of Africa and the Caribbean's place within it. Jamaica also participated in the attempt to bring down apartheid in Southern Africa, thanks to the leadership of people like PJ Patterson, Michael Manley, Fidel Castro, and Dame Nita Barrow—all icons of Caribbean civilisation who participated in the freedom of Africa." [Source: UWI News. www.mona.uwi.edu]

The Patterson Centre for Africa-Caribbean Advocacy (PC4ACA) thrums with the influence of Marcus Mosiah Garvey and his vision of Pan-Africanism! Oh yes, the establishment of the PC4ACA 80 years after Garvey's death is yet another example of the long and ongoing afterlife of his influence and legacy.

The Africa & Caribbean Summit

Another encouraging development in the strengthening and deepening of the relationship between Africa and the Caribbean that I think would please Garvey immensely was the convening of the inaugural CARICOM-Africa Summit on September 7, 2021. Previewing the summit, The Gleaner posited the following in its editorial of September 6, 2021: "It provides an opportunity for them [African and CARICOM leaders] to recast the debate on global governance, away from the narrow confines within which it has been set by the big global powers. Hopefully, they will grasp it – as kith and kin. But a meaningful effort, especially for the Caribbean, will require global policy activism of a kind that the region has not engaged in for over four decades, since the 1970s. It will demand speaking frankly, at times discomfortingly, with some of the region's better friends, including the United States."

The Gleaner continued: "The summit is taking place against the backdrop of interwoven and complex developments, the most obvious, and immediately compelling, of which is the COVID-19 pandemic. The coronavirus highlights the economic divide, and other inequities, between rich and poor countries, which includes most of those in the Caribbean and Africa."

The Gleaner ended its editorial on this note: "This summit, therefore, requires that the leaders of Africa and the Caribbean not only recognise their common concerns but begin to frame joint responses to looming global challenges. They must demand more than token places in the negotiating fora. And they must take to the table clear ideas and concrete reform proposals. The summit should also be a stepping stone from which the two groups, via other common institutions – such as the Commonwealth and the Association of African, Caribbean, and Pacific States (ACPS) – the Caribbean and Africa rally a wider cohort with common interests, to pursue a credible global reform agenda. More than four decades ago, the then leaders of many of the countries at the table this week had a vision for greater South-South cooperation – economic and other partnerships between developing countries to break the stranglehold of the power of rich nations. They made little headway. The idea, nonetheless, remains relevant. It should be seriously revived this week."

For her part, CARICOM Secretary General Dr. Carla Barnett provided the context for evaluating the virtual historic Africa-CARICOM Summit. She said: "We have had our moments of acting together to protect and advance our mutual interests, but today we are committing to forge a new more permanent alliance that has the potential to open new vistas of collaboration and cooperation."

The truth is that the relationship between CARICOM is ad hoc, with occasional expressions and token-like demonstrations of friendship. For example, CARICOM's trade with Africa accounted for a minuscule 3.2 percent of its total trade globally notwithstanding commitments to strengthening ties with the continent. For this to change meaningfully, concrete actions must be taken to ensure that there is the subsequent implementation of the proposals presented at the summit.

"The two regions account for approximately 1.4 billion people with great natural and wealth-creating resources, supplying vital commodities to the global community, and offering a strong market for the goods and services from Europe and North America. This is enriched by the bonds of cultural, historical, and political relations and bolstered by the prospects of the combined voting power of 69 nations in the United Nations and all its subsidiaries including the World Trade Organization. Prime Minister Ralph Gonsalves, St. Vincent & the Grenadines aptly summarized the potential: "We have global bargaining power but only if we use it effectively." The general agreement was that the new relationship emanating from the Summit must also extend to increasing trade and investment between Africa and CARICOM. Preliminary figures for 2020 indicate that total trade between Africa and the Caribbean, estimated at approximately US $29 Million is a drop of $10 Million from 2018." [Source: Global Frontier (GOFAD) Advisory and Development Services, September 9, 2021]

In an article titled **'Pursue Development though Economic Pan-Africanism'** published in The Gleaner on September 11, 2021, young public policy and management academician at the University of the West Indies David Salmon laid out several specific actions that could be taken between CARICOM and Africa, in support of his thesis: "Economic pan-Africanism can provide a solid foundation that guides subsequent interactions.

Pan-Africanism proposes that people of African descent have common interests that can be achieved with collaboration. While this relationship has often been seen through a cultural lens, in today's society economics presents the greatest opportunity for renewing our connection with Africa. In other words, investments have replaced apartheid as the linchpin of our relationship." Salmon's article is worth the attention and consideration of the leaders of CARICOM and their technocrats.

So, was there congruence between the expectations of the CARICOM Secretary General, The Gleaner, the recommendations of David Salmon, and the understandings and agreements reached at the summit?

Chairman of the summit, Uhuru Kenyatta, President of Kenya, said: "As we begin this journey, I would like to invoke the words of Martin Luther King Jr. And I quote: "We must learn to live together as brothers or perish together as fools". African and Caribbean cultural and political ties run deep based on a shared history, culture, as well as a sense of a common identity. Our common historical experiences of slavery and colonialism inspired Africa's founding fathers to form the Pan-African Movement in the 1900s. This movement was championed by the Africans in the diaspora, which established the foundations of a rich and vibrant African-Caribbean relationship." [Source: CARICOM Today, September 7, 2021]

Kenyatta outlined five key areas of cooperation namely, **blue economy, climate change, health and Covid-19, debt sustainability, and technology** which he said are crucial as the two regions initiate working partnerships. He also said the Covid-19 pandemic is a wake-up call for the developing nations to build their vaccine manufacturing and other critical medical supplies saying the outbreak has redefined health systems across the developing world. And he challenged the countries to embrace new technologies to create all-inclusive solutions and work together in formulating strategies to increase revenues and optimise their expenditures on activities that catalyse economic output. [Source CARICOM Today, September 7, 2021]

Prime Minister of Antigua and Barbuda who is also the current Chairman of CARICOM Gaston Browne challenged African and Caribbean nations to work together saying the countries wield formidable global bargaining power. Prime Minister Browne said the success of the African Union's Medical Supplies Platform (AMSP), which helped procure Covid-19 vaccines and other supplies for Caribbean and African nations had demonstrated the two regions' immense potential. "We must establish structures of cooperation to promote our mutual socio-economic interests; increasing investment and trade and people-to-people exchanges between Africa and the Caribbean. "We should resist being pushed to the margins of international decision-making and collaborate on decisions to restructure the global financial architecture, on global taxation, derisking, climate change and reparations among others." [Source: CARICOM Today, September 7, 2021]

For his part, Jamaica's Prime Minister Andrew Holness said, as reported by The Gleaner, he was truly honoured to address the historic inaugural event, which he described as "a timely dialogue which can only strengthen our fraternal bonds. The common historical experiences between Africa and the Caribbean have been enriched by cultural, economic, and political affinities. Potential untapped for centuries lies within our respective reaches, as we not only develop national capacities but engage opportunities for cooperation with each other and across continents and oceans."

Participants at the event included Heads of State and Government of the Caribbean Community and the African Union, Chairs of CARICOM and the African Union Commission, the Africa Regional Economic Communities, the Secretaries-General of CARICOM and the Organisation of the African Caribbean and Pacific States, and the President of Caribbean Development Bank. It is anticipated that the deliberations will institutionalise CARICOM-African Union collaboration. It is also expected that there will be an agreement to host summits of the CARICOM-African Heads of State and Government bi-annually. Expected outcomes could include greater economic trade and investment opportunities between Africa and the Caribbean, and solidarity in actions to address global challenges including climate change and the COVID-19 pandemic." [Source: The Gleaner, September 7, 2021]

There was strong support at the summit for multilateralism and the strengthening and reform of multilateral institutions to become more inclusive to reflect the post-colonial world. The Leaders reiterated their commitment to the Sustainable Development Goals. While welcoming the Debt Service Suspension Initiative, they emphasised the need for debt relief. They also called for an end to the illegal and unjust economic embargo against Cuba and the sanctions against Zimbabwe. The Heads of State and governments agreed to participate fully in the High-Level meeting of the UN General Assembly later this month to commemorate the 20th anniversary of the 2001 UN World Conference Against Racism, and to jointly use that event to advance the claim for reparations within the processes of the United Nations. The Summit ended with a mandate for the institutionalisation of co-operation between the CARICOM Secretariat and the African Union Commission. [Source: CARICOM Today, September 7, 2021]

In a post-summit editorial on September 21, 2021, The Gleaner noted: "Africa and Caribbean leaders touched on many of the relevant issues ... but given the urgency of many of the global developments with which they have to contend, the leaders were not sufficiently specific, and robust, about those on which they intend to develop joint initiatives. There was not the sense of urgency for which we had hoped. Having identified the issues of common cause, the issue now is how the AU and CARICOM deploy the power of their 69 global votes to prevent themselves, as CARICOM Chairman Gaston Browne put it at the conference's opening session, "being pushed to the margins of international decision-making".

The Gleaner concluded: "First, while we endorse the broad agenda, they have to bring greater clarity and specificity to the issues to be pursued. They have to address the textured differences on issues that will be natural between the two regions before they become points of friction at the global negotiating tables. That work has to start now, with the AU and CARICOM acting with urgency on "the institutionalisation of cooperation" with which they were charged. The secretariats should see, and welcome, intellectual inputs from independent analysts and think tanks in Africa and the Caribbean in fleshing out and articulating initiatives. The P.J. Patterson Centre for Africa-Caribbean Advocacy at The University of the West Indies is one institution that ought to be of value in this exercise. It would help, too, if there was a kindling of the historic, cultural, and ethnic links between the African diaspora in the Caribbean and their kin on the continent. Knowing each other better and embracing the relationship should bring energy and nuance to the cooperation. Which makes the summit's suggestion of a CARICOM-AU electronic mass media platform or mechanism to facilitate the flow of new information and artistic programmes between the two regions a sensible idea – as is the call for visa-free travel between CARICOM and Africa. The matter now is getting them done."

The first-ever CARICOM-Africa Summit is a beginning that should be acknowledged for its objectives and potential for great things to come. I will be watching to see if it bears fruit.

(Since independence, several African leaders have visited Jamaica: Haile Selassie I in 1966; President Julius Nyerere of Tanzania in 1975; President Uhuru Kenyatta of Kenya in 2019; and Paul Kagame in 2022).

Development Financing

Marcus Mosiah Garvey's 'richly stored mind' conceived the need for the provision of developmental financing to Black people to start businesses for wealth creation. Accordingly, to support nascent local industries, he advocated for the establishment of a Central Industrial Bank (Sources: Rupert Lewis, 1988; Sherlock & Bennett, 1998).

'Crowd-Sourcing' of Financing

Garvey was a pioneer in the crowd-sourcing financing model when he issued what was in effect an initial public offering (IPO) of shares to finance the establishment of the Black Star Line Steamship Corporation.

"Black Star Line Steamship Corporation was Garvey's greatest and most fateful project of economic self-reliance (by Black people). It was incorporated in 1919 and capitalized with stock. Garvey organized the Black Star Line to be the ultimate expression of Pan-African communal self-help. It would facilitate trade and immigration among Blacks in Africa, the Caribbean, and the United States, and transport some Blacks to Liberia in hope of forming an independent, Black-governed state, not unlike the Jewish-governed state of Israel. In the process, Garvey believed that the Black Star Line would positively influence the dignity and self-esteem of Blacks throughout the Diaspora by proving that Blacks could manage monumental endeavours independently. During this era of colonialism and Jim Crow, only a few decades removed from enslavement, many people of African descent were illiterate, impoverished, and regarded as less than human by most nations. Although some observers misinterpreted his rhetoric as Black supremacist in nature, Garvey merely helped to inspire in this community pride in their heritage that had been absent up to that point. Garvey once commented that "I thought if we could launch our ships and have our own Black captains and officers, our race, too, would be respected in the mercantile and commercial world, thereby adding appreciative dignity to our downtrodden people." [Source: Justin Hansford, 'Jailing a Rainbow: The Marcus Garvey Case', Miguel Lorne Printers and Publishers, 2016]

This from Justin Hansford is also instructive: "Everyone connected with the Black Star Line understood its higher purpose – including both employees and stock-holders. Often employees would work without asking for payment, simply because they knew that the Black Star Line was part of a greater plan to uplift the Black Diaspora. The stockholders contributed in the hopes that they could see the project come to fruition, not to reap financial profit for themselves. In the beginning, Garvey solicited funds as donations and turned to selling stocks later when the District Attorney urged him to incorporate the business. Garvey then appealed to the same people (UNIA members) for stocks as he did for donations. Consequently, it seems that even the sales of stocks were more like philanthropic contributions than profit-driven investments. The Black Star Line was a new kind of enterprise in the Black community; in its emphasis on joint ownership and community empowerment, today it would be called 'social entrepreneurship'."

****

Garvey The Newspaperman
=====================####===================

The Power of Media

Most adults get most of their information about politics and current affairs through the mass media. The media also exert tremendous power on society through its 'agenda-setting' and 'priming' effects.

Agenda-setting refers to the media's "ability to direct the public's attention to certain issues," while priming describes its "ability to affect the criteria by which viewers judge public policies, public officials, or candidates for office."

"The impact of media is not based exclusively on the explicit words, sentences, text, and images portrayed but also involves the implications, the nuances, the latent messages, and associative conclusions that can be drawn from the images, the text, and explicit statements. Media both reflect and construct cultural meaning, and influence understanding, opinion formation, and societal development. Those to whom the messages are conveyed invariably reach beyond the explicit, to uncover structures of meaning which may affect their opinions, their beliefs and ultimately the culture of their environment." [Source: Marjan de Bruin and Claude Robinson, 'Media & Violence in Jamaica' 2009]

Another dimension of Marcus Garvey's intuitive genius was his recognition of the importance of the written word as a vehicle for conveying his message and countering the lies and propaganda of opposing forces.

It is instructive to note here that Marcus Garvey recognized the importance of journalism and publishing – information power. The people who decide what we read and how we consume the news significantly shape how we see the world that we live in.

Role of the Free Press

According to the 'Noam Chomsky-Edward Herman propaganda model,' the (alleged) 'free press' serves the societal purpose of "protecting privilege from the threat of public understanding and participation."

Marcus Garvey founded the following local newspapers as 'alternative press' to The Gleaner (founded in 1834) that was aligned to the plantocracy: The **Negro Voice** and **The Blackman**. By 1920, his newspaper, **Negro World**, had a circulation of between 50,000 and 200,000.

Garvey averred that: "The function of the press is public service without prejudice and partiality, to convey the truth as it is seen and understood without favouritism and bias." (The Philosophy and Opinions of Marcus Garvey, p. 6)

The need of Black People for their own newspapers was also recognized by Blacks in the USA. "The first Black-owned newspaper in the United States was **Freedom's Journal**, which began, in New York City, in 1827, the year that the state officially abolished slavery. "Too long have others spoken for us," its founders declared. By the time Lincoln signed the Emancipation Proclamation, more than twenty other Black newspapers had been launched, including Frederick Douglass's the **North Star**, published in Rochester. These papers were essential to promoting the abolitionist cause, allowing free blacks to tell their own stories and to spread the stories of people still living in slavery." [Source: Casey Cep, 'The Legacy of a Radical Black Newspaperman', The Atlantic, November 18, 2019]

Media coverage of the Russia-Ukraine war versus the ongoing Israeli-Palestinian conflict, and the role of Fox News Network in the rise of Donald Trump and white nationalism in the USA, have forcefully confirmed in my mind that media are tools used to serve the ends of particular special interest groups. Marcus Garvey recognised this and became a 'newspaper man'.

Ironically, the members of the 'Garvey Must Go!' campaign in the USA used the media effectively against him.

******

Garvey The Politician

==================####==================

Garvey's People's Political Party (PPP)

I think the zenith of Garvey's philosophy is seen in his direct involvement in politics when he formed Jamaica's first, modern political party, the People's Political Party (PPP) on September 9, 1929 - well before the PNP and JLP that were formed in 1938 by Osmond Theodore 'OT' Fairclough and by Alexander Bustamante in 1943, respectively.

Garvey knew intuitively that whereas real change required activism and protest to highlight a problem, political machinery was needed to implement practical solutions and laws. He grasped that the intersection of consciousness-raising, psychological rehabilitation, and political action provided a winning combination for true emancipation and empowerment for historically marginalised Black people from their untenable situation.

The PPP's Manifesto

Garvey had some clear prescriptions as to how Jamaica should be governed. The PPP set out a 14-point manifesto—the first of its kind in the island's electoral history. The points contained in the PPP's manifesto were far-reaching and perceptive as illustrated by a few of them, such as:

- An eight-hour workday
- A minimum wage
- A larger share of self-government
- Protection for native industries
- A legal aid department for the poor

- Technical schools for each parish
- Land reform
- Libraries and civic improvement for parish capitals
- City status for Montego Bay and Port Antonio
- A National Park at the Kingston Race Course

Garvey: KSAC Councillor

Garvey contested and won a seat as a Councillor of the Allman Town Division of the Kingston and St. Andrew Corporation. But he lost his seat because he was imprisoned for "contempt of court" for daring to criticize the justice system as being "corrupt."

Jamaica Imprisoned Garvey

So, it wasn't only in the USA that Garvey was imprisoned. The land of his birth, Jamaica, also imprisoned him on a spurious charge.

Here is public relations consultant and writer Lance Neita's summary of the circumstances that led to Garvey's incarceration in Jamaica: "What happened was that Garvey was not popular with the hierarchy of the social order that ruled Jamaica in the 1920s. In July 1929, in a successful attempt to harass and distract him, the Jamaican property of the UNIA was seized on the orders of the chief justice. Garvey and his solicitor attempted to persuade people not to bid for the confiscated goods, claiming the sale was illegal. He was deemed to have gone one step too far when he referred to the justice system as stacked with corrupt judges. So, if we want America to issue a pardon for Garvey's incarceration there, then surely we should also issue a similar plea to strike out his prison record in Jamaica." [Source: Lance Neita, 'Garvey and today's generation', The Daily Observer, May 14, 2016]

This statement from Neita's account, "Garvey was not popular with the hierarchy of the social order that ruled

Jamaica in the 1920s", speaks volumes about the animus the establishment – crawling with colonial stooges and mimics - harboured against Garvey!

It is a significant tell that 'Contempt of Court' - the offence of being disobedient to or disdainful or disrespectful of a court of law and its officers – is on the books, but there is no law for contempt of the people by judges and other public officials.

(Another Jamaican, Alexander Bedward also had occasion, in 1921, to give a Jamaican Magistrate, Samuel Burke, a piece of his mind: "You use the force of law, Judge, to suppress the people. The laws and institutions are made by the few to keep the many in subjugation. No law, no judge, no newspaper, and no governor can stop the people's march forever. When the people are ready to move Judge, you and your soldiers and your policemen and your Governor had better step aside, or you will be trampled underfoot.")

In 1930, Garvey was re-elected as a KSAC Councillor, unopposed, together with two other PPP candidates. As a political representative, Garvey was seeking to manifest what Brazilian educator and philosopher Paulo Freire articulated: that "Education is politics and that the fundamental effort of education is to help with the liberation of people" (Freire clearly understood that education is a tool to resist and overcome oppression).

One sees that Garvey sought to connect learning to transformative action on the part of Blacks. And he realised, the prescient and radical genius that he was, that it was only by taking matters into their own hands that Blacks would truly liberate themselves. Starting with consciousness-raising regarding self-knowledge, racial pride, and self-esteem, and culminating in self-reliance that would be built on a foundation of education and secured through political action was "Garvey's Template."

****

Garvey The Entrepreneur
==============####============

Garvey was convinced that self-determination scaffolded on pride, fearlessness, self-confidence, and self-reliance were fundamental for the people of African descent to assert themselves and take their rightful place in the world as a proud race.

The Black Star Line

And in translating this vision into action, he established the Universal Negro Improvement Association (UNIA). The UNIA was a vehicle that would own and operate successful businesses. Most noteworthy was the Black Star Line, a steamship company to run between America, Africa, the West Indies, Canada, and South and Central America, carrying freight and passengers.

Other Businesses

There were other businesses as well such as cooperative grocery stores, restaurants, steam laundries, tailoring and dressmaking shops, and a publishing house (M. Curtin, B. Hamilton, and P. Patterson, 1987).

Garvey's aim was that Blacks would, through the operation of these businesses, experientially learn self-reliance.

This was vision finding method!

"The UNIA teaches our race self-help and self-reliance, not only in one essential but in all those things that contribute to human happiness and well-being. The disposition of the many to depend upon the other races for a kindly and sympathetic consideration of their needs, without making the effort to do for themselves, has been the race's standing disgrace by which we have been judged and through which we have created the strongest prejudice against ourselves. Prayer alone is not going to improve our condition, nor is the policy of watchful waiting. We must strike out for ourselves in the course of material achievements and by our own effort and energy present to the world those forces by which the progress of man is judged." [Source: The Philosophy and Opinions of Marcus Garvey, Centennial Edition]

"Garvey was so far ahead of his time, particularly concerning his promotion of entrepreneurship among Blacks" Owen James, Business Journalist, declared sagely on Twitter, on November 30, 2018.

I am sorely disappointed that Garvey's philosophy has not been mainstreamed in the minds of our people. I agree with economist, author, and lecturer Mark Ricketts when he said: "We can't forever cloak ourselves in an excuse-driven thought process which allows us as individuals, government, and the private sector, to make bad decisions, then tie everything to disadvantages arising from slavery, imperialism, and colonialism." [Source: The Gleaner, January 27, 2019]

Banishing the Psychology of Dependence

In Garveyesque fashion, and no doubt inspired by him, Michael Manley was seized by the import of the learned dependency syndrome among Blacks that was a feature of the 'ongoingness' (afterlife) of colonialism: "It might be as well to remind ourselves that colonial economies were conceived in the context of dependence. This economic pattern is so well documented and has been so accurately analysed and exhaustively discussed that it has often obscured a deeper consequence of colonialism which, not understood, can reduce to impotence the most skillfully devised plan for reshaping the economic system. I refer here to the psychology of dependence, which is the most insidious, elusive, and intractable of the problems which we inherit. The first task that a post-colonial society must tackle is the development of a strategy designed to replace the psychology of dependence with the spirit of individual and collective self-reliance. Until that exercise is successfully embarked upon every other plan will fail. Indeed, without the spirit of self-reliance, it is doubtful if a successful indigenous plan can be devised; instead, time and energy may be dissipated in the adaptation of other people's plans, designed for other situations, to solve other people's problems." [Source: The Politics of Change: A Jamaican Testament]

Michael Manley was possessed of unerring perspicacity. And he realized the futility of tinkering. "When one considers the magnitude of the economic and attitudinal restructuring which our condition demands, it becomes clear that the politics of conservatism and tinkering are not only irrelevant to our situation but represent an intolerable default of responsibility. Man can only adjust by tinkering but he cannot transform. Nothing less than transformation can provide answers to the dilemmas within which we are currently trapped." [Source: The Politics of Change: A Jamaican Testament]

I recall listening to a woman caller to a local radio talk show. The host found her interesting and wanted to get to know more about her, so he probed further. Here is how the conversation went:

"Do you work?" he asked.

"No," she answered.

"So, what do you do then?"

"I operate a restaurant," she replied.

"Oh, so you are a businessman, then," the host declared.

"Yes, my daughter and I run it," the woman added, with palpable pride.

I found the above-mentioned exchange revealing and instructive. The woman caller did not regard herself as being employed. She did not self-identify as a businesswoman, a bona fide entrepreneur, who had used her creativity and business acumen to orchestrate her family's livelihood! Sadly, many African-Jamaicans automatically think operating businesses is the natural aptitude and purview of other ethnic groups. "Work" for many Jamaicans is 'getting a job,' preferably a nice paper-handling one with the government, for life, and then retiring on a pension.

I saw a meme that showed two young Black men making posts on their Facebook pages; one posted that he had landed a job, and the news elicited tons of likes and congratulations from his friends. The other one posted that he'd started his own business, and the news elicited a mere handful of likes and congratulations.

Garvey and God

==================####==================

Even though Marcus Garvey warned Black people that: "Prayer alone is not going to improve our condition, nor the policy of watchful waiting" and that "we must strike out for ourselves in the course of material achievements and by our own effort and energy present to the world those forces by which the progress of man is judged," I don't think he sufficiently grasped the role of religion, and in particular Christianity, in instilling and perpetuating self-denigration, learned helplessness, and dependency in Black People. For all my admiration of Garvey, I think this was a significant 'oversight' by him.

Jamaica's National Anthem, for example, is a prayer:

Eternal Father bless our land,
Guard us with Thy Mighty Hand,
Keep us free from evil powers,
Be our light through countless hours.
To our Leaders, Great Defender,
Grant true wisdom from above.
Justice, Truth be ours forever,
Jamaica, Land we love.
Jamaica, Jamaica, Jamaica land we love.

Teach us true respect for all,
Stir response to duty's call, strengthen us the weak to cherish,
Give us vision lest we perish.
Knowledge send us Heavenly Father,
Grant true wisdom from above.
Justice, Truth be ours forever,
Jamaica, land we love.
Jamaica, Jamaica, Jamaica land we love.

Perhaps Garvey retained his religiosity from being "baptized, in 1890, into the Wesleyan Methodist Church" and "in 1895, he began attending the Church of England school in St Ann's Bay." [Source: Rupert Lewis, 2018]

These two bits of African wisdom are apropos of my point:

- "I tell you there will be nothing from heaven. We must all work hard to save ourselves from poverty and ignorance" – Jomo Kenyatta.
- "Do not stand in a place of danger trusting in miracles" – African Wisdom.

I am compelled to ask: was Garvey not aware that during the enslavement of Black People, it was illegal for them to read any book other than the Bible? And that anyone caught reading anything else faced severe punishment?

Why was this so?

The wily enslavers understood that the Bible was a tool to limit the thinking of Black People (enslaved Africans) and to keep them subservient. Cunningly, the enslavers knew that to keep enslaved Africans in servitude they had to make them accept their lot as the will of God and have them think about the end of days - these things will keep them in perpetual servitude.

The crafty enslavers refused to give our enslaved African ancestors anything good but they gave them Christianity and the Bible. Yet centuries later, the descendants of the enslaved Africans who were whipped, tortured, raped, and murdered, now confess total confidence in the same Bible.

Black people need to know that the Bible of the enslavers is a book that was hurriedly put together by Emperor Constantine in 325 AD when he decreed Christianity - an infusion of Roman paganism, Greek and Egyptian mythology - as the new State religion and his troops would violently convert most of the world's populations to this newly formed order by force and through violence.

The Bible was central to the success of trans-Atlantic slavery. Biblical verses used by vile enslavers to justify enslavement include the following:

- Ephesians 6:5: "Slaves, obey your earthly masters with respect and fear, and with sincerity of heart, just as you would obey Christ" lent divine credence to the predicament of slaves and consigned them to perpetual slavery.
- Ephesians 6:9: "And masters, treat your slaves in the same way. Do not threaten them, since you know that he who is both their Master and yours is in heaven, and there is no favoritism with him."
- Colossians 3:22: "Slaves, obey your earthly masters in everything; and do it, not only when their eye is on you and to win their favor, but with sincerity of heart and reverence for the Lord."
- Colossians 4:1: "Masters, provide your slaves with what is right and fair because you know that you also have a Master in heaven."
- Titus 2:9: "Teach slaves to be subject to their masters in everything, to try to please them, not to talk back to them."

- 1 Peter 2:18: "Slaves, submit yourselves to your masters with all respect, not only to those who are good and considerate but also to those who are harsh."

Enslaved Africans were made to believe that revolting against their oppressors was a direct rejection of God. Today, many Africans (including their descendants in Jamaica) know the Bible from the beginning to the end but they know little about themselves or ideas that can improve their lives. They can feel Jesus in their spirits and they are absolutely sure that Christianity is the only true religion. They are waiting for an apocalyptic climax to humanity where a blue-eyed, blonde-haired white saviour will appear from the sky at the sound of a trumpet, to save them from debilitating poverty, a dysfunctional system, diseases, and imbecility. The bottom line is that centuries after chattel enslavement was legally abolished, sadly and incredibly, Africans (including their descendants in Jamaica) are still languishing in deep ignorance and mental enslavement.

The damage has been done.

"He who defines you, controls you." ~ Dr. Leonard Jeffries

In the words of the late scholar Dr. Henrik Clark: "To control a people, you must first control what they think about themselves and how they regard their history and culture. And when your conqueror makes you ashamed of your culture and history, he needs no prison walls and chains to hold you".

I can't imagine how Garvey missed the import of religion as a tool in the arsenal of colonisers given that he had this insight: "The white man has succeeded in subduing the world by forcing everybody to think his way...The white man's propaganda has made him the master of the world, and all those who have come in contact with it and accepted it have become his slaves."

How then, could Garvey miss that a religion with a white god was meant for white people?

Did Garvey not ask himself where was the Blackman's God, or the race-neutral God, when Black People were being subjected to the bottomless barbarity and depravity orchestrated by white enslavers?

Did God not hear the cries of the enslaved when they were being mercilessly branded, whipped, and otherwise tortured?

"There were many times Desmond Tutu recalled when the apartheid rulers were strutting like cocks of the walk and his own people were being treated like rubbish, that he wanted to whisper in God's ear, "God, we know that you are in charge. Why don't you make it slightly more obvious?" ~ The Economist Magazine, January 1, 2022

Consider this barbaric incident: Describing it as a "pleasing duty," Julian Carr (a white Southerner) said this at the dedication ceremony of 'Silent Sam,' a monument in honour of Confederate Soldiers that was erected in 1913 on the campus of the University North Carolina, Chapel Hill: "I horse-whipped a negro wench until her skirt hung in shreds because she had publicly insulted and maligned a Southern lady."

Where was God when this and other ineffable cruelty was being inflicted on Black People?

Where was God when this was happening?

Where was God on August 28, 1955, when 14-year-old Emmett Till was abducted and tortured to death by white men in Money, Mississippi, USA?

Where was God when Thomas Thistlewood and the other sadistic enslavers were raping, whipping, and terrorising the Black people they 'owned'?

What is remarkable is that while the white enslavers were visiting ineffable cruelty upon Black People, they were blissfully worshiping their God. I adduce the following pieces of evidence:

- About her mistress, Harriet Ann Jacobs wrote in her book **'Incidents in the Life of a Slave Girl'** that, "She was a member of the church, but partaking of the Lord's supper did not put her in a Christian frame of mind." This behaviour gives much credence to C.S. Lewis' observation that "... a cold self-righteous prig who goes regularly to church may be far nearer to hell than a prostitute."

- Frederick Douglass noted in his autobiography – **'Narrative of the life of Frederick Douglass, An American Slave'** - that, "I assert most unhesitatingly, that the religion of the south (Southern USA) is a mere covering for the most horrid crimes – a justifier of the most appalling barbarity, a sanctifier of the most hateful frauds, and a dark shelter under which the darkest, foulest, grossest and most infernal deeds of slaveholders find the strongest protection. Were I to be again reduced to the chains of slavery, next to that enslavement, I should regard being the slave of a religious master as the greatest calamity that could befall me. For of all slaveholders with whom I have ever met, religious slaveholders are the worst. It was my unhappy lot not only to belong to a religious slaveholder but to live in a community of such religionists. I love the pure, peaceable, and impartial Christianity of Christ: I, therefore, hate the corrupt, slaveholding, women-whipping, cradle-plundering, partial and hypocritical Christianity of the land. Indeed, I can see no reason, but the most deceitful one, for calling the religion of this land Christianity. I look upon it as the climax of all misnomers, the boldest of all frauds, and the grossest of all libels. Never was there a clearer case of 'stealing the livery of the court of heaven to serve the devil in.' I am filled with unutterable loathing when I contemplate the religious pomp and show, together with the horrible inconsistencies, which everywhere surround me. We have men-stealers for ministers, women-whippers for missionaries, and cradle-plunderers for church members. The man who wields the blood-clotted cow skin during the week fills the pulpit on Sunday, and claims to be a minister of the meek and lowly Jesus ... The slave auctioneer's bell and the church-going bell chime in with each other, and the bitter cries of the heart-broken slave are drowned in the religious shouts of his pious master. Revivals of religion and revivals in the slave-trade go hand in hand together. The slave prison and the church stand near each other. The clanking of fetters and the rattling of chains in the prison, and the pious psalm and solemn prayer in the church, may be heard at the same time. The dealers in the bodies and souls of men erect their stand in the presence of the pulpit, and they mutually help each other. The dealer gives his blood-stained gold to support the pulpit, and the pulpit, in return, covers his infernal business with the garb of Christianity. Here we have religion and robbery the allies of each other—devils dressed in angels' robes, and hell presenting the semblance of paradise."

- The despicable Thomas Thistlewood, an enslaver, thanked God for sparing his life when 'Congo Sam,' an enslaved African he had viciously beaten, attacked him with a machete. Thistlewood was thanking his God – his white God. On December 27, 1752, Thistlewood recorded the encounter with "Congo Sam" in his diary as follows: "Attempting to take him, he immediately struck at me with a backed bill he had in his hand, and repeated his chops with all vehemence, driving me back into the morass, towards the river 25 or 30 yards from the road, but through the great mercy of God, his blows either fell short of me or were warded off with a pimento stick I had in my hand." Unfortunately, and to my immense disappointment,

Congo Sam was unsuccessful in killing the noxious, despicable son-of-a-bitch, because, in Thistlewood's words, "although he let on my jacket several times yet, as pleased God, I received no harm; the bill being new was not very sharp." By the way, Thomas Thistlewood was buried in the Anglican Churchyard in Savanna-la-Mar on December 1, 1786; by the values of Jamaican colonial society, he was considered worthy of being buried there.

In March 1969, **Ebony Magazine** was almost put out of business. Why? The March 1969 issue published a Black Jesus on the cover. So many in the Black community were upset to the point of threatening to cancel their subscription. They sent Johnson Publishing pictures of what some called the "True (White) Jesus."

It takes a special kind of genius and suite of deliberately devious directed technologies by the colonisers to so effectively brainwash a set of people. And countering this depth of distortion of the cognitive terrain (the psychitecture) of Black People is hard work. Arduous work.

Prominent scholars and the Archbishop of Canterbury, Justin Welby, have called for reconsideration of Jesus' portrayal as a white man.

This is the account of Sybil Hibbert, a Jamaican reporter, about visiting the inner sanctum of the Rev. Claudius Henry – head of the **African Reform Church** - at his compound in Kingston, in 1960: "I beheld the most exquisitely adorned altar in black and gold and at the top, looking down majestically, was a carving in wood of the Black Jesus. On a pedestal nearby was a similar carving of the Virgin Mary. Black scented candles glowed dimly as we tiptoed to other rooms where I saw breathtaking pieces of sculpture reminiscent of Africa and African culture."

Contrast Sybil Hibbert's account with what follows below.

In an article titled **'The Long History of How Jesus Came to Resemble a White European,'** published on July 22, 2020, in 'The Conversation,' Anna Swartwood-House, Assistant Professor of Art History at the University of South Carolina, USA, gives this account of images of Jesus Christ: "There have been 'evolving' images of Jesus Christ from A.D. 1350 to 1600. Some of the best-known depictions of Christ, from Leonardo da Vinci's "Last Supper" to Michelangelo's "Last Judgment" in the Sistine Chapel, occurred during this period. But the all-time most-reproduced image of Jesus is from another period – it is commercial artist Warner Sallman's light-eyed, light-haired "Head of Christ" that he did in 1940. Sallman successfully promoted this picture of Jesus worldwide. Through Sallman's partnerships with two Christian publishing companies, one Protestant and one Catholic, the Head of Christ came to be included on everything from prayer cards to stained glass, faux oil paintings, calendars, hymnals and night lights. Sallman's painting caps a long tradition of white Europeans creating and disseminating pictures of Christ made in their own image. As Europeans colonised increasingly farther-flung lands, they brought a European Jesus with them. Jesuit missionaries established painting schools that taught new converts Christian art in a European model. The historical Jesus likely had the brown eyes and skin of other first-century Jews from Galilee, a region in biblical Israel. However, no one knows exactly what Jesus looked like. There are no known images of Jesus from his lifetime. Pictures of Jesus historically have served many purposes, from symbolically presenting his power to depicting his actual likeness. Representation [and symbolism] matters and viewers need to understand the complicated history of the images of Christ they consume."

On July 11, 2018, John Paul Sunico published an article in The Christian Post titled **'More Christians Now Live in Africa Than in Any Other Part of the World.'** The article reports that Africa had 631 million Christians which accounted for about 45 percent of the continent's population. In the face of these statistics, in a piece titled **'How White Jesus and Black Satan have promoted skin bleaching among some Afrikans'** co-authors Nii Ashaley Asé Ashiley, while noting that, "The chief distinction between the modern-day Christianized white Jesus and black Satan serves as a considerable basis upon which the modern-day Afrikan Christian formulates his/her notion of good and bad, and of right and wrong," were compelled to ask the following potent questions:

- "What does it feel like to the modern-day Afrikan Christian who goes about his/her daily duties knowing s/he shares a common physical appearance with Satan 'The Black' - the chief arch-enemy of the white 'saviour' Jesus the Christ?

- And though the modern-day Afrikan Christian is encouraged within church premises teeming with large-framed pictures of white Jesus that Jesus's love for his 'children' is unconditional, what solution in a sermon is given to reconcile the striking difference in the physical appearance of the modern-day Afrikan Christian and the popular white-washed pictures of the acclaimed 'saviour' named Jesus The Christ?"

With a palpably heavy heart, Dr. Michael Abrahams in an article said: "While attending a funeral at a popular church, I recall looking up at the ceiling and walls and seeing numerous stained-glass paintings of Jesus, his disciples, angels, and other holy figures, and noting that they were all lily white. There is a reason why companies pay millions of dollars on advertising to have images of their products displayed on countless video boards, billboards, and other signs. It is because it works. Seeing images repeatedly does affect our subconscious. Similarly, going to church or Sunday or Sabbath school every week, and seeing images of a white Jesus, helps to further the agenda of reinforcing the concept of white superiority." [Source: The Gleaner, February 17, 2020]

I agree with Dr. Abrahams that this incessant subconscious conditioning is deliberately orchestrated to yoke Black People to be psychologically subservient.

Joel A. Rogers - Jamaican-American author, journalist, and historian (born in Negril, in the parish of

Westmoreland) - certainly didn't 'spare any lead' when he expressed his views on Christianity in his book from **"Superman" to Man**, which he self-published in 1917. Here's an excerpt: When the second main character, the Senator asks: "Then you do not advocate Christianity for the Negro?" The main character Dixon then answers, "The real Christianity, yes. The usual Christianity of the white Gentile with its egotism and self-interest, no." But," objected the senator, strenuously, "Christianity has done a great deal for the Negro. Look what a solace it was to him in slavery."

"Solace! Solace! did you say? To enslave a man, then dope him to make him content! Do you call THAT a solace? Would you call a chloroform burglar, for instance, a solace? No, that's the work of an arch-devil and a cowardly arch-devil at that." The honest fact is that the greatest hindrance to the progress of the Negro is that same dope that was shot into him during slavery. Many Negro sects, perhaps the majority, never stop to think about what they are doing. They have accepted the white man's religion pretty much in the same manner as, if they had remained in Africa, they would have worn his old tin cans, as a charm. As I sometimes watch these people howling and hullaballooing, I cannot but think that any other process, religious or otherwise, would have served just as well as a vehicle for the release of their emotions, and that, as far as Jesus is concerned, any other rose by that name would smell as sweet to them. The same holds true of the poor white mountaineers of Kentucky and Tennessee who are also violently religious and immoral.

The slogan of the Negro devotee is: Take the world but give me Jesus, and the white man strikes an eager bargain with him. The religious manifestations of the Negro, as a group, need to be tempered with hygiene, in the same manner that those of the whites need the spirit of Christ.

"Another fact, there are far too many Negro preachers. Religion is the most fruitful medium for exploiting this already exploited group. As I said, the majority of the sharpers, who among the whites, would go into other fields, go, in this case, to the ministry. In most Northern cities dinky Negro churches are as plentiful as dinky Negro restaurants. Many of these preachers are thorough-going rascals who have discovered a very easy way get money and to have all the women they want. Needless to say, they are a great hindrance to those earnest ones really working for the betterment of their people."

An African-Jamaican priest who goes by the moniker 'Blak Laka Taar' on Twitter, tweeted this: "One of the questions I am asked most frequently is some variation of: 'How do you reconcile being conscious about perennial Black struggles and being a member of an institution that's so intimately tied to the colonial Christianization of Black people?'"

It is well to remember that, in Africa, and elsewhere, "Out of sight of their countrymen back home, who continue to cloak the colonial mission in the language of Christian charity and improvement, the "pilgrims" became rapacious and cruel." [Source: David Denby, The Trouble with (Joseph Conrad's) "Heart of Darkness," The New Yorker, October 29, 2021]

Religion and religious thinking are psychological parasites of the higher cerebral sphere of the human brain. Not only does religion deplete the brain of its capacity for reason, but it also disrupts the application of reason to the understanding of phenomena and thus impairs the ability to devise creative solutions to challenges, substituting instead calls for "Lord Jesus, help us!"

If these are not examples of learned helplessness, then I do not know what is: "If we don't hear from you Lord, what will we do? If we do not hear from you Lord, there is no other way that we can live"; "We fight our battles on our knees in prayer."

"It's God's will ... I just have to pray for rain" ... is what a despondent Pastoralist in Kenya told a journalist interviewing him about a persistent drought that devastated large swathes of grazing land, resulting in the death of most of his cattle from starvation. In Madagascar where a severe drought precipitated a famine, a woman there told the BBC that, "despite my best prayers, there has been no rain."

Kenyan law professor and pan-African intellectual Professor Patrick Loch Otieno 'PLO' Lumumba got it right when he declared that "African problems that require technology will not be solved by theology!" This is also true of Jamaica.

What is more, "It is science that has made the old creeds and the old superstitions impossible for intelligent men to accept. It is science that has made it laughable to suppose the earth is the center of the universe and man the supreme purpose of the creation. It is science that is showing the falsehood of the old dualisms of soul and body, mind and matter, which have their origin in religion. It is science that is beginning to make us understand ourselves, and to enable us, up to a point, to see ourselves from without as curious mechanisms. It is science that has taught us the way to substitute tentative truth for cocksure error." ~ Bertrand Russell

This is apt and finds favour with me: "The emancipation of the mind from superstition is as essential to the progress of civilization as is emancipation from physical slavery." ~ Culbert Olson

This, too, is apposite: "The hope for life after death must be separated forever from the behavior control mentality of reward and punishment. The Church must abandon, therefore, its reliance on guilt as a motivator of behavior." ~ Bishop John Shelby Spong

My fellow African Jamaican, consider this tragic case: In her book, 'Archibald Monteath: Igbo, Jamaican, Moravian,' Maureen Warner-Lewis writes about an enslaved convert who claims to have washed himself of his ancestral roots. Given the name Aniaso in his native land of Ghana, Monteath eventually bought his freedom and became a pillar in the Moravian Church. A letter written by Monteath that appears in the appendix of Warner-Lewis' book reads in part, "What grace, what mercy, that the Lord brought me, a poor African, born a heathen, despised slave, to the light! With sadness, I look across from our land here, to the land of my birth, heathen, dark Africa! Oh, that the light in the Gospel may soon brighten it."

And one Rev. Jesse Lee Peterson delivered this of himself: "Thank God for slavery, because, you know, had not, then the blacks over here would have been stuck in Africa...Everybody and their Mama are trying to get out of Africa and come to America and so God has a way of looking out for folks and He made it possible by way of slavery to get black folks into this country...The ride over was pretty tough but you know it's like riding on a crowded airplane when you're not in First Class. It is a tough ride. But you're happy when you get to your destination...I thank God that he got me here and to show my appreciation to the Blacks who suffered as the result of coming here, and the Arabs and Blacks who sold us to the white man, the white man for going there, getting us, and bringing us here, I want to say, thanks."

I think the quotes above from Monteath and Peterson are compelling evidence of severely altered Black minds and I would not be surprised if scans of their brains would show real damage to their architecture.

With physical enslavement now outlawed, Black People must not voluntarily self-denigrate themselves as seems to be a requirement of Christianity. They must reject the self-denigrating and self-flagellating premise, often repeated by Christians, that they were "born in sin and shapen in iniquity" and therefore in need of "redemption." This narrative is psychological programming like the trope of the 'barbaric negro' invented and propagated by white colonialists and their surrogates to perpetuate intergenerational inferiority in Black People. How different is this from Blacks self-denigrating themselves as 'hoes' (whores), thugs, or gangsters?

I also find it ironic, and deeply sad, that the hymn **'Amazing Grace,'** written in 1772 by English slave trader John Newton, has become such a popular emblematic spiritual among so many Black people. The hymn begins thus: "Amazing grace! How sweet the sound ... that saved a wretch like me!" It continues "I once was lost, but now am found ... was blind but now I see."

I am not a wretch. Never has been. And I do not need to be 'saved.' Except from mental capture!

I had this exchange on Facebook with a childhood friend about the quote: "Born in sin and shapen in iniquity" and the words of the hymn 'Amazing Grace':

Friend: "What really matters are the words, what they mean to and who they connect us to. Black or white or whatever, guess what? we all need the saving grace of Jesus."

Me: "What do we all need to be 'saved' from?"

Friend: "Sin."

Me: "So, we are all sinners?"

Friend: "Yes we are ... we were born as sinners."

Me: "So, a newborn baby is a sinner?"

Friend: "Not by choice, but by nature it is an inherited trait ... every human born after Adam is a sinner .... just like how you have inherited the genes of your parents. Romans 5:12 says "wherefore as by one man sin entered into the world, and death by sin, and so death passed upon all men for that all have sinned."

My friend and other Blacks need to get that what they need to 'saved' and 'born again' from is white cultural, epistemological hegemony, and religiosity. As an entomologist, I understand the importance of metamorphosis. Many Black People need to undergo cognitive metamorphosis (Cognito-metamorphosis) of their cognitive architecture to grow or design out jejune thinking.

Dr. Frances Luella Cress Welsing, Afrocentric psychiatrist, with her acute understanding of the effect that conditioning has on the mind, averred, about Black People: "We're the only people on this entire planet who have been taught to sing and praise our demeanment."

Like Marcus Garvey, Dr. Cress Welsing discerned that Black People were suffering from mental illness induced by colonisation.

"To control a people, you must first control how they think about themselves and their history and culture. Once they have been made ashamed of themselves and culture you no longer need chains to hold them" ~ Dr. John Henrik Clarke

If you can condition and train people to demean and degrade themselves, and even kill each other, then you can oppress them forever. Mental poisoning is real. So, too, is conditioning.

"Classical conditioning (also known as Pavlovian or respondent conditioning) is learning through association and was discovered by Pavlov, a Russian physiologist. In simple terms, two stimuli are linked together to produce a new learned response in a person or animal. The most famous example of classical conditioning was Pavlov's experiment with dogs, which salivated in response to a bell tone. Pavlov showed that when a bell was sounded each time the dog was fed, the dog learned to associate the sound with the presentation of the food. John Watson proposed that the process of classical conditioning (based on Pavlov's observations) was able to explain all aspects of human psychology. Everything from speech to emotional responses was simply patterns of stimulus and response. Watson famously said: "Give me a dozen healthy infants, well-formed, and my own specified world to bring them up in and I'll guarantee to take anyone at random and train him to become any type of specialist I might select - doctor, lawyer, artist, merchant-chief and, yes, even beggar-man and thief, regardless of his talents, penchants, tendencies, abilities, vocations and the race of his ancestors." [Source: Dr. Saul McLeod, Simple Psychology, updated 2021]

Religion and religious thinking act kind of analogous to how malware ('viruses') take over the operating system of computers and makes them do their bidding!

Fortunately, the antidotes to which these psychological parasites – religion and religious thinking - are remarkably susceptible are critical thinking (the objective analysis and evaluation of an issue to form a judgement) and common-sense (practical judgement or a basic ability to perceive, understand, and judge things for what they are).

This quotation is worth investment of one's time to consider: "One need not be well researched in history, one need not be a rebel, one need not even to be exposed to other religions; on the contrary, the only mental exercise one needs to employ for Christianity or any other major world religions' 'truths' and versions of history to be brutally shattered is common sense. Any doctrine, that asks you to suspend logic and critical analysis in the way of 'faith' should automatically be met with well-deserved skepticism and cynicism, and should under no circumstances be taken as facts, or documented, verifiable events in history. And likewise, it can be said with somewhat of a degree of certainty, although a generalization, that anyone who has an unbiased cognizance of history tends typically to not be a person who would consider themselves 'religious.'" [Source: Sean Coleman, 'Black People Can't Unite as One While Following Religions from the Oppressor,' Tru Dreadz, June 21, 2019]

As a Black man, I find the self-denigration and cultural erasure that Christianity imposes on my race offensive in the extreme.

The primary objective of missionaries in the colonies was 'civilisation' of the 'African savages.' To be Christian was to be 'civilised.' White colonizers used the cloak of religion and violence as cover to prey on Black People, and other non-white people.

It was the Portuguese who first saw enslaving Africans as missionary work – a mission from God to help civilize and Christianise the African 'savages' and save their 'wretched souls'. Jason Reynold and Ibram X. Kendi posited in their book **'Stamped: Racism, Antiracism, and You'** that Gomes Eanes de Zurara was the world's first racist. They note that Zurara's book **'The Chronicle of the Discovery and Conquest of Guinea'**, written in 1450, was the first defence of African slave trading by Europeans. "Zurara's book became an anthem. A song sung across Europe as the primary source of knowledge on unknown Africa and African peoples for the original slave traders and enslavers in Spain, Holland, France, and England. Zurara depicted Africans as savage animals that needed taming. This depiction over time would even begin to convince some African people that they were inferior. Zurara's documentation of the racist idea that Africans needed slavery to be fed and taught Jesus, and that it was all ordained by God, began to seep in and stick to the European cultural psyche. And a few hundred years later, this idea would eventually reach America."

This bit of truth from Desmond Tutu supports my position that Christianity has been an unmitigated disaster for Black People: "When the missionaries came to Africa, they had the Bible and we had the land. They said 'Let us pray.' We closed our eyes. When we opened them, we had the Bible and they had the land."

Besides, after stealing the land, wealth, and people the Europeans gave them a book that says "thou shalt not steal." And to seal the deal, also included the instruction to "forgive your enemies 70 times 7!" And guess who, historically, have been the worst enemies of Black People?

I find this potent braindrop from James Baldwin apt: "If there was power in the name of Jesus, slaves (enslaved persons) would not have been introduced to the Bible."

So, when next you hear the term 'missionary zeal,' it is to be reinterpreted to mean "great enthusiasm" to exploit and denigrate Black People in the most extreme fashion imaginable!

In addition, Martinican poet, politician, and intellectual Aime Cesaire, in **'Discourse on Colonization: A Poetics of Anticolonialism'** argued that the chief tool of colonialism was Christian pedantry, which laid down these two historically dishonest equations: Christianity = Civilization; Paganism = Savagery, and from these "there could not but ensue abominable colonist and racist consequences, whose victims were to be the Indians, the Yellow peoples, and the Negroes. Between colonization and civilization, there is an infinite distance."

During slavery "Africans had to equate all of their inherited traditions with a sinful past (from which they had to 'repent') if they were to convince the missionaries of their authentic conversion to Christ" ~ Jason 'Timbuktu' Diakite

I have to hand it to Jamaica's Rastafarians whose religion, according to Jamaican educator Stanley Redwood, "is a conscious rejection of the hegemonic cultural aspects of white religions."

I will dilate a bit more on Rastafarians below.

Writing in the Jamaica Observer on July 29, 2022, Lloyd B. Smith averred that "it would be remiss of the Jamaican Government of the day not to fully recognise and pay tribute the Rastafarian movement which is indeed an integral part of the nation's indigenous culture. A close-up view of this religion will reveal that it has influenced as well as made its way into the Jamaican psyche, in terms of language, cuisine, music, fashion, politics, and the embracing of Afrocentric ideology."

In addition, Professor Carolyn Cooper notes that "The emergence of the Rastafari movement is another classic example of the continental consciousness of Jamaicans. Rooted in the Pan-African philosophy of Marcus Garvey, Rastafari created God in the image of the Ethiopian Emperor Haile Selassie. The revolutionary vision of Rastafari is also manifested in their mystical language. In the spirit of our African ancestors who created the Jamaican language by adapting English to suit our own tongues, Rastafari has subverted the vocabulary of English to articulate new modes of overstanding. Rastafari livity has spread across the globe. Reggae music is a primary medium through which the message of Rastafari has been transmitted." [Source: Carolyn Cooper, The Sunday Gleaner, August 29, 2021]

And it is the case that Jamaica's Rastas have consistently embraced Africa as the Motherland, and, above and beyond all other Jamaicans, have kept Marcus Garvey's message and legacy alive! For this, they deserve maximum respect for their consciousness and steadfastness. What is remarkable is that the Rastafarians have demonstrated fixity of purpose despite decades of derision from Jamaica's upper classes, including some Blacks.

Alas, Rastafarians have also taken the brunt of preternatural police brutality in Jamaica; they have been routinely harassed, including having their locks cut off, sometimes with knives or broken glass! At that time, Rastas were regarded as enemies of the State.

"It is well known that the history and evolution of Rastafarianism (in Jamaica) has been a turbulent and controversial one. One recalls the infamous Coral Gardens massacre in Montego Bay on Good Friday, April 11, 1963. Following a violent altercation at a gas station, the police and military were ordered by then Prime Minister Sir Alexander Bustamante to detain Rastafarians throughout the country, killing and torturing many in the process while detaining well over 100 of them in subhuman conditions, violating, in the process, many of their constitutional rights." [Source: Lloyd B. Smith, The Jamaica Observer, July 29, 2022].

When he unleashed the police on the Rastafarians, Bustamante is alleged to have issued this order: "Who the jail cannot hold, the morgue will hold!" This is the same Bustamante who declared that "not one drop of negro blood runs through my veins."

More from Lloyd Smith's article: "Perhaps the most seminal and lasting contribution that Rastafarianism has made to Jamaica's culture is its lasting and strong influence on the development of reggae music, which gained global attention thanks to the iconic superstar Bob Marley, who unashamedly and unabashedly espoused and preached the doctrine of Rastafarian to the masses all over the world. He along with the Wailers took the world by storm with their blockbuster award-winning album Rastaman Vibrations. Many of the teachings and practices of Rastafari can have a very positive and productive influence on the Jamaican people. Their mantra of peace and love, especially at a time when this country has become so violent and fractious, needs to be fully embraced. And when it comes to healthy eating and lifestyle as is being promoted by the Ministry of Health and Wellness, "ital" cooking presents a most attractive alternative for a desirable and tasty cuisine."

Today, Rastafari culture, like Jamaica's reggae music, may be found all over the world, practically among all races and cultures. Pan-Africanism and African solidarity are central to Reggae as the lyrics from Bob Marley's song 'Africa Unite' prove:

How good and how pleasant it would be
Before God and man, yeah
To see the unification of all Africans, yeah
As it's been said already
Let it be done, yeah
We are the children of the Rastaman
We are the children of the Iyaman
So, Africa unite
'Cause the children wanna come home, yeah
Africa unite
'Cause we're moving right out of Babylon
And we're grooving to our Father's land
So, Africa unite
Unite for the benefit (Africa unite) of your people!
Unite for it's later (Africa unite) than you think!
Unite for the benefit (Africa unite) of my children!
Unite for it's later (Africa uniting) than you think!
Africa awaits (Africa unite) its creators!

Africa awaiting (Africa uniting) its creator!
Africa, you're my (Africa unite) forefather cornerstone!
Unite for the Africans (Africa uniting) abroad!
Unite for the Africans (Africa unite) a yard!"

Jamaican Rastafarian reggae musicians, through their potent and uncompromising lyrics, were leaders in the struggle against the abominable and obscene system of Apartheid in racist South Africa. Some examples are: 'Fight Apartheid' (1977) by the unapologetically militant Peter Tosh; 'Invasion S.A.' by Robert 'Brigadier Jerry' Russell, and 'Botha the Mosquito' by Neville 'Bunny Wailer' Livingston.

The book **'Rastafari: Roots and Ideology'** by Professor Barry Chevannes of The University of the West Indies chronicles in scholarly fashion the development of the Rastafarian religion that was birthed in Jamaica.

This is how the publisher describes 'Rastafari: Roots and Ideology': "The first comprehensive work on the origins of the Jamaica-based Rastafaris, including interviews with some of the earliest members of the movement. Rastafari is a valuable work with a rich historical and ethnographic approach that seeks to correct several misconceptions in the existing literature— the true origin of dreadlocks, for instance. It will interest religion scholars, historians, scholars of Black studies, and a general audience interested in the movement and how Rastafarians settled in other countries."

In Jamaica, Christianity is one of the legacies of colonialisation, and Christianity has long been a weapon to 'batter-bruise' Black People both physically and psychologically. At the psychological level, it was mainly about instilling compelling self-hate in Black People, as in: "Lord, wash me, and I shall be whiter than snow."

Is it any wonder there is a veritable epidemic of skin-bleaching in Jamaica?

And yet, "Melanin is the black pigment which permits skins to appear other than white (black, brown, red and yellow). Melanin pigment coloration is the norm for the hue-man family." ~ Dr. Frances Cres-Welsing

Professor Carolyn Cooper's column in the Sunday Gleaner of August 8, 2021, was a eulogy to poet Jean 'Binta' Breeze, in which she is quoted as follows: "When I started going to primary school in the sixties, I was the brown-skin girl with long hair and if my pencil dropped someone would pick it up for me." Cooper continued "By the time Breeze got to Rusea's High School in Lucea, she fully understood that the deference of an anonymous Black 'someone' to brown skin was an essential element of the demeaning legacy of colonialism in Jamaica."

On May 30, 2022, on a popular radio talk show in Jamaica, the host asked one of his regular callers, a woman, to describe herself. After mentioning her height, weight, etc., the woman turned to her complexion and declared: "Mi dark-coloured, but mi nuh jet black."

In Jamaica, a space where Black misery is largely ignored and Black beauty dismissed, there is a veritable epidemic of skin-bleaching by Black Jamaicans.

And "Yu black and ugly lakka tar baby" is an epithet light-skinned [i.e., rape-coloured skin] Black children and adults often hurl at melanin-richer Blacks. A 'tar baby' is never a beautiful baby.

And there is also the ubiquitous self-esteem-sapping epithet, "Nothing too black nuh gud."

I posed this question on my Facebook page: So, who or what is a 'tar baby'? It provoked the following responses/comments:

- "Someone that has a very dark complexion. I used to call my little sister tar baby because she is very dark when I was a kid and knew no better. Since we got older, I apologize for ever calling her that."
- "Don't you know the tar baby story that was in one of our reading books?"
- "It is a slur, akin to the N-word in the United States, which was used to perpetuate colorism in Jamaica and defile, belittle and malign black or dark complexioned people. It was a tool or a weapon used to separate a nation of many people. It conditioned children into thinking that black is undesirable, as to be black means you are a tar baby. Not only are you unseemly black but you are ugly and things stick to you. These are the subliminal messages that they sent to children to indoctrinate them and guide their life choices. Cue how Buju Banton (mark Myrie) loves his 'browning' because the tar baby just would not fit into the sequence of his "car, bike, money an ting". The US rappers have shifted the negativity behind the N-word and made it a power icon, so Jay-Z rolls with his N..ga. The Jamaican entertainers still fear the tar baby, so it has not found its way into ballads and pop culture. The tar baby is still undesirable. Jay-Z made up a term to rhyme with n..gga (Jigga) but what would rhyme with tar baby? Come into my arms my tar baby. Mek wi go dung town an par maybe."

In her book, **'Growing Out: Black Hair & Black Pride in the Swinging Sixties'**, journalist and Rastafarian Barbara Blake-Hannah writes this about her father, Evon Blake in these terms: "He was best remembered for having desegregated the pool of the city's leading hotel – the Myrtle Bank – by simply going for a swim there one day and refusing to come out despite the unwritten rule that forbade Black Jamaicans from enjoying the water. "Call the Police, call the Manager, call God" was his only comment when they told him to come out. He says he did it because a white employee of his could swim there and he – the man's employer – couldn't. You would have thought that a father like this would have been the source of inspiration for my Black consciousness. Hardly so. What my father tried to drum into my head – successfully – was the thought that Black people could only be accepted by white ON THE BASIS OF HOW WELL THEY IMITATED AND FITTED IN WITH WHITE CUSTOMS AND MANNERSIMS, HOW WHITE THEY COULD BE. My father encouraged me to straighten my hair and shave my legs. He constantly lamented the 'broadness' of my nose, and in his eyes I was considered quite un-pretty. His preference was always for white female partners, by comparison with whom I certainly fell short. This did not exactly give me confidence in myself or my looks as a Black female. By the time I was a young woman, I saw myself as ugly, thin, and Black with 'bad' hair. Ever hoping to please my father, I did my best to try to be as white as possible."

Marcus Mosiah Garvey valiantly attempted to counter vulgar denigration of Blackness with, "The Black skin is not a badge of shame, but rather a glorious symbol of national greatness." Also, South African anti-apartheid activist and scholar Bantu Stephen Biko ['Steve Biko'] popularized, '**Black is Beautiful**' under the banner of his Black Consciousness Movement launched during the late 1960s.

The song '**Princess Black**' by Jamaican Reggae singer Eddie Fitzroy (Fitzroy Edwards) is a paean to Black women and a lasting and positive part of his legacy.

She's a precious, precious, precious woman
Princess Black
She always, always, always say no
she tougher than a nut
She's a precious, precious, precious woman
Princess Black
She always, always, always say no
she tougher than a nut
She don't like to stay at home, living on dependency
She say she have to strive out dey yah, just like a man you
see
Anything that is progressive, she always inna that
Works and able to fight to keep her system alive

I found this valiant pushback pleasing: "As a member of The Gleaner Company (Media) Limited's board, Ayana Samuels – MIT graduate, Aerospace Engineer, and International Development Consultant - did not think twice about voicing strong views about the newspaper's reference to issues about Jamaica's COVID-19 fight using the word 'Black'. "It had to do with a story headlined 'COVID black market.' It was a headline of three successive Sunday papers and in one of the headlines it was in red. For me, especially in this space, in a post-George Floyd world, to use that term in which nefarious activities are taking place, we are unfortunately exuding a definition of black that is not positive," she explained, referring to the African-American man whose death at the hands of police officers in the United States last year sparked global protests. While a red or blue market denotation would not have the same meaning, the term 'black market' remains offensive, she said. "I am concerned with the black sheep, black market, blacklist, and dark days and the negatives they connote. Unfortunately, when you look in the Oxford English Dictionary at the word 'black', it speaks to the fact that black belongs to a certain race of people, but they also indicate that it means heinous activities, evil, venom – lots of definitions that show that there is systematic racism inbuilt in the definitions," she charged. Seeds of belief must be sown to children, but for a long time she bemoans there is a severe drought. "So often we have been told that we are inferior because of our colour. So, we have the bleaching phenomenon, and I think that what The Gleaner represents, it can play a role in helping us to remove a layer of the narrative that our people have been told for centuries. That is a big part of my deep concerns with the use of the word 'black'," she explained. Samuels believes that there is a collective failure for not instilling in dark-skinned people that the dictionary definitions were carefully crafted to denounce black people. Jamaicans, she said, have demonstrated the capacity to befuddle those who expect the worst. "I am a feminist. I am Jamaican; a proud black woman, a daughter, mother, wife, and a spiritual person. I was raised with the specific philosophy that no one is better than anybody else. Everything taught about us being inferior and that we have reduced mental capacities that we don't even try for things. It is not so, but that is the narrative that has been reinforced and, unfortunately, many believe that," she bemoaned." [Source: The Sunday Gleaner, February 14, 2021]

On the morning of March 17, 2021, I heard this on-air exchange between a popular melanin-rich broadcaster and a popular melanin-rich academician (they were discussing an item in the radio station's just-ended major newscast):

Broadcaster: "So, is it a case of blackmail?"

Academician: [Hypervigilant and 'woke'] "You mean extortion? Your term – blackmail - is not a term that I use."

Broadcaster: [Blissfully oblivious] "It seems to me that it is a clear case of blackmail."

I texted the Academician after the on-air exchange ended and commented that I noted how his attempt to correct the broadcaster's learned and internalized denigration of blackness just flew over his head and was a classic example of dysconsciousness among many Black People. The academician dolefully agreed with me.

The epidemic of learned self-hate and anti-Blackness is a Jamaican verity that has 'skin-bleachers' believing they are ugly and the one thing that will surely save them is light skin (that is, being white-adjacent). This is one of the awful results of centuries of denigration of Blackness. Sadly, many Blacks prefer to lighten their skins rather than enlighten their minds.

Here is a parallel to skin-bleaching: one of the Black characters, Pecola Breedlove, in Toni Morrison's novel **'The Bluest Eye'** was tortured by the preposterous and hard-to-eradicate fallacy and falsity of racial inferiority, and earnestly believed the one thing that would save her from her ugliness was blue eyes like those of white people.

The blurb of Morrison's novel reads: "Pecola Breedlove, a young black girl, prays every day for beauty. Mocked by other children for the dark skin, curly hair, and brown eyes that set her apart, she yearns for the blond hair and blue eyes that she believes will allow her to finally fit it."

In the Foreword, Morrison states "The origin of the novel lay in a conversation I had with a childhood friend. We had just started elementary school. She said she wanted blue eyes. I looked around to picture her with them and was violently repelled by what I imagined she would look like if she had her wish. The sorrow in her voice seemed to call for sympathy, and I faked it for her, but, astonished by the desecration she proposed, I "got bad" at her instead. Until that moment I had seen the pretty, the lovely, the nice, the ugly, and although I had certainly used the word "beautiful," I had never experienced its shock – the force of which was equaled by the knowledge that no one recognized it, not even, or especially, the one who possessed it. It must have been more than the face I was examining: the silence of the street in the early afternoon, the light, the atmosphere of confession. In any case, it was the first time I knew beautiful. Had imagined it for myself. Beauty was not simply something to behold; it was something one could do."

Morrison continued: "The Bluest Eye was my effort to say something about that; to say something about why she had not, or possibly ever would have, the experience of what she possessed and also why she prayed for so radical an alteration. Implicit in her desire was racial self-loathing. And twenty years later, I was still wondering about how one learns that. Who told her? Who made her feel that it was better to be a freak than what she was?" Who had looked at her and found her so wanting, so small a weight on the beauty scale? The novel pecks away at the gaze that condemned her."

Morrison went on: "The reclamation of racial beauty in the sixties stirred these thoughts, made me think about the necessity for the claim. Why, although reviled by others, could this beauty not be taken for granted within the community? Why did it need wide public articulation to exist? These are not clever questions. But in 1962 when I began this story, and in 1965 when it began to be a book, the answers were not as obvious to me as they quickly became and are now. The assertion of racial beauty was not a reaction to the self-mocking, humorous critique of cultural/racial foibles common in all groups, but against the damaging internalization of assumptions of immutable inferiority originating in an outside gaze.

Morrison then said: "I focussed, therefore, on how something as grotesque as the demonization of an entire race could take root inside the most delicate member of society: a child; the most vulnerable: a female. In trying to dramatize the devastation that even casual racial contempt can cause, I chose a unique situation, not a representative one. The extremity of Pecola's case stemmed largely from a crippled and crippling family – unlike the average black family, and unlike the narrator's.

But singular as Pecola's life was, I believed some aspects of her woundability were lodged in all young girls."

Pecola desperately wanted an appearance that soothed and agreed with the concluded solution her restless, tortured, and wounded mind conjured.

As a people, we must not just mourn, but must radically reject and actively re-write this odious and false narrative of Black inferiority, and white superiority.

Barack Obama, 44th President of the USA, in his New York Times bestseller book **'Dreams From My Father: A Story of Race & Inheritance'** (that predated his presidency by nearly a decade) also mentioned how one of his female friends, Ruby, exchanged her "normally warm, dark brown eyes that matched the colour of her skin" with an "opaque shade of blue contact lens" that transformed her into looking "as if someone had glued plastic buttons over her irises."

Obama mentioned that he was bothered by what Ruby felt compelled to do to her eyes. He continued: "When I mentioned the incident (with Ruby) to a Black friend of mine, she bluntly asked: "What are you surprised about? That black people still hate themselves?"

Obama answered: "No," I told her. "It wasn't exactly surprise that I was feeling. Since my first frightening discovery of bleaching cream in Life Magazine, I'd become familiar with the lexicon of colour consciousness within the Black community – good hair, bad hair; thick lips or thin; if you're light, you're all right, if you're black, get back. In college, the politics of black fashion, and the questions of self-esteem that fashion signified, had been a frequent, if delicate, topic of conversation for black students, especially among the women, who would smile bitterly at the sight of the militant brothers who always seemed to be dating light-skinned girls – and tongue-lash any Black man who was foolish enough to make a remark about Black women's hairstyles."

In March 2020, Michael Schulman of The New Yorker asked now-retired actress Pam Grier this question: "Your look onscreen was also ground-breaking. You wore an Afro at the same time that Angela Davis did. What impact do you think that had culturally?"

Grier's response was: "Well, I was poorer, so I had the cheap Afro. Other people had it more refined. They could get it coiffed."

And in a Facebook post on January 29, 2020, that she called a 'revelation,' which generated numerous comments, prominent Jamaican journalist Janet Silvera 'revealed' that "Miss Sarah (her mother) sent me to Infant school very late in life because she was afraid the children would tease me because of my picki, picki head."

And I overheard a woman telling her friend that she had an emergency in the form of the urgent need to get to the hairdresser because her "hair was tough," to which the friend replied, "It look tough fi true!"

There is only one logical conclusion to be drawn from seeing Black women wearing false hair. They hate their natural hair. One of my brave male friends posted this on his Facebook page, "Black women's biggest 'hair problem' is that they think their hair is a problem."

Jena McGregor on September 19, 2019, discussed the issue of Black hair in America, in an article in the Washington Post titled **'More States are Trying to Protect Black Employees Who Want to Wear Natural Hairstyles at Work'.** "Several states have taken steps to push employers, schools and the broader culture to move with them, and help dismantle a culture of discrimination experienced by Black women and men who say they continue to face implicit or explicit pressures to conform, unwelcome comments or even outright discrimination."

The Black nose is another object of derision and exaggerated attention. Stacy-Ann Smith, author of the book **'Time Does Not Heal'** disclosed in a radio interview that her grandfather used to affix a clothespin to her nose to give it a "better shape." And of course, the 'reconstruction' of Michael Jackson's face and nose is a case study.

Here's the thing. The history of ideas is far from being neutral. A main project of colonialism and settler colonialism was to produce academic knowledge and methodologies to justify ineffable violence against Black and Indigenous people. And, like the odour from a mature skunk, the residue of those methodologies lingers.

Even in a modern and supposedly "objective" discipline as computer science, racism and anti-Blackness shape the contours of coding because the human beings who create artificial intelligence (AI) recreate racism in digital hardware and software discipline. It was discovered, for example, that facial recognition software failed to see Black People as humans!

Consider this: "Facebook has disabled its 'topic recommendations' after the artificial intelligence-powered feature mislabeled a video of Black men as "primates." Facebook users who watched a video by the Daily Mail dated June 27, 2020, of Black men in altercations with white civilians and police officers, were asked whether they wanted to "keep seeing videos about Primates." After it was brought to Facebook's attention the company apologized. "This was clearly an unacceptable error and we disabled the entire topic recommendation feature as soon as we realized this was happening so we could investigate the cause and prevent this from happening again," Facebook spokesperson Dani Lever said. "As we have said, while we have made improvements to our AI we know it's not perfect and we have more progress to make. We apologize to anyone who may have seen these offensive recommendations. Facebook didn't catch the problem itself but rather a former content design manager at the company got a screenshot from a friend and she posted it to a forum for current and former employees, reports the New York Times. She also posted it on Twitter. This is the latest controversy involving artificial intelligence that has displayed gender or racial bias. In 2015, for example, Google Photos labeled pictures of Black people as "gorillas." Google said it was "genuinely sorry." Then in 2016, Microsoft shut down its chatbot Tay after it started using racial slurs. Last year, Facebook said it was analyzing whether its algorithms that were trained using artificial intelligence were racially biased. Within Facebook there has also been controversy regarding racial issues. A few years ago, CEO Mark Zuckerberg called on employees at the company's Menlo Park, California headquarters to stop scratching out "Black Lives Matter" and writing "All Lives Matter" in a public space in the company." [Source: Daniel Politi, Facebook Apologizes After its AI Mislabels Video of Black Men as "Primates," Slate Magazine, September 4, 2021]

When a Black professor, Nalova Westbrook, was denied tenure in the department of education at Calvin University (founded by the Christian Reformed Church) in Michigan, USA, the department chair noted in a letter that "Professor Westbrook brings variation to the classroom and that sometimes creates dissonance for students who are accustomed to professors of similar backgrounds and ways of being." In other words, the department chair took refuge behind transparent sophistry to say that because Westbrook was Black, her Blackness made the white students uncomfortable.

The 'psychological constitution,' 'cognitive bandwidth' (i.e., the mind, intelligence, and IQ), and physical features of Africans, and people of African descent, have long been prominent subjects of relentless denigrating colonial cultural and pseudo-scientific debates, designs, and racist ideologies [e.g., Joseph Conrad's **'Heart of Darkness'** (1899); Joyce Cary's **'Mister Johnson'** (1939); and Charles Murray's **'The Bell Curve'** (1994)].

In the chapter 'The Negro and Psychopathology,' Frantz Fanon in his searing book **'Black Skin, White Masks,'** presents brief, yet deep psychoanalyses of colonized Black People, and thus proposes the inability of Black People to fit into the norms (social, cultural, racial) established by white society (the colonizer). To wit:

- That "a normal Negro child, having grown up in a normal Negro family, will become abnormal on the slightest contact of the white world." That, in a white society, such an extreme psychological response originates from the unconscious and unnatural training of Black People, from early childhood, to associate "Blackness" with "wrongness".

- That such unconscious mental training of Black children is effected with comic books and cartoons, which are cultural media that instill and affix, in the mind of the white child, the society's cultural representations of Black People as villains. Moreover, when Black children are exposed to such images of villainous Black people, the children will experience a psychopathology (psychological trauma), which mental wound becomes inherent to their individual, behavioral make-up; a part of his and her personality.

- That the early-life suffering of said psychopathology – Black skin associated with villainy – creates a collective nature among the men and women who were reduced to colonized populations." [Source: Wikipedia]

This is the back cover blurb of Fanon's masterpiece: "Few modern voices have had as profound an impact on the black identity and critical race theory as Frantz Fanon, and **'Black Skin, White Masks'** represents some of his most important work. A major influence on civil rights, anti-colonial, and black consciousness movements around the world, Black Skin, White Masks is the unsurpassed study of the Black psychitecture in a white world. Hailed for its scientific analysis and poetic grace when it was first published in 1952, the book remains a vital force today from one of the most important theorists of revolutionary struggle, colonialism, and racial difference in history."

There is also Social Darwinism, which "is an application of the theory of natural selection to social, political, and economic issues. In its simplest form, Social Darwinism follows the mantra of "the strong survive," including human issues. This theory was used to promote the idea that the white European race was superior to others, and therefore, destined to rule."

Professor Clinton Hutton, speaking at an online forum **'Black Boys Education: Currency, Practices and Social Interventions in Jamaica'** that was hosted by Mico University College on March 19, 2021, mentioned that another canard thrown at Blacks by Europeans was that they possessed, "Arbitrary sexual will that fetters their intellect and creativity and is denoted by very large genitalia." This sexual envy of Blacks fuelled fear and hate in whites who think that if given a chance Black men would breed whiteness out of existence! Therefore, it was not surprising that the castration of Black men was a frequent punishment inflicted by whites during enslavement.

The weaponization of thought and the conscription of complicit 'intellectuals' were done in service of a vile racist ideology that sought to enhance the value of whiteness, and the simultaneous devaluing of Blackness to legitimize the capitalist exploitation of Black and indigenous peoples. Indeed, to make Blacks pliable subjects of continued exploitation one evil enslaver bragged of a desire to breed inferiority in Black People down to the 6th generation!

Alas, the desire to instill inter-generational inferiority in Black people has been successful. As recent as July 11, 2022, a Black lawyer who was hosting a morning current affairs television show averred that he was surprised so many Jamaicans were scared of the monkey pox disease, implying that they should be comfortable with monkey references and/or comparisons. He's a sorry specimen of internalised self-hate and self-loathing.

That "Racist lie must end!" This was what UN Secretary-General António Guterres declared on International Day of Remembrance of the Victims of Slavery and the Transatlantic Slave Trade. The United Nations (UN) International Day of Remembrance of the Victims of Slavery and the Transatlantic Slave Trade is observed on March 25 each year. It honors the lives of those who died as a result of slavery or experienced the horrors of the transatlantic slave trade. On March 25, 2021, Mr. Guterres declared, "Although the transatlantic slave trade ended more than two centuries ago, the ideas of white supremacy that underpinned it remains alive. We must end the legacy of this racist lie," Guterres declared.

While recalling the resilience of those who endured the "brutal yoke" of slavery, Guterres condemned the trade as creating and sustaining "A global system of exploitation that existed for more than 400 years." The UN chief underscored the need to address the "pernicious and persistent consequences" of slavery and called for renewed commitments to "a world where all can live in peace with dignity and opportunity." Guterres also acknowledged the "immense contributions" that the enslaved have brought to culture, education, and economies. "We honour the memory of the victims of the transatlantic slave trade by educating about its history and acknowledging its impact on our world today," he said, urging everyone to "tackle racism, injustice, and inequality and build inclusive communities and economies."

UN General Assembly President Volkan Bozkır painted a picture of enslaved people reduced to chattels and stripped of their freedom, dignity, agency, and identity, summing up that "violence replaced autonomy." "Not only do the descendants of the 15 million victims of the transatlantic slave trade have to grapple with the pain and grief of their ancestors, but every day they navigate a world built by them, but not for them," he said. "And as they suffered, working stolen lands and raising the children of their abusers, free men and women benefited from the Industrial Revolution enabled by their slave labour," he added, attesting to the "complicity of those who profited, but did not stand up for the oppressed." [Sources: UN News, March 28, 2021]

This description by Lloyd Garrison on May 1, 1845, of Frederick Douglass upends the vile lie of the 'barbaric Negro': "In labours he has been most abundant; and his success in combatting prejudice, in gaining proselytes, in agitating the public mind, has far surpassed the most sanguine expectations; He has borne himself with gentleness and meekness, yet with true manliness of character. As a public speaker, he excels in pathos, wit, comparison, imitation, strength of reasoning, and fluency of language. There is in him that union of head and heart, which is indispensable to an enlightenment of the heads and a winning of the hearts of others."

Garrison continued: "Let the calumniators of the coloured race despise themselves for their baseness and illiberality of spirit, and henceforth cease to talk of the natural inferiority of those who require nothing but time and opportunity to attain the highest point of human excellence."

Yet, "the colonizers' sense of superiority, their sense of mission as the world's civilizers, depends on turning 'the Other' into a barbarian. (Thus) the invention of the 'barbaric Negro' - and by extension the fabrication of whiteness and all the racial boundary policing that came with it – required immense expenditures of psychic and intellectual energies of the West. An entire generation of 'enlightened' European scholars worked hard to wipe out the cultural and intellectual contributions of Egypt and

Nubia from European history, to whiten the West to maintain the purity of the 'European' race. They also stripped all of Africa of any semblance of 'civilization,' using the printed page to eradicate their history and thus reduce a whole continent and its progeny to little more than beasts of burden or brutish heathens. The result is the fabrication of Europe as a discrete, racially pure entity, solely responsible for modernity, on the one hand, and the fabrication of the Negro on the other." [Source: Cedric Robinson, 'Black Marxism: The Making of the Black Radical Tradition, cited in Aime Cesaire's 'Discourse on Colonialism: A Poetics of Anticolonialism']

The foregoing is yet another example of the weaponization of thought and the conscription of complicit intellectuals in service of a vile racist ideology that is unable to resist the assault of bald facts: "To wit, the invention of arithmetic and geometry by the Egyptians. To wit, the discovery of astronomy by the Assyrians. To wit, the birth of chemistry among the Arabs. To wit, the appearance of rationalism in Islam at a time when Western thought had a furiously pre-logical cast to it [Source: Aime Cesaire, Discourse on Colonialism].

"They want Black people to be who they want them to be, as opposed to who they are" ~ John Singleton.

So devastating has been the mental control of the mind of Africans and people of African descent that they have become both objects and architects of their own scare and denigration. Manifesting their psychic disarray, many try to flee from their reflection in the mirror ... from their racial identity and features through, for example, skin-bleaching.

The renaming of enslaved persons, branding and flattening them into becoming property (mere wealth-producing 'machines'), and other forms of systematic dehumanization were acts of 'identity-stripping' – early forms of identity theft! Erasure of their humanity and dignity – and supplanting them with an alien Eurocentrically constructed imperial 'reality.' Yes, it's the cruel and systematic destruction of an entire culture.

"It is through language, symbols, laws, religion, entertainment, sex, politics, and economics that blackness is defiled and rendered expendable." ~ Dr. Glenville Ashby

"I grew up in a world where a woman who looks like me, with my kind of skin (Black) and my kind of hair (kinky), was never considered to be beautiful. And I think that it is time that stops today. I want children to look at me and see my face, and I want them to see their faces reflected in mine." ~ Zozibini Tunzi of South Africa, Miss Universe 2019

Frantz Fanon had this experience: Born into a middle-class family in Martinique in 1925, Fanon had been a proud citizen of the French Republic. He grew up reading Montesquieu and Voltaire, and, like many Black men from French colonies, fought with the Allied forces during the Second World War. Wounded in Alsace, he was awarded the Croix de Guerre. It was only in postwar France, where he went, in 1946, to study psychiatry that he discovered he was little more than a "dirty nigger" in the eyes of whites - a "savage" of the kind he had previously assumed lived only in Africa.

In "Black Skin, White Masks," he narrates his experience of a formative trauma common to many anti-colonial leaders and thinkers. In his case, it was a little girl in Lyon exclaiming, "Maman, look, a Negro; I'm scared!" Being "overdetermined from without," as he described it, shocked him out of any complacent assumptions about equality, liberty, and fraternity. "I wanted quite simply to be a man among men," Fanon wrote, but the "white gaze, the only valid one," had "fixed" him, forcing him to become shamefully aware of his Black body, and of debasing white assumptions about his history, defined by "cannibalism, backwardness, fetishism, racial stigmas, slave traders." [Source: Pankaj Mishra, Frantz Fanon's Enduring Legacy, The Atlantic Magazine, November 29, 2021]

In his Gleaner newspaper column of January 13, 2020, Dr. Garth Rattray shared this experience: "I spoke at a function several years ago. As I exited the building, an elderly lady stopped me. She introduced me to two of her sons, grasped both my hands firmly, smiled, looked me straight in the eyes, and said in a solemn voice "Although yuh black and ugly, continue to hold up yuh head ...what she meant was this: although the colour of your skin is a handicap, continue doing well and being proud of who and what you are. In her early 20th-century world, there was no descriptive term for simply being Black; it was always Black ... and ugly. The two were inseparable. To be 'Black' (dark-skinned) meant that you were thought of as being 'ugly.' And, sadly, eventually, many 'Black' people saw themselves as ugly because of how they were treated by the privileged in society."

Concerning the inequities in how Black bodies are assigned value, an advertisement for a popular brand of skin bleaching cream that I saw was revelatory. It promised Black users that "one jar will improve your complexion."

Jamaicans of a certain age will remember when the regnant belief in the country was that Black Jamaicans were unsuitable for work as receptionists, bank tellers, or any work, except as gardeners and domestic helpers, that involved interaction with the middle- and upper-class people in that era. An old advertisement for a job at the now-defunct Air Jamaica airline made the rounds on Facebook – it required that applicants be Jamaican citizens and have "good complexion and attractive hair."

The article **'The Fight to Integrate Commercial Banks'** in Jamaica by historian Arnold Bertram, which was published in The Gleaner on December 7, 2017, is a must-read. Here is an excerpt: "The four foreign-owned commercial banks - the Bank of Nova Scotia, established in 1832; Barclays Bank in 1837; the Canadian Imperial Bank of Commerce in 1867; and the Royal Bank of Canada in 1869 - reserved clerical positions for whites and near-whites. Blacks were relegated to menial jobs. In 1949, journalist Evon Blake published a series of articles in his Spotlight Magazine, drawing attention to the absence of black Jamaicans working in the commercial banks, except in menial positions. That same year, Bishop

Percival James Gibson, the headmaster of Kingston College, responding to a request from Barclays Bank for a clerk, asked for indications of interest from the sixth form. All the boys, either white or near-white, raised their hands. Roy McFarlane, an outstanding student who was black, did not raise his, and on being asked why, replied, "You said a bank, sir, and they don't employ black boys like me." Bishop Gibson gave McFarlane a letter of recommendation to the bank and informed the manager that depending on his response, he would hear about the matter further from the pulpit of St George's Church. Roy McFarlane was hired. Once [several decades later] when a black man was to act for a white manager who was going on long leave, the question was raised as to whether the furniture in the house would be changed when the manager returned. In 1977, when the PNP administration, led by Michael Manley, nationalised Barclays Bank to create the National Commercial Bank (NCB), the appointment of Don Banks as general manager was entirely predictable. Over the next decade, Don Banks and his team of professionals - all black - including Rex James, Jeffrey Cobham, Dunbar McFarlane, Theo Golding and Denzil Barnes made NCB Jamaica's premier commercial bank. In the process, the bank rescued the agricultural sector, facilitated the expansion of entrepreneurship in the middle class, and demonstrated the extent to which racist policies had retarded Jamaica's growth and development."

Anti-Blackness remains in Jamaica!

Remarkably, in 2011 reports surfaced in Jamaica that some employers have asked the national training agency - HEART Trust/NTA - for brown or light-skinned trainees to fill vacancies at their companies.

Pervasive anti-Blackness led Dr. Garth Rattray to offer these thoughts: "[It is] baffling that a chemical (melanin) that has the natural advantages of being protective, has somehow given an entire race of people an extreme socio-economic disadvantage. $C_{18}H_{10}N_2O_4$ isn't even skin deep; it is only as deep as the upper layer of skin. $C_{18}H_{10}N_2O_4$ does not confer any moral or attitudinal characteristics. $C_{18}H_{10}N_2O_4$ does not predispose anyone to laziness, nastiness, dishonesty, or violence. Although the hue of the skin is socially inconsequential, it has become a liability in many countries; surprisingly, even in some of those countries in which there is a significant preponderance of people with melanin-producing integument. In many countries, people with a high expression of $C_{18}H_{10}N_2O_4$ are sometimes systemically disenfranchised, impoverished, undereducated, targeted by the police, deprived of equal health and social opportunities, and therefore more likely to end up the victims of various disease and involved in criminal activities. In those countries, they are disproportionally under-represented at the management levels, representational politics and the judicial system. They are also disproportionally over-represented in the unemployment lines and penal institutions. $C_{18}H_{10}N_2O_4$ must be toxic because it can damn people to poverty, lack of amenities, ill health, societal and institutional brutality. I often wonder how such a wonderful and protective chemical can lead to such pain, suffering and death for so many people and for so long." [Source: Dr. Garth Rattray, Can Melanin Be Toxic? The Gleaner, March 1, 2021]

The 'melanin toxicity' query of Dr. Garth Rattray came just a week before the explosive interview Prince Harry and his wife Meghan Markle (who by conventional racial calculus is deemed a Black person – go figure) gave to Oprah Winfrey that was aired on March 7, 2021, in which Meghan dropped the bombshell that, when she was pregnant ('gestating while Black'), there were concerns in Buckingham Palace about how dark the skin of her unborn baby might be. The disclosure reverberated globally, shocking millions of people. Oprah's mouth was agape for several seconds. But I wasn't shocked. Did fate orchestrate the 'planting' of Meghan inside the so-called British 'Royal Family' so that she could expose their veneer of civility?

In a column in the Jamaica Observer on March 2021, the Reverend Dr. Clinton Chisholm weighed in on the saga: "Call the guarded disclosures a collective bombshell if you wish, but there is a deeper bomb that should have been exploded in Britain ages ago by the archbishops and other leaders of the Anglican church to which denomination Her Britannic Majesty belongs. I am talking about the Anglican Church's tacit support of the damnable notion of 'royal blood', and the related view of all who are not members of the royal family being seen and treated as commoners. The royal blood notion is an indictable 'better than', not simply 'other than' or 'different from' idea which readily breeds its kindred negative idea of others being less than or inferior to self. Such sentiments do not simply die; they have to be killed by cogent corrective logic. I know that my little piece here will not reach Harry or Meghan. Yet, they both must have broached a live possibility that their courtship and marriage would trigger negative sentiments generally, and especially within the so-called Firm. A key sentiment would be that their relationship was a veritable double invasion of white/royal privilege — marrying a 'commoner', and a black one at that! I commend Harry, though, for equalling or exceeding the stance of his ancestor King-Emperor Edward VIII, who abdicated the throne for his intended 'commoner' bride, Wallis Simpson, who was divorced from her first husband and in train to divorce her second husband. Harry's decision to marry a black woman and step away from royal/white privilege to protect his family is highly commendable in my view."

For me, Meghan Markle is like the proverbial fish bringing a 'first-person' message from below the surface of the water about what resides down there! Besides, I see the so-called British 'Royal Family' for exactly what it is – a racist institution comprising the heirs, successors, and beneficiaries of colonialization and the horrendous crime of slavery. And it traumatized Meghan (and Harry, one of its own, for marrying her) that they had to literally flee for their lives. Meghan also disclosed in the Oprah

Winfrey interview (watched by more than 15 million people globally) that she contemplated suicide.

Oprah asked Harry if racism was the reason the couple left the UK; he replied: "It was a large part of it."

'Melanin toxicity' can be explained by the psychological disorder called phobogenesis.

In response to the jaw-dropping revelations from the Harry and Meghan interview, Buckingham Palace issued this statement: "The whole family is saddened to learn the full extent of how challenging the last few years have been for Harry and Meghan. The issues raised, particularly that of race, are concerning. While some recollections may vary, they are taken very seriously and will be addressed by the family privately. Harry, Meghan, and Archie will always be much-loved family members."

I think the statement from Buckingham Palace is remarkable – in the same sense that a train wreck is a remarkable thing. It's kind of like when, as a child, you do something and your mother wants to 'fix your business' with a spanking but she is pretending not to be very upset so that she can collar you when you drop your guard.

Piers Morgan has claimed that "several members of the Royal Family" have sent him messages of "gratitude" following his criticism of Meghan Markle. Interesting!

By the way, let me declare here that no one, and I mean no one, can get me to subscribe to the same religion under whose imprimatur my ancestors were subjected to unspeakable trauma by being kidnapped, oppressed, brutalised, terrorised, subjugated, dehumanised, tortured, and murdered!

Exodus 21:20-21 (NIV) states, "Anyone who beats their male or female slave with a rod must be punished if the slave dies as a direct result, but they are not to be punished if the slave recovers after a day or two, since the slave is their property."

Internalising, embracing, and perpetually practising white people's religion is the primary means by which Black People remain enslaved even after the legal abolition of chattel slavery in Jamaica and elsewhere.

About the UK, this is what Yoel Omowale, a Black medical doctor, and author of the essay '**The Nightmare of Blackness in Britain,**' posted on his Facebook page on August 16, 2021: "We abide a nation that used Christian missiology to legitimize their racial prejudice and envy of indigenous people worldwide, giving them religion and taking away their dignity and resources as a divinely mandated exchange. Churches were schools of cultural indoctrination for the enslaved to abandon their own spiritual practice to become more like white people for their salvation." I concur!

Omowale also posits that "Christianity in the Caribbean is thoroughly colonized by either old British imperialism and/or new American neo-colonialism. Either way, unless there is an active or ongoing intentional project of decolonization, most of what is considered righteousness or holiness by Christians from the Caribbean is based on Victorian codes of morality or American Evangelical (Republican) moral priorities." I agree!

From my teens, I realised that religious receptors were not present in my psychitecture. I refuse to volunteer for mental enslavement, which I define as the deliberate capturing by a dominant group, often by cunning, of the cognitivesphere of an oppressed group of people and holding them as de facto inmates in a state of psychological unfreedom that induces bizarre behavioural patterns in the inmates, chief among which is the inability to think for themselves. I will not spend my life living in mental enslavement ... in a psychological cage.

I have thought long and hard about the cognitivesphere of Black People and I have been lured to draw two conclusions about it:

- The miseducation of Black People, especially through religion, has laid waste to the cognitive apparatus of millions of Black People.
- The complete and permanent ditching of white people's religion is a condicio sine qua non (a precondition) for Black Empowerment. I am convinced there can be no authentic, complete, and permanent cognitive liberation of Black People unless this is done!

Frederick Douglass noted in his autobiography – **'Narrative of the Life of Frederick Douglass, An American Slave'** - that, "I assert most unhesitatingly, that the religion of the south (Southern USA) is a mere covering for the most horrid crimes – a justifier of the most appalling barbarity, a sanctifier of the most hateful frauds, and a dark shelter under which the darkest, foulest, grossest and most infernal deeds of slaveholders find the strongest protection. Were I to be again reduced to the chains of slavery, next to that enslavement, I should regard being the slave of a religious master as the greatest calamity that could befall me. Of all slaveholders with whom I have ever met, religious slaveholders are the worst. It was my unhappy lot not only to belong to a religious slaveholder but to live in a community of such religionists."

This question naturally arises in my mind: what is the nature of the Heaven that would accept the horrible and despicable sort of people Douglass mentioned? And others like them?

In his book '**The Future of an Illusion**' (1927) Sigmund Freud wrote, "Religion is comparable to a childhood neurosis. Our knowledge of the historical worth of certain religious doctrines increases our respect for them but does not invalidate our proposal that they should cease to be put forward as the reasons for the precepts of civilization. On the contrary! Those historical residues have helped us to view religious teachings, as it were, as neurotic relics, and we may now argue that the time has probably come, as it does in an analytic treatment, for replacing the effects of repression by the results of the rational operation of the intellect."

This bit of truth is dressed like the emancipation statue ('Redemption Song' by Laura Facey) that adorns the entrance of Emancipation Park in Kingston: "We have not as yet figured out a way to lionise people whose accolades flow directly from their intellectual prowess and pursuits, similar to how we celebrate and extol our athletes and entertainers and even, sometimes, politicians. This is a matter that should be worked on – as a deliberate project of the Government and civil society institutions. This suggestion is not because we believe Jamaica's sportsmen, artists, and entertainers are undeserving of great accolades. That, on the evidence of the genius of many in this group, would be fatuous. Rather, we are for the recognition of all of our especially talented people, appreciating that the output of academic intellect will be crucial if Jamaica is to build a competitive 21st-century economy." [Source: The Gleaner, Editorial, August 9, 2021]

It has been said that scientist Mary Somerville's "uncommon gift for seeing clearly into complexity came coupled with a deep distaste for dogma and the inherent divisiveness of religion, the supreme blinders of lucidity. Above all, Somerville possessed the defining mark of the great scientist and the great human being — the ability to hold one's opinions with firm but unfisted fingers, remaining receptive to novel theories, and be willing to change one's mind in light of new evidence."

Somerville's daughter recounted this about her: "It is not uncommon to see persons who hold in youth opinions in advance of the age in which they live, but who at a certain period seem to crystallise, and lose the faculty of comprehending and accepting new ideas and theories; thus, remaining at last as far behind, as they were once in advance of public opinion. Not so my mother, who was ever ready to hail joyfully any new idea or theory, and to give it honest attention, even if it were at variance with her former convictions. This quality she never lost and it enabled her to sympathise with the younger generation of philosophers, as she had done with their predecessors, her own contemporaries." [Source: brainpickings.org]

This cognitive posture is apposite: "I have always kept an open mind, a flexibility that must go hand in hand with every form of the intelligent search for truth." ~ Malcolm X

In my late teens, a family friend forgot one of his books at the house of one of my sisters. Always one to gravitate to books, I picked it up. It turned out to be the "Autobiography of Malcolm X." I devoured it. It resonated with me on several levels. In particular, I was awed by his militancy and boldness regarding his views on racism and the antidote as he saw it, as well as the searing honesty of his account of his life! I think the unvarnished manner in which I have written my own autobiography ('It All Began With The May Rains: An Introvert's Remarkable Journey) was influenced by my reading of Malcolm X's autobiography.

Childhood is a fantasy-filled life stage. Adulthood is the life stage for mental 'spring cleaning' when we should evict from our mind myths, untruths, and other cognitive detritus and pollutants put there when we were children! Adulthood is the life stage to learn new ways of seeing the world and acting within it. Axing beliefs that feel like old friends or which are just 'part of a tradition,' is often difficult but necessary.

I contend that Marcus Garvey failed to excise his childhood religious inculcation, and the result of not doing so was that, in his project of empowerment of Black People, he missed addressing religion as an important variable, one of the weapons of colonialization, that was, and still is, a formidable retardant to the psychological liberation of Black People!

A friend of mine shared this on social media: "Religion is a formal social institution. Its purpose is to psychologically socialize people into conforming to establishment norms ... even if those norms are racist, classist, and exploitative. We saw that clearly during slavery."

Here is a reflection by Prof. Kei Miller that he shared on Facebook on June 28, 2020, about his childhood religious experiences: "Christian youth culture is its own thing. It's the culture I grew up in. And in every season, there was a new popular song which we would blast from our radios or sing gustily in Praise and Worship sessions. We were young and passionate and earnest to a fault. In one such season, the big song was 'Shout to the Lord' which is how I was introduced to Hillsong Worship. For a time almost any song coming out of the Hillsong catalogue would travel from Australia and become a big thing in Christian Youth groups all over the world. For a time, that's all I imagined Australia as being – a place where there were kangaroos, and this big Hillsong church, and maybe even the kangaroos themselves were singing songs like 'Shout to the Lord'. Last October I was in Australia again, and this time had more meaningful conversations with writers who were from indigenous communities. Their stories were painful. Oftentimes they had been taken away from and forced to grow up separate from their families. And the backdrop of their lives was all those stories you kind of expect to come out of a place so deeply touched by colonialism and apartheid: mass incarceration of dark-skinned people; their deaths in prison; alcoholism in their communities; a history that is never in the past but in the present and every day; land that is still occupied; names that have been erased; languages they attempted to erase; belief systems that were mocked and demonised and on and on. And then that name from my youth came up. Hillsong. And for so many it was an example of how the past is made present – a symbol of colonialism and whiteness and a belief system that tries to colonize all others. It doesn't help that the present Prime Minister is a member of Hillsong Ministries. And even for me, that was hard – the reckoning that it forced in me, that something from my past that had mostly positive connotations – that I now had to rethink it from another perspective, I had to look at it through the eyes of the 'least of these'. I had to confront a racism I had simply never recognised but had participated in it all the same. I listened back to some of those songs and the ones that declared 'dominion over the earth' made me wince, the terrible implications of that idea suddenly hitting me, how it made musical justification of the very philosophy that made some of my new friends grow up without their families. I get it. I get the denials. I get the head in the sand reflex. I get the defensiveness. Reckoning with the past is difficult. Reckoning with the things we didn't fully understand, didn't know enough of, and things that we experienced positively – yeah. It can be painful."

Prof. Miller's 'backward glance' on his childhood underscores the necessity and usefulness of interrogating this life stage through an adult lens.

As an adult, I've interrogated some aspects of my childhood and found them to be wanting, so I jettisoned them from my cognitivesphere. I was exposed to religion as a child but did not assimilate it – my brain got in the way.

As a parent, I have deliberately engaged in myth-free parenting of my child, who was mainly home-schooled to be a lifelong, critical-thinking autodidact. I had my own curriculum. The formal education system was just an 'add-on.' I'm entreating Black parents to do likewise. (I also recall someone gifting my child a doll that depicted none of her racial features; I promptly got rid of it.)

"Have you the power of reason? Why then not use it? When it performs its proper office, what more do you require? ~ Marcus Aurelius (161-180).

"Education is not the learning of facts, but training the mind to think." ~ Albert Einstein

"A well-organized education should not be one which prepares students for a good remuneration alone. It should be one that can help and guide them towards acquiring clear thinking, a fruitful mind, and an elevated spirit." ~ Haile Selassie

The human brain – the organ responsible for all patterns of logic, thought, speech, action, and emotional response – is an organ of the nervous system that evolved over thousands of years. Its purpose has been to decode and solve problems. So, instead of wasting time futilely praying (to the white God of colonisers), Black must use their damn brains to solve problems!

Blacks must routinely embrace the concept of "active thinking," and in particular critical thinking, as a concrete and discrete activity; something that is isolatable, can be given priority, deliberately developed, and even cherished as a valuable pursuit for its own sake. And Blacks must stop outsourcing their thinking.

I have often wondered why it was necessary for there to be a 'King James Version' (KJV) of the Bible. I got an answer in an article by William Saletan titled **'There Is No Such Thing as the Bible - The Messy Scripture on Display at the Museum of the Bible'** which was published in Slate Magazine on November 21, 2017. The article stated that "'the'" Bible as a single, clear, definitive text is a myth. There is no such thing as the Bible," David Trobisch, director of collections at the Museum of the Bible (which opened in Washington, Dc, USA, on November 17, 2017, said matter-of-factly. When Trobisch says there's no such thing as "the" Bible, he's alluding in part to the seven versions displayed along a wall on the museum's fourth floor: Hebrew, Samaritan, Catholic, Protestant, Eastern Orthodox, Oriental Orthodox, and Assyrian. Each has its own selection of texts, a sign on the wall observes, "yet each one is a Bible." In display cases, you can read about the Gospel of Thomas, the Gospel of Philip, and other texts that haven't made the cut. But don't count them out. Such "Apocrypha," another note explains, have been appended to various Bibles, on and off, for centuries."

Saletan continued: "The Museum of the Bible [is] a real museum, exploring the messy history and shifting contents of the Judeo-Christian canon. The more closely you look at the history of Scripture, the more you see how fluid it is. In the New Testament, the gradual canonization of text is obvious. "In time, writings widely associated with the apostles' teaching came to be regarded as scripture," says one display. But you also learn how Jews layered texts over the Torah, adding narrative speculations and "expanding the Scriptures" through the Middle Ages. Interpretation is just one avenue of expansion. Archaeology is another. The Dead Sea Scrolls were unearthed only decades ago, and "discoveries are still being made," say one exhibit."

This was a most remarkable part of Saletan's article: "The most striking concession is the museum's account of the debate over slavery. Scripture was crucial to the movements for abolition and civil rights. But the collection also shows how verses such as Ephesians 6:5 ("Servants, be obedient to them that are your masters ... as unto Christ") and Genesis 9:25 ("a servant of servants shall he be unto his brethren") were deployed to rationalize human bondage. One case displays an 1808 book titled **'The Negro Bible: Parts of the Holy Bible, Selected for the Use of the Negro Slaves.'** A note explains that the volume features passages about obedience but "omits all entries that express themes of freedom," including the story of the Exodus."

"The slave Bible is an edition of the Bible specifically made for educating slaves. Its full title was: Select Parts of the Holy Bible for the use of the Negro Slaves in the British West-India Islands. It was produced in England in 1807 for use in the British West Indies. Such bibles had all "references to freedom and escape from slavery" excised, while passages encouraging obedience and submission were emphasized. It was originally published in London on behalf of the Society for the Conversion of Negro Slaves, an organization dedicated to improving the lives of enslaved Africans toiling in Britain's lucrative Caribbean colonies. The clarion call for human freedom is found in many forms and in various stories throughout the Bible, but all of these ideals were stripped from and carved out of the Slave Bible. The Slave Bible, also called The Negro Bible, is one of the most powerful examples ever witnessed of manipulation using a controlled narrative. The fact that the Christian faith, a religion one-third of the world relied on to bring comfort, spiritual rest, peace, and salvation was the narrative being controlled makes the Slave Bible the ultimate propaganda tool and the greatest lie ever told. [Sources: Wikipedia; rarebooksdigest.com; getconscious.org]

In addition, there is the publication **'How to Make a Negro Christian.'** It is "a reprinting of the religious instruction of the negroes and other works of Dr. Reverend Charles Colcock Jones" (with commentary and analysis by Kamau Makesi-Tehuti). Here is a quote from it: "[What will be the benefit of giving enslaved Afrikans Christianity?] "It is a matter of astonishment, that there should be any objection at all; for the duty of giving religious instruction to our Negroes, and the benefits flowing from it, should be obvious to all. The benefits, we conceive to be incalculably great and [one] of them [is] there will be greater subordination ... amongst the Negroes (page 52)."

I am compelled to repeat - based on the excerpt above from William Saletan's article and the references from Wikipedia and the other mentioned sources (juxtaposed with other information I have read and processed) - that no one, and I mean no one, can get me to subscribe to the same religion under whose imprimatur my ancestors were subjected to unspeakable trauma by being kidnapped from their homeland by white people, transported under the most horrible conditions across the Atlantic ocean (more than 36,000 trips) and thereafter oppressed, brutalised, terrorized, subjugated, dehumanised, tortured, and murdered on plantations in service to the said white people!

It is no wonder the white enslavers took such harsh measures to prevent our enslaved ancestors from being able to read!

If a supposedly 'holy book' provides instructions on how to treat slaves, how does it qualify to be used as a moral code? How?

Here is another example of how fecklessness was deliberately encouraged by enslavers in enslaved persons of African descent: "The days between Christmas and

New Year's Day are allowed as holidays. The staid, sober, thinking, and industrious ones among our number would employ themselves in making corn brooms, mats, horse collars, and baskets; another class of us would spend the time hunting. But by far the larger part engaged in such sports and merriment as playing ball, wrestling, running foot races, fiddling, dancing, and drinking whisky; and this latter mode of spending the time was by far the most agreeable to the feelings of our masters. A slave (enslaved person) who would work during the holidays was considered by our masters as scarcely deserving them. It was deemed a disgrace not to get drunk at Christmas; and he was regarded as lazy indeed, who had not provided himself with the necessary means during the year, to get whisky enough to last him through Christmas." [Source: 'Narrative of the Life of Frederick Douglass, An American Slave']

Christmas as a 'time of merriment' for victims of social violence continues to be an embedded feature of Jamaica's socio-economic architecture (invisible scaffolding). For example, there is this thing called 'Christmas Work' in which, two weeks before the day, there is a flurry of 'make work' activities – overgrown verges of roadsides are bushed and curbside walls painted, and clogged drains are cleaned by an army of persons unemployed, under-employed, or involved in 'hand-to-mouth' existence throughout the year.

The purpose of the 'Christmas work' is to give these marginalized persons a little pittance for temporary merriment, after which they return to their precarious existence, and the cycle continues. Of course, if the people had steady employment all year round and the local authorities routinely and effectively performed their functions, there would be no need for a flurry of 'Christmas Work.'

******

Teaching Garveyism
================####================

Other countries make sure their children learn about their heroes and philosophers. Not so in Jamaica. Instead, we teach our students about the exploits of European villains (e.g., Christopher Columbus, Napoleon Bonaparte) and revere the so-called 'classics' of English literature that thrum with racist stereotypes. So, at graduation ceremonies and other formal occasions, children and adults deem it appropriate and reflect being 'educated', to preface or festoon their remarks with quotes from Shakespeare or other dead white men while foregoing the profound wisdom and insights from, for example, our own Marcus Mosiah Garvey.

Dr. Lisa Tomlinson, lecturer in literary and cultural studies at The University of the West Indies, argued that while Garvey is recognised as a national hero in Jamaica, his pan-Africanist antecedents have not gotten the attention they deserve. Dr. Tomlinson said bluntly in a Gleaner interview that Jamaica has done a poor job of highlighting the teachings of Garvey in schools. In her opinion, locals are not sufficiently seized of their Afrocentric roots. "We are very divorced from that," Tomlinson said. "We have no problems using terms like Indo-Jamaicans or Chinese-Jamaicans, but African-Jamaican raises an eyebrow." [Source: The Gleaner, April 14, 2022]

Someone on Twitter tweeted this profundity: "You know what a weird contrast was? Being in high school doing Caribbean History, Caribbean Studies, and Sociology and learning about colonialism, but having to conform to school rules which reinforce colonial values." Another person tweeted, "Schools in Jamaica will see the students' hairstyle or attire but can never see their depression or abuse!"

The message fed to generations of Black children in our schools is hegemonic Eurocentricity and its implicit superiority.

"Even though Jamaica, Barbados, and Trinidad & Tobago, call themselves "free" from British colonialism we have all maintained a philosophy and method of education which is contrary to our so-called 'independence project,' be it as a Republic or a member of the Commonwealth. The old British philosophy of education, as I have discovered it, and which the English-speaking Caribbean unfortunately still uses in its educational system, is that education is actually not for all, as Michael Manley intended it to be in Jamaica. A thorough education remains available only for a portion within the larger society." [Source: Martin J. Schade, 'Know Thyself! The Imperative for Tertiary Education and Beyond,' 2008]

Sadly, most of the people teaching and leading Jamaican schools have absorbed and learned to identify with the sources of oppression, not the resistance to them. Yes, it is truly sad that the malware of colonialism remains embedded in their cognitive operating system.

The fetish for colonialization in our education system must go! And replaced with a decolonized curriculum.

This needs to be fixed: "Although gaining independence from British colonialism in 1962, the country (Jamaica) still struggles with the impact of its colonial past. Such impact is seen in an education system in which the colonizer aimed to create schools to fit people into their world, creating an estrangement from their culture and heritage, and reinforcing European traditions." [Altbach, P. G., & Kelly, G. P. (1992). Education and colonialism (2nd ed.), Piscataway, NJ: Transaction Publishers, cited by Hope Mayne & Raymond Dixon, **The Epistemological Dilemma: Student Teachers Shared Experiences of Jamaica's National Standards Curriculum (NSC),'** Journal of Curriculum and Teaching, Vol 9, No 4, 2020]

Here's the unvarnished truth: "Britain had introduced slavery into, and colonised, 20 Caribbean countries for three centuries. Many Caribbean citizens thus grew up on a staple diet of British education and culture. They embraced the Mother Country and were told that they were members of the Commonwealth, entitled to carry British passports. They thus wore their Sunday best, sang 'God Save the King' and 'Rule Britannia', and unfurled the Union flag every Empire Day on May 24. They read Shakespeare, Dickens, Kipling, and Wordsworth; their history was about how Churchill had vanquished Hitler; their geography about British seas and shires; and their economics about Bristol iron and Sheffield steel. West Indians also played cricket, football, rugby, tennis, and bridge; they attended churches with British priests; and they admired English gentlemen in bowler hats and umbrellas. Many Caribbean citizens, however, never made the connection between the widespread destitution and poverty on their islands and British slavery and colonialism. Indeed, many adopted deferential and subservient attitudes to white people. Many Anglophile Caribbean citizens thus wholeheartedly imbibed British culture, despite the widespread professional and social discrimination baked into British colonial rule on their islands. As Waveney Bushell, a Guyanese immigrant noted: "We were indoctrinated into feeling that Britain was the place in the world ... I felt everything English was the best." [Source: Professor Adekeye Adebajo, Director of the University of Johannesburg's Institute for Global African Affairs in South Africa, The Gleaner, April 9, 2021]

We need education consciously designed to counter the entrenched Eurocentric epistemic and cultural hegemony- that the ideas, thoughts, beliefs, and actions of Europeans are inherently superior to people of African descent and their ideas, thoughts, beliefs, and actions.

I agree with Dr. Louis E. A. Moyston that "We need to recalibrate the curriculum - to rid it of its 'null' and 'hidden' qualities - towards an emancipatory project. Dr. Joseph Robert Love called for education in Jamaica to be grounded in the "Black man's point of view," a call to displace the colonial philosophy of education."

What Dr. Love has articulated is of such fundamental importance that it cannot be overstated. We must 'indigenise' the curriculum!

One of the greatest failures of Jamaica's education system is that it hasn't exorcised colonialism as its default scaffolding philosophy nor has it deepened the consciousness of the Jamaican people and our confidence in ourselves and not merely to confirm other people's distortions, lies, and myths about us and 'subject identities' imposed on us.

Through systematic efforts, colonizers infiltrated the minds of colonized peoples through the creation of 'subject identities' the acceptance of which by colonized peoples represented a significant triumph for the colonizers – the subjugation of their minds.

Being the intuitive genius that he was, Marcus Garvey perceived the cunningness of the colonizer and the import of this mental conquest. Citing Hill 1973, Lewis, 1988, noted that "In 1937, Garvey, in a speech at the regional conference of the UNIA in Nova Scotia, Canada, dubbed this process mental slavery. And in a brilliant sentence, which Bob Marley later put to music, he said, "We are going to emancipate ourselves from mental slavery because whilst others might free the body, none but ourselves can free the mind. Mind is your only ruler, sovereign. The man who is not able to develop and use his mind is bound to be the slave of the other man who uses his mind."

How we think is life-changing — it affects our ability to make informed choices and solve life problems.

On the subject of mindset, another one of Jamaica's social engineers, Michael Manley, said, concerning his push for a fundamental change in Jamaican society: "I have deliberately chosen to consider the question of the psychological elements first because of the conviction that all human achievement flows from states of mind without which technical elements in human performance cannot develop. For Jamaica, the two critical elements are to be found in the areas of confidence and attitude. Because colonialism undermined confidence, the great need now is to develop a mood of national confidence in which the people at large assume that they have both the duty and the capacity for great achievement." [Source: The Politics of Change: A Jamaican Testament].

"A man cannot directly choose his circumstances, but he can choose his thoughts, and so indirectly, yet surely, shape his circumstances. Mind is the Master power that molds and makes. And Man is Mind, and evermore he takes the tool of Thought, and, shaping what he wills, Brings forth a thousand joys, a thousand ills, He thinks in secret, and it comes to pass: Environment is but his looking glass." [Source: 'As a Man Thinketh', James Allen]

Jamaica's education system had not mainstreamed and carried on in a deliberately systematic way Marcus Garvey's project of centering racial identity, pride, and a settled racial outlook, and thereby abolish the cultural and identify formulation colonialisation imposed on Black People, which continue to stalk and menace too many of our people.

On June 1, 2021, I attended a conference hosted by the education faculty of a leading local university. One of the sessions was a panel discussion by masters and doctoral students reflecting on their lived experiences as students of Jamaica's education system. 'The power of the belt' was the reflection of one of the students who said being beaten at school was "still etched in my mind."

During the 'question and answer' segment, I asked the students whether, on reflection, as they were asked to do in the assignment, they had now become more aware of the ongoingness of colonialism in the Jamaican education system. One student acknowledged that the education system was "built on a colonial foundation" but he found that all things considered, the "Judeo-Christian values and other positives aspects of colonialism outweighed the bad aspects."

I found this response shocking and took it as an indication of how much work still needed to be done at the level of the cognitivesphere of our people, by our education system and thought leaders. Our education system must stop producing 'parrots' and mimics conditioned to be simulacrums of our colonisers.

Professor Kei Miller scored a bullseye with this brain drop: "We have become a mouthpiece for the very history that hated everything about us." The blunt truth is many of us have .... many willingly ... and many unwittingly .... become what Professor Kei Miller says we have become.

One of my critiques of our education system is that it has been an abject, unmitigated failure in that it has not deepened the consciousness of our people and our confidence in ourselves, rather than merely confirming other people's racism-informed formulated myths about us. And neither has our education system mainstreamed in a deliberately systematic way Marcus Garvey's project of centering racial identity, pride, and a settled racial outlook.

Consider this: "For the 468 years of slavery and post-slavery colonialism, the schooling and educating of our people, informally and formally, were aimed at framing an identity and an agency to conform to a belief system rooted in white superiority and black inferiority. Put another way, for 468 years schooling and education in Jamaica were not centrally rooted in the three 'Rs', but on the shaping of Black identity as an agency in the service of whiteness. They were rooted in a philosophy, a curriculum, and pedagogy of Black self-denial: That sense of value and agency of worth realisable only to the extent that black people became masters of the imagery, psychology, and notion of blackness designed by whiteness." (Clinton Hutton, Jamaica Observer, Sunday, June 6, 2021)

Over the years, there have been calls and lamentations about the need for the teaching of Garveyism in our school curriculum. We teach about our national heroes, so I don't see what the fuss is about. Teachers simply need to just do it. But the real problem is that the curriculum of Teacher training institutions is not designed to produce teachers as change agents in the mold that Paulo Freire, bell hooks, or James Baldwin advocate.

But I was pleased, though, to read the enthusiastic account of public relations consultant and writer Lance Neita about his attendance at a St. Ann Schools Elocution Competition held at the St. Ann Parish Library in St Ann's Bay: "The schools had been given a Garvey quotation on which to build their five-minute speech. "A people without knowledge of their history, origin, and culture, are like a tree without roots."

Here is what 11-year-old Bianca Rose of Discovery Bay Primary School had to say: "Just as important as the roots are to the tree, so is the knowledge of our history, culture, and origin to us. We are sustained, supported, and exist out of the knowledge of our ancestry.

"A Yoruba proverb reads, 'If we stand tall, it's because we stand on the backs of those who came before us.'

"Therefore," asked little Bianca as she stared her audience in the eye, "how can we, children of African descent, stand tall with so little knowledge of our past?

"The knowledge of our ancestry," she went on to say, "is what can bring us wealth, health, prosperity, peace, and stability."

Hmmm, I thought, that sounded so much like Garvey's clarion call to his Negro race to stand up and be counted as among the world's best.

The audience was all smiling. Were Garvey's words coming to pass? But hold the applause. There was more to come, as Drew-Gayle Fletcher of Steer Town Primary and Junior High had her own light to shed on the subject.

"Let us delve into our own history and strive to understand where we came from. Let us embrace every aspect of our culture so that the message of our ancestors will forever occupy a space in our hearts and our minds."

My goodness, these young visionaries of the 21st century, born some 60 years after Garvey's death, were telling us that they recognised Garvey as one of their ancestors, a man whose inspirational quotations have helped to give them a positive outlook on life.

It took the eventual winner, Ajanae Boswell, from Columbus Prep (the irony), to seal the issue for us when she told us why Garvey is still relevant today; why this generation and others to come should continue to value his teachings; and why Garvey's history and philosophy need to be taught in schools.

"Marcus," she said, "does not want his African brothers and sisters to forget their roots. He envisioned the rise of his African brothers and sisters as world beaters, not only in athletics and music, but also as philosophers, scientists, writers, and innovators."

She closed with Garvey's original words: "So why should the Black man not be aware of his roots? This is Garvey's message to our generation. Without our roots, we may become squatters because we don't know we have royal blood running through our veins. Don't allow yourselves to be trampled under the feet of your competitors. Stand firm."

I left the hall satisfied. I got a fresh perspective of what Marcus Garvey means to the younger generation." [Source: The Daily Observer, May 14, 2016]

In my case, I am pleased to say I have incorporated Garveyism in my andragogy. You see, I teach topics in innovation and entrepreneurship from time to time to students pursuing master's and doctoral degrees, and I always start with the question: "What lessons can nascent innovators and entrepreneurs draw from Marcus Garvey? On these occasions, I find that a few of the students are familiar with Garvey's life and work while others, at this advanced level of education, are only aware of his name. The latter situation is a further indictment of the Jamaican education system.

Anyway, in my discussion with the students, I seek to get them to 'connect dots' between the mindset nascent innovators need to have and the corresponding philosophical or tangible aspects of Garvey's life. For example, Garvey said, "without confidence one is twice defeated in the race of life." Nascent innovators and entrepreneurs need to be doggedly confident to reap success in their endeavours.

In addition, I draw the students' attention to the fact that nascent innovators and entrepreneurs often need financing for their endeavours. I then link this point to the fact that Garvey also used 'crowd-sourced financing' well before it was in vogue, by selling shares in the Black Star Line shipping company to fund its startup and operating expenses.

I also draw my students' attention to the fact that nascent innovators and entrepreneurs must also be excellent communicators capable of persuading actors of various kinds to support their activities, and in this regard, they can draw lessons from Garvey who was a skilled orator.

And then there's the matter of courage; Garvey was a profile in courage. He also demonstrated grit, determination, and anti-fragility in the face of tremendous challenges, hostility, and opposition – all attributes nascent innovators and entrepreneurs need to possess to be successful.

I am immensely pleased to state here that Kamau Mahakoe has produced a set of three workbooks on the life, legacy, and impact of Marcus Garvey. Mahakoe is the principal and co-founder of the Kemet-Maasai Academy, a primary-level educational institution located in Portmore, Jamaica. She has been an educator for more than two decades and is the 2014 recipient of the UNIA (Jamaica Chapter) Marcus Garvey Centennial Award for contribution to the field of education.

Of course, Garveyism may be taught through other media such as film. And in this regard, I am delighted that Jamaica-born filmmaker Roy T. Anderson has made a Docufilm on Garvey - **'African Redemption: The Life and Legacy of Marcus Garvey.'**

"I appreciated Garvey before, but I have a deeper appreciation now of all that this man was able to achieve," Roy Anderson told The Sunday Gleaner. "Garvey affects and influences from the little boy in the streets to the top leaders in Africa. He was a catalyst for the African leaders who led their countries to independence." He noted that Garvey's signature "up you mighty race" was a clarion call to the black man to reclaim his best self and not be left out of mainstream society. One hour and 25 minutes long, African Redemption: The Life and Legacy of Marcus Garvey is both riveting and redemptive. It accords Garvey all the honour of which he is truly deserving. **"Who would have thought that a simple country boy, born 50 years after the abolition of slavery, would go on to provide the most comprehensive blueprint for the liberation of his people?** The Black man's messiah was born Malcus Mosiah Garvey; he later changed his name to Marcus," the narrator, Emmy-award-winning actor Keith David (Greenleaf, Mr & Mrs. Smith, Crash) says early in the feature-length documentary film that "chronicles the life and legacy of the world's foremost pan-Africanist, considered by many to be the greatest mass leader of the 20th century". For the non-scholars of Garveyism, 'African Redemption: The Life and Legacy of Marcus Garvey' is a textbook chock-full of information, as Anderson and his team peel away the layers for this exposé. In his powerful director statement about the film, Anderson said, in part: "For all his greatness, Marcus Garvey has often been portrayed as a caricature, and someone marginalised by history. Foremost in our minds was telling a story of this oft-misunderstood man, in a way that was not only objective and balanced, but insightful and engaging. Our film sheds light on the world's foremost pan-Africanist, and look at the extraordinary achievements of a great man considered by many as the greatest mass leader of the 20th century, as expressed to us by noted scholars, public officials, and laypersons. The story unfolds in places like the Caribbean and Central America, Europe, and the North American continent; it also takes place on the African continent where, sadly, Marcus Garvey was not permitted by colonial officials to set foot. Our visual style for the film blends live action with breathtaking still photography, archival images, and illustrations to provide a window into the life of a man rarely seen in contemporary culture. Garvey's omniscient voice and oratory are the spine that holds these story elements together. The docufilm is interspersed with interviews and conversations with those who have been touched by the philosophy of Marcus Garvey, among them reggae artistes Sean Paul and David Hinds, lead singer for Steel Pulse; award-winning American actors Louis Gossett, Jr and Danny Glover; retired United States Congressman Charles Rangel; Leonard Jeffries, past chairman City College of New York; Samia Nkrumah, Professor Carolyn Cooper, and Professor Sir Hilary Beckles, vice-chancellor of The University of the West Indies. Making the film took Anderson to Canada, the UK, Jamaica, Africa, and Costa Rica, where Division 300 in Limón is the most active Universal Negro Improvement Association (UNIA) division in the world. In Africa, Anderson interviewed Samia Nkrumah, daughter of Kwame Nkrumah, who revered Garvey. "It was very emotional for Samia who I interviewed at the mausoleum," Anderson shared. Recalling how this docufilm came in the making, Anderson shared that as far back as 2014, he was contacted by Garvey's son, Dr. Julius Garvey. "He reached out to me after my first film Akwantu [an award-winning docufilm on the Jamaican Maroons], about doing a documentary since it was the 100th anniversary of the Universal Negro Improvement Association. But I was finishing up work on Nanny, and I had to tell him that I couldn't do it at the time. Fortunately, we reconnected, and several conversations led to the framework." [Source: The Sunday Gleaner, October 16, 2021]

Dr. Louis E.A. Moyston has made an important point with which I agree. And it is the need to include other persons who made tremendous contributions to the Black self-improvement project in Jamaica.

Dr. Moyston: "The practice of selecting one man as a representative of Black Nationalism in Jamaica is not a good conception of history. We need to develop the history and curriculum of Black Nationalism in Jamaica, not from any single individual, but a programme rooted in this rich tradition of Black Nationalism from Bogle to Bedward, Dr. Robert Love, and the others. Some of those persons are Dr. T.E. S. Scholes, Sandy Cox, Una Marson, W.A. Domingo, W. A. Roberts, Leonard P. Howell, St William Grant, and A.G.S. 'Father' Coombs" [Source: 'The Forgotten One (s),' Jamaica Observer, August 20, 2020].

I agree with Dr. Moyston. But Garvey is special. The depth, breadth, and durability of the influence of his philosophy make him peerless.

****

Marcus Garvey Technical High School
==================####==================

"Marcus Garvey, himself a truly educated, if not degreed man, was a great advocate of the power of education. Garvey was a great proponent of liberating education. "Education is the medium by which a people are prepared for the creation of their own particular civilisation and the advancement and glory of their race." But he also emphasised the importance of practical and technical education for industry and enterprise. Three of the 26 propositions of Marcus Garvey's People's Political Party were directly concerned with education, and were far-reaching for the time, 1929. Garvey proposed a Jamaican university and polytechnic; a government high school in every parish capital for free secondary education with a night continuation school; and a public library in each parish capital. Garvey said. "The only time you [should] stop learning is when you die." [Source: Martin Henry, The Gleaner, August 23, 2015]

Garvey revered scholarship and emphasized education and knowledge as the foundation of self-awareness and productivity. Most fittingly, therefore, a school – the Marcus Garvey Technical High School – has been named in his honour.

The Marcus Garvey Technical High School is located in St. Ann's Bay, St. Ann, which is about 15 minutes from Ocho Rios. The school (formerly St Ann's Bay Junior Secondary) was established in September 1971, with 14 teachers and 780 students enrolled from grades seven to nine.

The present principal of the Marcus Garvey Technical High School is Mrs. Anniona Hunter Jones.

Unfortunately, the school has faltered and has not lived up to bearing the name of a national hero and world-class philosopher. In fact, in 2011, the school was among four institutions singled out for intervention by the Ministry of Education, Youth, and Information due to persistent underperformance.

Thankfully, the situation is changing for the better and Marcus Garvey Technical High School (MGTHS) is now on a trajectory to become one of Jamaica's top high schools. That's how it will truly honour the mighty intellectual giant whose name it bears.

I am pleased to say I have a 'connection' to the renaissance now underway at MGTHS. Mrs. Anniona Hunter Jones – the current principal, whose tenure began in 2018 – is a former student of mine. She was one of the pioneering students in a new degree programme I played a pivotal leadership role in developing in 1998 as Dean of the Faculty of Science at the College of Agriculture, Science, and Education (CASE), Jamaica's premier multi-disciplinary college. Her academic aptitude and potential and leadership abilities were obvious from day one.

Mrs. Hunter-Jones and I spoke when she was appointed principal of MGTHS and I told her that taking up the leadership of a 'challenged school' was a massive opportunity to make a difference! She invited me to make a presentation to her academic staff members. I pointed out to the staff that the students were simply products of their environment and circumstances, and I entreated them to make the students believe in themselves, as the foundation for improved behaviour and academic performance.

I also advised the staff that they should, and also encourage the students to do so, embrace and internalize reverence for scholarship as Marcus Garvey did. I also reminded the principal and staff that Marcus Garvey was a first-rate orator, and I challenged them to make their school the top school in Jamaica in debates! They accepted my challenge and I left feeling confident that a new day had dawned at MGTHS!

In a Jamaica Information Service (JIS) feature written by Garwin Davis on July 13, 2020, Mrs. Hunter Jones dilated on her vision for leading the transformation of the school. I now share it hereunder:

"Principal at the Marcus Garvey Technical High School, Anniona Jones, is leading the transformation of the St. Ann's Bay-based institution, named in honour of the country's first national hero. Ms. Jones, who was appointed principal in 2018, has embarked on an improvement programme aimed at turning around the performance of the school.

"When I got here and saw the rich talent pool we have at our disposal, I promptly declared the dawn of a new day at the institution and have set about making it more reflective of the national hero in whose honour it is named."

She says that her job from the get-go has always been about the rebranding of the school, adding that along the way, the educational focus has expanded to include entrepreneurship and skills training. Ms. Jones notes that traditionally, Marcus Garvey has been a school that receives students who are performing below average.

"It was viewed by residents in the community as a troubled institution, which had disciplinary challenges, and examination passes were below expectations."

"That was the mindset and that was what we were up against. I told our teachers that we would not accept that stigma as a given and that we would work hard and dedicate ourselves to changing that narrative, and, for the most part, I think we have succeeded."

Nearly two years into the post, Ms. Jones has stamped her mark as a transformational leader who is focused on success and has got the full support of the entire school community, including staff, students, and parents. Ms. Jones says that in getting the buy-in of the students, they had to be convinced that they were the bearers of the legacy of one of the most influential civil rights activists of the 20th century, and that Marcus Garvey Technical is potentially as good as any other high school in St. Ann.

She tells JIS News that the next step was to unleash the creative spirit of the students and noted that focus was not only placed on skills development but also on how to use those skills to learn, in keeping with Garvey's belief in promoting black wealth.

"So, as it stands today, entrepreneurship, as well as skills training, is a main part of our focus where some of the older kids are enrolled in disciplines such as hospitality management where they will earn associate degrees. We have two associate degree programmes that we started along with the University of the Commonwealth Caribbean. We also have the Centre of Occupational Studies that is partnering along with us for that programme," she points out.

Ms. Jones tells JIS News that the school will only get better and will be a force to be reckoned with in terms of academic excellence and sports. She notes that the institution's Mansfield campus in Ocho Rios, which accommodates junior students, will be used as an incubator to address academic deficits and, more importantly, shift the children's mindset to more positive thinking.

"We believe that as a technical institution it doesn't matter where our students are coming from. We know we have some children that come in reading at about grade four... [and] we plan to take these children towards their purpose using skills development and shifting the mindset. Once we understand where we're coming from and we firmly set our eyes on where our kids can go, the staff that I have here are qualified and trained, and they can get the kids there," she notes. "So, we're not going to quit on them, once they don't quit on us," she adds.

'Former 'failed school' hits it big in CSEC, CAPE passes' was a banner headline in The Gleaner on October 6, 2021. The news item was about Marcus Garvey Technical High School. Gleaner Writer Carl Gilchrist provided the following details about the remarkable turnaround that had occurred:

"Once denigrated to the level of 'failed school' that needed immediate intervention, the Marcus Garvey

Technical High School in St Ann's Bay has this year achieved an academic level never before reached in its 33-year history. The school recorded excellent results in Caribbean Secondary Education Certificate (CSEC) and Caribbean Advanced Proficiency Examination (CAPE), with the CAPE results being particularly impressive, as it was the first results since the sixth-form level was introduced at the school.

Additionally, come November, the school will graduate the first set of students who have successfully completed the associate degree programmes that principal Anniona Jones introduced, leaving her overwhelmed with the progress that has been made since she became principal in 2018.

"Here is the thing that has me so excited. Teachers of tourism, management of business, and physical education at CAPE, they're doing it for the first time and we had 100 percent passes for tourism, physical education, entrepreneurship, and then [a] 75 percent pass [rate] for management of business," Jones told The Gleaner. Communications studies had a pass rate of 93 percent.

For the CSEC exams, all the students who sat passed visual arts, theatre arts, technical drawing, mechanical technology, office administration, religious education, geography, and physical education. Mathematics recorded a 120 percent rise, English literature improved by 67 percent, while English language, physics, and biology recorded a 50 percent increase in passes. +Some students passed as many as eight subjects.

"In the history of the school, this is the lowest absentee rate we ever had (for CSEC). We used to have kids pay for their exam and just don't turn up, but for most subjects, we had 100 percent of the children who had entered, sitting the exam. We never had that before," Jones pointed out.

"Last year, it was 108 kids, on average, who used to leave Marcus Garvey without a CSEC. For the first time in the history of the school, we only had 23 students who left without a CSEC. This year, we had children with eight subjects and over 50 percent of our cohort could actually go on to tertiary study."

Meanwhile, for the first time, 15 students will graduate next month after completing their associate degree in hospitality and tourism management, which concluded with internships in Negril. In addition to the associate degree, the students will pick up two additional certificates – a diploma from the American Hospitality and Lodging Institute and a diploma in customer service. Already, efforts are being made to place them in institutions, locally and overseas, to complete their bachelor's degree. Jones outlined to The Gleaner just how she and her team have been able to achieve success at Marcus Garvey Technical High.

"Here is what we did differently. When every other school decided that they were going to do just online, even when school was reopened and the teachers were just going to meet them once or twice, what we did was we called out every teacher from grade seven to sixth form. So, every teacher came in and they just broke the children into small groups, and the teachers just literally went back through – review. We were not depending on one teacher to do 10 or 15 kids, so they got more time with a teacher as the groups were smaller, and that is what works."

She continued: "We zeroed in on using corona (COVID-19) to pull our team together and to make our relationship and the kids stronger. We zeroed in on a single goal – we're going to use learning to manage behaviour, learning to tie the team together, learning to motivate the children, and that is how we were able to see the kind of significant improvement that we are witnessing. We decided on a single aim; we were going to pour everything that we had into these kids, and the kids were going to give us a hundred percent, and that was how we were able to achieve excellence."

Jones said she is humbled by the change taking place at Marcus Garvey Technical High and refused to take all the credit, showering her entire staff with praise for their input. "I have a phenomenal team," Jones said. "My team has made me a better human being, a better person, a better leader. They're teaching me so much about love and passion and disappointment and grace and mercy, and I am such a better person for having had the opportunity to lead this team at Marcus Garvey Technical. I have an amazing 109 academic staff, I have the most talented 22 administrative staff, not to mention my ancillary workers. They've been at work every day; every day. We've not had to shut down the school once. We've been able to offer exemplary service to our population because of the work of my administrators and my ancillary staff."

When I read the story, it warmed my heart to see evidence that MGTHS was on a trajectory to truly honour the mighty intellectual giant whose name it bears by becoming a space and symbol for the empowerment of children that look like him.

****

Marcus Garvey's Courage
==================####==================

Garvey was uncommonly courageous. He called out local Judges and criticized Jamaica's legal system, which he reportedly described as "oppressive," and called for laws to "punish Judges who acted unfairly." He was charged and convicted of contempt of court. He was fined £100 and sentenced to three months in prison.

But you know, it is not an accident that Garvey took on the Justice system frontally. In Jamaica after emancipation, the plantocracy used laws to maintain their advantage over the newly freed African Jamaicans.

Besides, a Jamaican Court is one of the most intimidating spaces! The Judges behave like gods, especially when dealing with regular, Black Jamaicans from which they spring! It is worth noting that many of the fore parents of our present-day Black judges were higglers, maids, farm hands, etc. And yet.

Here is how Paul Beale, highly-acclaimed writer, director, producer, described, in a passionate Facebook post on August 17, 2019, titled **'A Typical Jamaican Court Session - What Justice?'** the posture typical of many local judges: "Many poor youths who do not answer the Judge with the alacrity expected by the judge or perhaps if they fidgeted too much, could incur the wrath of these 'justice' officials, intoxicated with power. It is really amusing to observe the presumptuous, complacent, self-satisfied, smug position of these purveyors of justice who so nonchalantly brush aside the rights of the individual while reveling in the power that they have annexed to themselves. Unfortunate citizens have their rights violated every day and get no protection from the State. No wonder the constant cry of the downtrodden inner-city youths is 'we want justice'. This is a cry that for the most part goes unanswered. Even some of the lawyers, especially the younger ones, are not spared the overbearing self-importance of the court and seemed petrified and even tongue-tied in the presence of the almighty honourable judge, perched on his bench. God help the poor unfortunate accused youngster without the benefit of a lawyer. It is almost sacrilegious to attempt to represent oneself, as Garvey once did. There's a level of impatience and intolerance when these defendants try to explain themselves. One gets the feeling they were wasting the court's time by trying to present their cases, some laden with innocence."

I recall in 1981, while I was a student at the secondary level, being taken on a visit as part of my Sociology class to observe the proceedings of a Resident Magistrate's Court (now Parish Court). The visit was based on the principle of 'open justice' which is a central tenet of the justice system that establishes the right of parties directly involved in legal proceedings, together with the wider public and media, to attend and observe legal proceedings. The rationale for the principle has been explained in different ways, but the core of it rests in the benefits to the proper administration of justice arising from public scrutiny of judicial proceedings.

During my visit to the Resident Magistrate's Court in Port Antonio, in 1981, my then 18-year-old brain was befuddled (puzzled) by the strange way the lawyers conversed in legal jargon with their colleagues ("my learned friend") and how they addressed the Judge ("Your Honour"). Additionally, the way the policemen used the maximum capacity of their lungs and vocal cords to bellow the names of persons who had matters before the court perplexed me.

It is a form of violence.

The sight of young men handcuffed together and herded into the Courthouse by policemen, who held ('draped') them by the waist of their pants and the brusque way the Judge spoke to the accused persons, were also deeply troubling to me. I formed the impression the proceedings were more about 'showing who was boss', rather than dispensing justice.

My experience observing the court session in 1981 had an imprinting impact on me. I found the court visit interesting and simultaneously troubling and puzzling. The references to "Her Majesty Queen Elizabeth" and "God Save the Queen" at the start of the proceedings seemed exceedingly offensive and contradictory in a supposedly independent country. In truly independent jurisdictions, it's "The People" vs. accused persons. The puzzling and undignified reality is that Queen Elizabeth of brutish Britain is still the Head of State of Jamaica – the 'hovering power'! And homage is paid to her daily in every Court across the length and breadth of Jamaica! Jamaica negotiated its independence from Britain and kept the colonial laws and institutions intact!

The history of laws in Jamaica provides insights into why justice often eludes the 'little people': "In most societies, laws are directed downward. This was certainly true of Jamaica. The vagrancy laws were seen as such ... the ganja laws ... and laws regulating vending are also regarded by many as anti-poor and oppressive. In the colonial period, the law was a tool for controlling the 'dangerous classes.' Despite the changes since Independence, these are the lens through which the present laws and law enforcement are viewed by many" [Source: Anthony Harriott, 2009].

The above perspective from Prof. Harriott comports with the view of many philosophers that there is no moral order imposed on humans by divine decree. What obtains is that the strong will impose their will upon the poor and then establish a moral code to justify what they've done or intend to do.

Attorney-at-Law Frank Phipps reminded in an article in the Jamaica Observer newspaper on June 25, 2020, that "Emancipation was for freedom from colonial rule, with the otherwise status quo preserved to be in conformity with what was accepted and that all had grown accustomed to, which was for the plantation owners to keep their wealth while the former slaves get nothing — only contrived obedience enforced by the Jamaica Constabulary Force."

"The masses getting the right to vote in Jamaica was a hard fight. In post-emancipation Jamaica, the House of Assembly, which was dominated by the white planter class, passed laws to stymie land ownership by African Jamaicans. Laws that equated political power and the right to vote with land ownership. For instance, African-

Jamaicans could get registered to vote if they owned property worth £6, or paid £30 in rent, or £3 in direct taxes!" [Source: 'The Story of the Jamaican People' by Sherlock & Bennett].

Coercive policing and iniquitous laws were essential to colonial rule. It is instructive to note here that the law mentioned above is an example of how many laws in Jamaica were passed with the purpose being to suppress or 'keeping the dangerous masses in their place.'

Someone, perhaps a cynic, once said: "The State calls its own violence 'law,' but that of the individual, 'crime.'"

******

Marcus Garvey's Travails

=================####=================

"To jail Marcus Garvey would dim romance; like jailing a rainbow" ~
New York Journal, January 18, 1922

The 'Empire Strikes Back'

Those who wish to maintain the status quo of oppressive systems and structures deliberately conflate activism with trouble-making.

The powerful concedes nothing voluntarily.

Activists for positive change cannot be fearful about offending the powerful but must be prepared to speak truth to power – and be prepared for the consequences of their conscience and conviction.

When one is doing the right thing, consequences be dammed!

Besides, many persons now celebrated as national heroes or icons were once regarded as rabble-rousers, rebels, malcontents, and non-conformists.

And it was so with Marcus Garvey. He is one of those historical figures, flawed because they are human but full of promise for the same reason, who are maligned.

Villainisation of persons who attempt to change the status quo is a part of the playbook of those who desire to maintain the status quo that is beneficial to them.

In classical psychological warfare, one of the approaches taken is to criticise, demonize, and denigrate relentlessly the object of one's ill intent. It's a form of psychological evisceration, the objective of which is not just to break the spirit of the victims, but to destroy them.

In Jamaica, "the planter and merchant elite saw Garvey as a threat to their privileged way of life and hounded him mercilessly. Gleaner editor H.G. Delisser led the vilification campaign, which was sadly so successful that many still believe Garvey never had a large following in his native land." [Source: Kevin O'Brien Change, The Gleaner, 'Marcus Garvey: Black Champion of Vision and Destiny,' August 3, 2012]

In addition, when Dr. Robert Morton, who succeeded Booker T. Washington as President of Tuskegee Institute in Alabama, USA, visited Jamaica in 1916, the British colonial government (BCG) in Jamaica, seeing Garvey as "a threat to the colonial order," advised Dr. Morton not to contact Garvey because he was a 'trouble-maker.' Translated, this means the BCG perceived Garvey as subversive of a natural order in which Black People were to remain forever subordinate and marginalised.

Garvey's tenacity is best understood when one considers that the "empire always strikes back." And struck it did back at Garvey. Hard. And devastatingly.

According to Sherlock and Bennett (1998), Garvey was: "A man who through his life lived his message; and did so through triumph and disaster, in the face of derision and oppression, of imprisonment and of rejection. Those in the centers of white power and influence in Jamaica, in the United States, and Europe saw Garvey as a formidable threat and used all means in their power, the law included, to obstruct and vilify him; they projected the image of a black racist subversive, a rabble-rouser, a confidence man, and trickster (p. 293)."

This is thought-provoking: "...Garvey is now a National Hero... the official society had to make Garvey the hero, but they used it to their own ends - those who had condemned, now praise. They wanted to make the mulatto, William Gordon, a National Hero and then they had to give in to the demand that it was the Black Paul Bogle who was the real hero of the 1865 Morant Bay Rebellion. So they try to use the honouring of Bogle, like that of Garvey, to their own cause..." [Source: Richard Small, in Introduction to "Groundings with Brothers" by Walter Rodney]

Professor Rupert Lewis notes that "Throughout Garvey's life (1887-1940), controversy about his ideals and his leadership meant that he functioned in perpetual ideological, cultural, political, and economic minefields as he sought to challenge the racial subordination and economic exploitation being experienced by black people." [Source: 'Life, times, and legacies of Marcus Garvey,' The Sunday Gleaner, May 22, 2022]

Not taking punitive action against the white, racist South African government, then UK Prime Minister the heartless Margaret Thatcher once called Nelson Mandela a terrorist for having the guts to fight against the evil, reprehensible, and vulgar system of apartheid in South Africa.

Throughout his life beginning in the 1950s, Malcolm X endured surveillance from the Federal Bureau of Investigation (FBI) for the Nation of Islam's supposed links to communism. And yet, his legacy is impactful: "Malcolm X has been described as one of the greatest and most influential African Americans in history. He is credited with raising the self-esteem of black Americans and reconnecting them with their African heritage. He is largely responsible for the spread of Islam in the Black community in the United States. Many African Americans, especially those who lived in cities in the Northern and Western United States, felt that Malcolm X articulated their complaints concerning inequality better than did the mainstream civil rights movement. One biographer says that by giving expression to their frustration, Malcolm X "made clear the price that white America would have to pay if it did not accede to Black America's legitimate demands. In the late 1960s, increasingly radical Black activists based their movements largely on Malcolm X and his teachings. The Black Power Movement, the Black Arts Movement, and the widespread adoption of the slogan "**Black is Beautiful**" can all trace their roots to Malcolm X. In 1998, Time Magazine named 'The Autobiography of Malcolm X' one of the ten most influential nonfiction books of the 20th century " [Source: Wikipedia].

(Malcolm X was assassinated in 1965. Two men, Muhammad Aziz and Khalil Islam, who were convicted after a trial in 1966 and sentenced to life imprisonment, were exonerated on November 18, 2021, their convictions overturned by Justice Ellen Biben of the State Supreme Court in Manhattan. The Manhattan district attorney, Cyrus Vance Jr., had submitted a 43-page motion written with the lawyers for the two men asking that she vacate the convictions. When she did so, the courtroom burst into applause. The extraordinary moment came after a 22-month review of the case initiated by Vance's office and conducted jointly with the men's lawyers. It found that they had not been given a fair trial. It reached the same conclusions that historians and scholars had arrived at years earlier: The case against the two men was dubious. No physical evidence tied Aziz and Islam to the murder. Both had alibis. It was proven that in the trial the FBI and the New York Police Department withheld exculpatory evidence. "I do not need this court, these prosecutors, or a piece of paper to tell me I am innocent," Aziz declared in a stern voice that did not shake or falter. "I am an 83-year-old man who was victimized by the criminal justice system." I hope the same system that was responsible for this travesty of justice also takes responsibility for the immeasurable harm it caused to me," Aziz said, adding that his conviction was part of a corrupt process "that is all too familiar to Black people, even in 2021." [Source: The New York Times, November 19, 2021). This is yet another example of Black persecution – 'judicial lynching' - in the USA.

In 1968, American sprinters Tommie Smith and John Carlos raised their Black-gloved fists while the USA's national anthem was being played during the 200-metres medal ceremony at the Mexico City Olympics – "Smith had won the gold medal with a world-record time of 19.83 seconds and Carlos the bronze. Smith and Carlos had agreed, a priori, to use their medal wins as an opportunity to highlight the social issues roiling the United States at the time. Racial tensions were at a height, and the Civil Rights movement had given way to the Black Power movement. African-Americans like Smith and Carlos were frustrated by what they saw as the passive nature of the Civil Rights movement. They sought out active forms of protests and advocated for racial pride, Black Nationalism, and dramatic action rather than incremental change. Their action killed their careers. They would not only eventually be sent home but ended up being ostracized by the Olympic Movement for nearly half a century. They received death threats. Many Americans saw them as traitors, as villains, or, at least, as un-American, unpatriotic. For Smith, who was in the ROTC at the time that was the end of his military aspirations. Both experienced major personal challenges. Their marriages fell apart. Carlos had difficulty getting employment for many years. Not until 2016 did the United States Olympic Committee (USOC) bring them to an official event. Not until 2019 did it enshrine them in its Hall of Fame." (Sources: The Associated Press; History.com; Douglas Hartmann, 'Race, Culture, and the Revolt of the Black Athlete: The 1968 Olympic Protests and Their Aftermath')

In addition, Jesse Owens, a Black American track and field athlete who won four gold medals at the 1936 Summer Olympics in Berlin, Germany, - in the 100 meters, long jump, 200 meters, and 4 × 100-meter relay. He was the most successful athlete at the Games and, as a Black American man, was credited with "single-handedly crushing Hitler's myth of Aryan supremacy." In Germany, Owens had been allowed to travel with and stay in the same hotels as whites, at a time when African Americans in many parts of the United States had to stay in segregated hotels that accommodated only Blacks. When Owens returned to the United States, he was greeted in New York City by Mayor Fiorello LaGuardia and there was a Manhattan ticker-tape parade in his honor along Broadway's Canyon of Heroes. After the parade, Owens was not permitted to enter through the main doors of the Waldorf Astoria Hotel, New York, and instead was forced to travel up to the reception honoring him in a freight elevator. And then President of the USA, Franklin D. Roosevelt (FDR), never invited Jesse Owens to the White House to congratulate him following his triumphs at the Olympic Games. Owens initially refused to support the black power salute by African-American sprinters Tommie Smith and John Carlos at the 1968 Summer Olympics. He told them: "The black fist is a meaningless symbol. When you open it, you have nothing but fingers – weak, empty fingers. The only time the black fist has significance is when there's money inside. There's where the power lies." Four years later in his 1972 book 'I Have Changed,' he revised his opinion: "I realized now that militancy in the best sense of the word was the only answer where the black man was concerned, that any black man who wasn't a militant in 1970 was either blind or a coward." [Source: Wikipedia]

Also, Muhammad Ali was vilified and suffered for his opposition to the unjust Vietnam war – "no Vietnamese ever called me a nigger ... I have no reason to join a war to kill them, so you all might as well just take me to jail right now," he declared with his characteristic bravado. Here is Ali's full statement: "I ain't draft dodging. I ain't burning no flag. I ain't running to Canada. I'm staying right here. Do you want to send me to jail? Fine, you go right ahead. I've been in jail for 400 years. I could be there for 4 or 5 more, but I ain't going no 10,000 miles to help murder and kill other poor people. If I want to die, I'll die right here, right now, fightin' you, if I want to die. You are my enemy, not no Chinese, no Vietcong, no Japanese. You are my opposer when I want freedom. You are my opposer when I want justice. You are my opposer when I want equality. You want me to go somewhere and fight for you? You won't even stand up for me right here in America, for my rights and my religious beliefs. You won't even stand up for my right here at home. "

Wikipedia notes the following: "Ali refused to be drafted into the military, citing his religious beliefs and ethical opposition to the Vietnam War. He was found guilty of draft evasion so he faced 5 years in prison and was stripped of his boxing titles. He stayed out of prison as he appealed the decision to the Supreme Court, which overturned his conviction in 1971, but he had not fought for nearly four years and lost a period of peak performance as an athlete (In speaking of the cost on Ali's career of his refusal to be drafted, his trainer Angelo Dundee said, "One thing must be taken into account when talking about Ali: He was robbed of his best years, his prime years"; age 25-29)."

And concerning the impact of Ali's anti-war stance and refusal to be drafted, this is what Wikipedia records: "Ali's example inspired many black Americans and others. However, initially, when he refused induction, he became arguably the most hated man in the country and received many death threats. People who supported Ali during this time were also threatened, including sports journalist Jerry Izenberg, whose columns defended Ali's decision not to serve. He wrote, "Bomb threats emptied our office, making the staff stand out in the snow. My car windshield was smashed with a sledgehammer." The New York Times columnist William Rhoden wrote, "Ali's actions changed my standard of what constituted an athlete's greatness. Possessing a killer jump shot or the ability to stop on a dime was no longer enough. What were you doing for the liberation of your people? What were you doing to help your country live up to the covenant of its founding principles?"

Recalling Ali's anti-war position, [basketball legend] Kareem Abdul-Jabbar said: "I remember the teachers at my high school didn't like Ali because he was so anti-establishment and he kind of thumbed his nose at authority and got away with it. The fact that he was proud to be a Black man and that he had so much talent made some people think that he was dangerous. But for those very reasons, I enjoyed him."

Civil rights figures came to believe that Ali had an energizing effect on the freedom movement as a whole. Al Sharpton spoke of his bravery at a time when there was still widespread support for the Vietnam War. "For the heavyweight champion of the world, who had achieved the highest level of athletic celebrity, to put all of that on the line—the money, the ability to get endorsements—to sacrifice all of that for a cause, gave a whole sense of legitimacy to the movement and the causes with young people that nothing else could have done. Even those who were assassinated certainly lost their lives, but they didn't voluntarily do that. He knew he was going to jail and did it anyway. That's another level of leadership and sacrifice."

Ali was honored with the annual Martin Luther King Award in 1970 by civil rights leader Ralph Abernathy, who called him "a living example of soul power, the March on Washington in two fists." Coretta Scott King added that Ali was "a champion of justice and peace and unity."

[Boxing analyst and commentator] Bob Arum did not support Ali's choice at the time. More recently, Arum stated that "when I look back at his life, and I was blessed to call him a friend and spent a lot of time with him, it's hard for me to talk about his exploits in boxing because as great as they were they paled in comparison to the impact that he had on the world," and "He did what he thought was right. And it turned out he was right, and I was wrong."

"Shut up and just dribble" was the rude 'instruction' hurled at Basketball star **LeBron James** by the racist and entitled Fox News host Laura Ingraham when James, exercising his social conscience and freedom of speech, commented on the palpable and embedded racial injustice in the USA. Zlatan Ibrahimović, a striker for the Italian football club AC Milan, also had the temerity to tell

James to stay out of politics and "do what you're good at doing."

This was James' forceful retort that I think would make Garvey proud: "I will never shut up about things that are wrong. I preach about my people and I preach about equality, social justice, racism, and voter suppression - things that go on in our community. I'll use my platform to continue to shed light on everything that's going on around this country and around the world. There's no way I would ever just stick to sports because I understand how powerful this platform and my voice is. I speak from a very educated mind." [Source: MSN News, February 27, 2021]

James, describing the 'Black Lives Matter' movement as a 'lifestyle,' decided to use his voice and platform as a basketball star to speak out and take action about injustice against Black people in the USA. For example, James is one of the founding members of the 'More Than a Vote' organization that is focused on combating systemic, racist voter suppression in the USA. James has also established a school for more than 200 at-risk youths in his hometown of Akron, Ohio.

I salute LeBron for his activism and good works and decision not to "shut up and dribble." The likes of Laura Ingraham and Zlatan Ibrahimović need to understand and hug up the reality that their kind are no longer overlords entitled to issue orders to Blacks. The order I am issuing to Ingraham and Ibrahimovic in my Jamaican language ('Patwa') is this: gweh! (that is, go away, get lost!)

Afro-centric psychiatrist **Dr. Frances Cress-Welsing** is another champion for Black people who has been vilified for her activism. She was derisively, disrespectfully, and condescendingly described as that "controversial Black Doctor." In 1975, Cress-Welsing, then an assistant professor of pediatrics, was denied tenure at Howard University and was subsequently fired.

"Dr. Welsing is perhaps best known for her 1991 book, '**The Isis Papers: The Keys to the Colours**,' which came about after 20 years of research and analysis from her private practice. It is considered required reading for those interested in the psychological origins and manifestations of white supremacy." [Source: The Root, January 2, 2016]

When I got and read a copy of Dr. Welsing's book, I found it remarkably insightful in helping me to understand clearly the diabolical nature of white supremacy and its foundational objective – the annihilation (or in the alternative, perpetual oppression and subjugation) of Blacks (and other non-white) people to ensure white genetic survival.

Consider, too, the vaunted Harvard University's treatment of an outspoken scholar. It denied **Cornel West** tenure because it "has a problem with outspoken, principled faculty who take public positions that question university policy, challenge authority, or might ruffle the feathers of big donors. And when the faculty members in question are scholars of color, their odds of getting through the tenure process are slim to none." [Source:

Robin D.G. Kelley, 'Why Cornel West's Tenure Fight Matters,' The Boston Review, March 3, 2021]

Behold systemic racism at play! Cornel West's case is an example of what its grotesque face looks like!

There was also the troubling case in June 2021 of **Nikole Hannah-Jones**, a Pulitzer Prize winner and MacArthur Foundation "genius" grantee, who, although she had the strong backing of the faculty, her dean, and, reportedly, the administration, was denied tenure by the trustees of the University of North Carolina, Chapel Hill, USA.

"It is widely suspected that she's been targeted for her reporting on race, which challenges conventional narratives about the USA's history of slavery and its cruel treatment of Blacks (and other people of colour). Hannah-Jones, who is Black, is most known for her work on The New York Times Magazine's "1619 Project," which re-examines (i.e., gives a more accurate and complete account) the role of race in the nation's founding, and which has been criticized by detractors, including a major donor (newspaper publisher Walter Hussman) to UNC, and former president Trump as being unpatriotic and marinated in critical race theory. Backlash against the project fueled some of the current legislation against teaching critical race theory in public schools, colleges and universities." [Source: Inside Higher Ed, May 25, 2021; June 27, 2021]

Walter Hussman said "he was given pause by some prominent scholars' criticism that Hannah-Jones distorted the historical record in arguing that the protection of slavery was one of the USA's Founding Fathers' primary motivations in seeking independence from the British." [Source: NPR, July 6, 2021]

Nikole Hannah-Jones' case is another example of what systemic racism looks like and it also shows the extent to which white racists will go to punish Black people for speaking the truth about America's history!

'Marked' & Imprisoned

"I was going to Jericho and fell among thieves. Christ died to make men free; I shall die to give courage and inspiration to the race." ~ Marcus Garvey

Unfortunately, Marcus Garvey was imprisoned (Prisoner #19359) for five years at the Atlanta Penitentiary in 1925, at age 38, following his conviction for mail fraud. The trial by an all-white jury reflected the systemic racial bias of the justice system and followed a pattern of punitive measures against him.

The charges brought against Garvey related to the sale of stock in the Black Star Line Inc., a corporation then existing under the laws of Delaware. Garvey's imprisonment was to be for five years, but in 1927 President Calvin Coolidge (who appointed J. Edgar Hoover) commuted his sentence and had him deported to Jamaica as an alien with a felony record. Garvey is the most famous Jamaican deportee – there have been many - from the USA.

The Federal Bureau of Investigations (FBI) in the USA closely followed Garvey. On its website, the FBI acknowledges seeking to "deport him as an undesirable alien." (In March 2021, it was announced that Actor Winston Duke is set to play Marcus Garvey in the film,

'Marked Man.' The film will be made by Amazon Studios and will be directed by Andrew Dosunmu. Kwame Kwei-Armah wrote the film's script which was developed initially by Esther Douglas. The film is also based on the Garvey biography, **"Negro With a Hat: The Rise and Fall of Marcus Garvey"** by Jamaican-British historian Colin Grant. Set in the 1920s, 'Marked Man' follows a young Black man who joins J. Edgar Hoover's Federal Bureau of Investigation and then infiltrates Garvey's UNIA organization. "'Negro With a Hat' restores Garvey to his place as one of the founders of black nationalism and a key figure of the 20th century.")

"Like many visionaries, Garvey was not the most practical of businessmen. His Black Star Line Steamship Corporation, conceptualised to transport Blacks back to Africa, proved a financial disaster. It also gave American authorities, who saw Garvey as a threat to the Jim Crow status quo, the opportunity to neutralise him. He was charged with fraud, given a five-year sentence, and deported back to Jamaica in 1927. Thousands hailed Garvey's return. **The Daily Gleaner** reported that "no denser crowd has ever been witnessed in Kingston .... Deafening cheers were raised." [Source: Kevin O'Brien Chang, The Gleaner, August 3, 2012]

Betrayed

In addition, a 'Bag-O-Wire' contributed to Garvey's troubles. The term is a slang expression for someone who is a betrayer. This term is used to describe a close friend/relative of Marcus Garvey who betrayed him by giving away a lot of details about his plans before disappearing.

From Prof. Rupert Lewis: "Garvey faced betrayal from many opponents to his message, even from within the Black community. Hoover was assisted by black agents such as Dr. Arthur Ulysses Craig, who, like Dr. W.E.B. DuBois, came from the intellectual section of the middle class. According to historian Theodore Kornweibel Jr, after Dr. Craig attended two UNIA mass meetings, "his middle-class sensibilities were shaken by the fervour of the working-class (and heavily West Indian) crowds which widely applauded every call for racial change. As a member of the race's educated, upwardly mobile, and assimilationist 'Talented Tenth', Craig concluded that the 'spirit of these meetings is decidedly unAmerican'. (Kornweibel, Seeing Red, 103). Craig became a technical adviser to the Black Star Line's Captain Joshua Cockburn, helping him inspect the leaky boilers on an old steamer that was purchased". Craig and others systematically sabotaged the Black Star Line. But it was a Jamaican who got close to Garvey and developed a personal relationship. His name was Herbert S. Boulin, special confidential informant P-138. Garvey developed confidence in Boulin as a fellow Jamaican, and Boulin exploited this relationship to provide J. Edgar Hoover with considerable intelligence on Garvey's activities." [Source: 'Life, Times, and Legacies of Marcus Garvey', The Sunday Gleaner, May 22, 2022]

'Garvey Must Go!'

"Marcus Garvey's style of Black nationalism clashed with that of the 1920s Black establishment, notably with William Edward Burghardt (W.E.B.) Du Bois, head of the National Association for the Advancement of Colored People (NAACP). Garvey was both a racial purist and a Black separatist, whereas the establishment hoped for a self-sustaining Black ecosystem within a predominantly white America." [Source: Encyclopedia Britannia].

In their book **'Stamped: Racism, Antiracism, and You'**, Jason Reynolds and Ibram X. Kendi give an interesting profile of DuBois. Reader, I strongly recommend that you read the profile and the rest of the book!

Justin Hansford in his book **'Jailing a Rainbow: The Marcus Garvey Case'** gives a compelling and lucid step-by-step analysis of the 'Garvey Must Go!' campaign that implicated the leadership of the National Association for the Advancement of Coloured People (NAACP) as key antagonists of Garvey. After detailing the motive of the campaign as being rooted in ideological, financial, and personal jealousy of Garvey by the likes of W.E.B Dubois, Hansford enumerates the following systematic and calculating steps the diabolical and evil 'Garvey Must Go!' campaign followed:

- **"Step 1: Manipulating the Media Narrative** – The coalition began its campaign to discredit Garvey in the media using the media's 'agenda-setting' and 'priming' effects. Agenda-setting refers to the media's "ability to direct the public's attention to certain issues," while priming describes its "ability to affect the criteria by which viewers judge public policies, public officials, or candidates for office." Most of the coalition (against Garvey) members were editors or contributing writers to influential African-American newspapers and magazines such as **'The Crisis'** (the NAACP's primary publication edited by W.E.B. Dubois), **'The Crusader'** (edited by Cyril Briggs), **'The Messenger'** (edited by Chandler Owen and A. Phillip Randolph). Between 1921-1924, both 'The Crisis' and 'The Messenger' published five vituperative articles a piece criticizing Garvey. In one article, Dubois even referred to Garvey as a "little, fat Black man; ugly, but with intelligent eyes and big head." (Garvey, not one to take things lying down, hit back and described Dubois as an "unfortunate mulatto who bewails every drop of Negro blood in his veins"). In another article, Dubois wrote that "The American Negro has endured this wretch [Garvey] too long with fine restraint and every effort of cooperation and understanding. But the end has come. Every man who apologises for or defends Marcus Garvey from this day forth writes himself down as unworthy of the countenance of decent Americans. As for Garvey himself, this open ally of the Ku Klux Klan should be locked up or sent home."

- An article by the NAACP's Reverend Robert W. Bagnall entitled, 'The Madness of Marcus Garvey," published in **'The Messenger'** magazine described Garvey as "A Negro of unmixed stock, squat, stocky, fat and sleek, with protruding jaws, and heavy jowls, small bright pig-like eyes, and a rather bull-dog-like face. Boastful, egotistic, tyrannical, intolerant, cunning, shifty, smooth and suave, avaricious; as adroit as a fencer in changing front, as adept as a cuttle-fish in beclouding an issue he cannot meet, prolix to the 'nth degree in devising new schemes to gain the money of poor ignorant Negroes; gifted at self-advertisement, without shame in self-laudation, promising ever, but never fulfilling, without regard for veracity, a lover of pomp and tawdry finery and garish display, a bully with his own folk but servile in the presence of the [Ku Klux] Klan, a sheer opportunist and a demagogic charlatan. When Garvey was found guilty at a recent trial, [Superior Court] Judge [Jacob] Panken of New York excoriated him, ending with these words—"There is a form of paranoia which manifests itself in believing oneself to be a great man." In this he infers that Garvey is afflicted with this form of insanity. If he is not insane, he is a demagogic charlatan, but the probability is that the man is insane. Certainly the movement is insane, whether Garvey is or not." The magazine even included a picture of Garvey with devil's horns.

- **Step 2**: **Supporting and Legitimizing J. Edgar Hoover's View of Marcus Garvey.** The 'Garvey Must Go!' coalition did not need to engage much lobbying in order to persuade the US Government to put Garvey under surveillance and pursue charges against him. Indeed, the US federal government had already begun to do so. In a 1919 correspondence, J. Edgar Hoover spoke of Garvey in these terms: "Garvey is particularly active among the radical elements in New York City in agitating the Negro movement. Unfortunately, however, he has not as yet violated any federal law whereby he could be proceeded against on the grounds of being an undesirable alien, from the point of view of deportation. It occurs to me, however, from the attached clipping that there might be some proceeding against him for fraud in connection with his Black Star Line propaganda." Eight members of the 'Garvey Must Go!' coalition also made a direct appeal for Garvey's arrest in a letter delivered to the U.S. Attorney General, Harry Daugherty. The letter urged Daugherty to "use his full influence completely to disband and extirpate this vicious movement," and implored him to "vigourously and speedily push the government's case against Marcus Garvey for using the mails to defraud." The letter amounted to a twenty-nine paragraph legal brief requesting that the federal government prosecute Marcus Garvey. (Garvey described the letter as "the greatest bit of treachery and wickedness that any group of Negroes could be capable of.") The letter was signed by William Pickens, Robert Bagnall, Chandler Owen, Robert Abbott, George Harris, John E. Neil, Julia P. Coleman, and Harry H. Pace.

- **Step 3**: **Biasing the Legal Narrative.** This witch's brew of political intrigue is what ultimately led Garvey to Court with the future of the Black Star Line and the communal self-help idea for racial liberation hanging in the balance. To add to Garvey's dismay, he would soon find that the coalition's influence would extend into the courtroom itself. To fully understand how the 'Garvey Must Go!' coalition influenced the federal district court, one should first consider the reasons that the coalition chose to do so. Judicial influence, if it can be accomplished, is one of the most effective methods of influencing public policy. Although media and federal agency influence affected public opinion and the government's investigation, respectively, only through judicial capture could the campaign have had Garvey jailed, deported, or both. By extending their campaign to the judiciary, the 'Garvey Must Go!' coalition ensured that this rivalry would put the opponent's own personal wellbeing and freedom in peril. But why did they choose the judiciary as the venue where they would attempt to inflict the final blow to Garvey and his philosophy? First, they choose the judiciary because it was the most clandestine mode of governmental interference they could seek. As one scholar noted, "Typically, factions have some concern about their own public image – they may depend on the public as consumers or for contributions. Special interest appeals to the legislature or agencies may appear to be ... seeking quasi-corrupt political favours." In the context of this particular case, it is clear that Garvey's competitors would have ruined their own careers if they openly appealed to Jim Crow government officials in the hopes of eliminating a fellow Black leader from political competition. However, the lack of transparency provided by the judicial process ensured that the coalition could cloak their actions and thus maintain the respect of their constituency. Second, apparently the coalition knew that, in order to eliminate their competition they would have to do more than simply imprison Garvey – they had to destroy his credibility. The United States government has prosecuted many African-American leaders on criminal charges. Generally, the Black community has continued to support its leaders and has been inclined to see the government indictments as manifestations of racial injustice. If Garvey went to prison for tax evasion or violation of the Mann Act, it is possible that the community might have rallied around him even more in response. In contrast, by manufacturing an indictment alleging that Garvey's flagship project was actually a money-generating fraud preying on poor Blacks, the coalition may have predicted that they could destroy the credibility of Garvey's vision in the eyes of his followers. Leaving them no option but to follow their direction instead. Though they had already attacked his credibility through their publications, they might have believed that the legitimacy of a judicial opinion would justify their accusations." Ultimately, Garvey (who represented himself, after firing his lawyer who wanted him to cop a guilty plea deal with the government) was found guilty - by an all-white jury in a trial presided over by a biased and compromised judge - on one count of mail fraud and was given the maximum penalty under the law of five years in prison plus a fine of $1000.

The 'Garvey Must Go!' campaign deployed one of the classic approaches used in psychological warfare against a target, which is to first demonize it as a prelude to destroying it.

In classical psychological warfare, one of the approaches taken is to criticise, demonize, and denigrate relentlessly the object of one's evil intent. It's a form of psychological evisceration, the objective of which is not just to break the spirit of the victims, but to utterly destroy them.

Whenever people are mobilized into resenting and hating an individual, it is difficult for that person to prevail. The first step is to "other" the intended target. Peasants, aristocrats, and leaders have been discredited, defamed, demonised, and dehumanised through the deployment of this form of psychological warfare. This wilful destruction of the dignity and reputation of another is one of the worst crimes imaginable. It makes possible the normalization of vulgar abuse.

The website Jamaica Travel and Culture.com sums up Marcus Garvey's trial and sentencing in these terms: "Towards the end of 1919, the FBI hired its first five African-American Agents to investigate Marcus Garvey and the activities of the UNIA. A trial for using the postal service to commit mail fraud was constructed in January 1922 and in May 1923 the trial began. The basis for the trial was that the Black Star Line had mailed out brochures for the company with a picture of a ship named "Phyllis Wheatley" on the cover. The Black Star Line was in the process of negotiating the purchase of the ship but the purchase had not been made by the time the charges were brought. The result of the trial was that Garvey was found guilty and sentenced to five years in prison; however, many believe the trial to be fraudulent with one key witness even admitting that he had been told to lie by the Postal Inspector. In 1927, Garvey had the remainder of his sentence commuted by President

Calvin Coolidge and, in accordance with US federal law, he was deported to Jamaica."

Marcus Garvey's Letter from Prison

Journalist and historian Joel A. Rogers, himself a Jamaican, was one of the few people beyond Garvey's inner circle permitted to visit him in prison and act as a conduit of information to his followers.

In **'Negro With a Hat: The Rise And Fall Of Marcus Garvey'**, Colin Gran wrote "Once past the heavy iron-barred door, Rogers was greeted by a stocky figure clad in ordinary workmen's clothes, 'nothing to indicate a prisoner in popular belief – but an unbelievable contrast to the figure in the glittering uniform, gold epaulettes, plumed hat, sword and spurs on the prancing steed, who as leader of 400,000,000 Negroes of the World,' led his followers through the streets of Harlem. Though Garvey had lost a lot of weight, Rogers confirmed for the readers of the New York Amsterdam News that his zest and imagination were unbounded. '"When I get out of here," he [Garvey] said, with all that old fire that had held his great audiences spellbound in Madison Square Garden, "I mean to do a thousand times more.'"

Grant continued: "Garvey, who always had a clear idea of his worth, had set his face at defiance by the time he entered the Atlanta Penitentiary. He would not, he said, be beaten by state-sponsored persecution and the indignities of his imprisonment; he would not be 'dwarfed and dulled by deadly routine'. Marcus Garvey was built to lead and, even from the confines of the Atlanta Penitentiary, he would inspire. On the first night of his incarceration, when the malodour of defeat closed in on his darkening cell, Marcus Garvey sat down to write, and roused himself to a height of eloquence previously unsurpassed."

Below is Garvey's letter:

February 10, 1925

"Fellow Men of the Negro Race, Greetings:

I am delighted to inform you, that your humble servant is as happy in suffering for you and our cause as is possible under the circumstances of being viciously outraged by a group of plotters who have connived to do their worst to humiliate you through me, in the fight for real emancipation and African Redemption. I do not want at this time to write anything that would make it difficult for you to meet the opposition of your enemy without my assistance. Suffice to say that the history of the outrage shall form a splendid chapter in the history of Africa redeemed. When the black man will no longer be under the heels of others but have a civilization and culture of their own. The whole affair is a disgrace, and the whole black world knows it. We shall not forget. Our day may be fifty, a hundred, or two hundred years ahead, let us watch, work, and pray, for the civilization of injustice is bound to crumble and bring destruction down upon the heads of the unjust. My work is just begun, and when the history of my suffering is complete, then the future generations of the Negro will have in their hands the guide by which they shall know the "sins" of the twentieth century. I, and I know you, too, believe in time, and we shall wait patiently for two hundred years, if need be, to face our enemies through our prosperity. All I have, I have given you. I have sacrificed my home and my loving wife for you. I entrust her to your charge, to protect and defend her in my absence. She is the bravest little woman I know. She has suffered and sacrificed with me for you, therefore, please do not desert her at this dismal hour, when she stands alone. I left her penniless and helpless to face the world, because I gave you all, but her courage is great, and I know she will hold up for you and me. After my enemies are satisfied, in life or death I shall come back to you to serve even as I have served before. In life I shall be the same; in death, I shall be a terror to the foes of Negro liberty. If death has power, then count on me in death to be the real Marcus Garvey I would like to be. If I may come in an earthquake, or a cyclone, or a plague, or pestilence, or as God would have me, then be assured that I would never desert you and make your enemies triumph over you. Would I not go to hell a million times for you? Would I not like Macbeth's ghost, walk the earth forever for you? Would I not lose the whole world and eternity for you? Would I not cry forever before the footstool of the Lord Omnipotent for you? Would I not die a million deaths for you? Then, why be sad? Cheer up, and be assured that if it takes a million years the sins of our enemies shall visit the millionth generation of those that hinder and oppress us. If I die in Atlanta my work shall then only begin, but I shall live, in the physical or spiritual to see the day of Africa's glory. When I am dead, wrap the mantle of the Red, Black and Green around me, for in the new life I shall rise with God's grace and blessing to lead the millions up the heights of triumph with the colors that you well know. Look for me in the whirlwind or the storm, look for me all around you, for, with God's grace I shall come and bring with me countless millions of black slaves who have died in America and the West Indies and the millions in Africa to aid you in the fight for liberty, freedom and life. The civilization of today has gone drunk and crazy with its power and by such it seeks through injustice, fraud, and lies to crush the unfortunate. But if I am apparently crushed by the system of influence and misdirected power, my cause shall rise again to plague the conscience of the corrupt. For this again I am satisfied, and for you, I repeat, I am glad to suffer and even die. Again, I say cheer up, for better days are ahead. I shall write the history that will inspire the millions that are coming and leave the posterity of our enemies to reckon with the host for the deeds of their fathers.

With God's dearest blessings, I leave you for a while."

While he was imprisoned, Garvey was further humiliated by being forced to carry out cleaning tasks. But he didn't take it lying down; on one occasion he was reprimanded for alleged insolence towards the white prison officers. In prison, Garvey's health deteriorated; he became increasingly ill with chronic bronchitis and lung infections. Two years into his imprisonment he would be hospitalized.

Considering its history, Garvey's treatment in the USA should not be surprising at all.

"The foundation of the United States is structural racism. It is built into all of the institutions. It is built into the culture, and in that sense, we've all absorbed the ideology. We've all absorbed the practices of systemic racism, and that's what I mean when I say we are racist. I don't mean that individuals have conscious awareness of anti-Blackness, or that they intentionally seek to hurt people based on race. That's not what I'm referring to when I make a claim like all white people are racist. What I mean is that all white people have absorbed racist ideology, and it shapes the way we see the world and the way we see ourselves in the world, and it comes out in the policies and practices that we make and that we set up." [Source: The New Yorker Conversation: Robin DiAngelo on 'Nice Racism,' July 14, 2021]

Should Garvey Be Exonerated?

Many historians and legal scholars have doubted the legality of Garvey's conviction. Over the years, they have been calls for Marcus Garvey to be exonerated for his unjust persecution in the USA. This has generated a lot of debate, with arguments being posited 'for' and 'against' Garvey's exoneration.

The arguments 'for' exonerating Garvey may be summarised as "A great wrong and horrible injustice were perpetrated against him with malice aforethought and therefore must be erased." And the arguments 'against' exoneration may be summarised as: "Exoneration will not erase that crime against Garvey and his conviction should stand to remind us of the sacrifice he made."

The advocacy for Garvey's exoneration continues: "Julius Garvey, Marcus Garvey's youngest son, led an exoneration campaign/petition drive during the course of Barack Obama's second term. There was overwhelming support for the petition, but disappointingly Obama did not seem to show any apparent interest in considering it. Then, in 2016, when it was assumed that Hilary Clinton would win the presidential race against Donald Trump, there was an effort to resurrect the petition drive. Now, with Joe Biden in office, it has been deemed another appropriate time to push for the exoneration and the requisite expungement of his criminal record. This particular drive is being spearheaded locally by the Marcus Garvey Institute (led by Julius Garvey) and the P.J. Patterson Centre for Africa-Caribbean Advocacy, as well as the Centre for Reparation Research, and importantly has the blessing of the National Council on Reparation and the Jamaican Government. It must be emphasised that it is an exoneration that is being called for, and not a presidential pardon, on the basis that Marcus Garvey was not guilty of a crime in the first place, and that he was unjustly criminalised." [Source: Dr. Michael Barnett, 'Unfettering Marcus Garvey, Part 2, The Jamaica Observer, February 21, 2022]

Justin Hansford in his book **'Jailing a Rainbow: The Marcus Garvey Case,'** dissected the case that was made out against Garvey by the US Government, and laid bare the terrible miscarriage of justice perpetrated against Garvey.

In two articles published in The Jamaica Observer on February 20 & 22, 2022, Dr. Michael Barnett of the University of the West Indies, summarised the blatant legal and other aberrations, as catalogued by Justin Hansford, which characterised Garvey's trial:

> "One of the leading experts on the court case/trial is Justin Hansford, a graduate of Georgetown University Center and is presently a professor of law at Howard University. According to an early article written on the trial (2011, Liberty Hall Street Journal) Justin is able to make the case by analysing the circumstances surrounding the trial and making key legal insights that Marcus Garvey was wrongly convicted, and has thus in effect proved to be a strong proponent in the drive for Marcus Garvey's posthumous exoneration.
>
> According to Justin Hansford, it was in February 1922 that Marcus Garvey, as well as Orlando Thompson, then vice-president of the Black Star Line Steamship Corporation; George Tobias, the treasurer; and Ellie Garcia, the secretary, were all indicted for mail fraud. Immediately after the indictment, the Government seized all the books and records of both Garvey's UNIA and the Black Star Line Steamship Company.
>
> The trial did not begin until over a year later in May 1923. Garvey notably dismisses his attorneys when they try to enter a plea of guilty. Feeling that these attorneys were setting him up for a legal trap, and intent on professing his innocence, Garvey decided to defend himself. Leaning on the legal knowledge that he was able to amass from attending some law lectures at Birbeck

College, University of London, when he was in England in 1912, Garvey does the best that he can to defend himself during the trial.

Hansford points out that, from the outset of the trial, the courtroom atmosphere was permeated with hostility and scorn. Notably, the trial judge, Julian Mack, jokingly remarked several times that he had to conduct a regular law school for Garvey's benefit, displaying a certain amount of contempt for Garvey.

Notably, at the end of the trial, Garvey is the only defendant who is convicted, the other three officers of the Black Star Line Steamship Company, were found innocent on all counts. Garvey was ultimately found guilty on just one count (out of a total of 13 initial counts) of using the mail to defraud. For this, he was given the maximum penalty under the law, five years imprisonment and a US$1,000 fine, which was a considerable amount of money at that time.

Hansford argues that for one thing, Judge Mack should have recused himself from the case because of an obvious bias — that of being a member of the National Association for the Advancement of Coloured People (NAACP), which was a rival organisation to Garvey's and his consistent financial contributions to it.

The second legal issue that Hansford raises is that of Judge Mack erring in not addressing perjured testimony by the key prosecution witness, Schuyler Cargill. The sole count on which the Government convicted Garvey rested on the allegation that Garvey caused to be mailed a letter soliciting Benny Dancy's purchase of Black Star Line Steamship Company shares when the organisation was near insolvency, depended heavily on Cargill's testimony, as he was the 19-year office boy/Black Star Line Steamship Company employee, who had allegedly mailed the letter soliciting Dancy's purchase.

Cargill was the only Black Star Line Steamship Company employee who testified that he was an actual participant in the sending of false advertisements by US mail. But apparently in his cross-examination, he admitted that the prosecutor (Maxwell Mattock) had told him to lie on the stand. According to Hansford, specifically, Mattock instructed Cargill to say that he had worked for the Black Star Line Steamship Company in 1919 and 1920.

However, when cross-examined Cargill revealed that he did not even know who was the mailing supervisor at those times, and reluctantly admitted that it was the prosecutor who advised him to mention those dates.

Hansford points out that in 1923, at the time of Garvey's trial, the perjury rule authorised courts to grant a new trial, if one could prove that a witness willfully and deliberately had testified falsely. It follows then that as Cargill had willfully and deliberately testified falsely (at least to the years that he had worked for the Black Star Line Steamship Company), and because Judge Julian Mack had failed to strike this testimony and instruct the jury to disregard it, or even offered to grant a new trial, the district court's conviction of Garvey could have been legally expunged according to the perjury rules in existence at the time. Unfortunately, Garvey as a layman representing himself was most likely not aware of this, otherwise it is almost certain that he would have pushed for a new trial or pushed for the expungement of his conviction.

Of important note is that the only physical evidence that was tendered that ultimately led to Garvey's conviction on the charge of mail fraud was an empty envelope addressed to Benny Dancy and stamped with the Black Star Line Steamship Company seal on the back — but with no accompanying letter or company-related materials whatsoever. In fact, none of the purported contents that were purported to have been mailed to Dancy on the instruction of Garvey were ever furnished before, during, or after the trial. Where, then, was the tangible proof that the envelope that was allegedly mailed from the BSL office contained materials for the express purpose of soliciting funds from Benny Dancy? This is just one of the questions that reverberate not only within my head but also in the heads of many who have scrutinised Garvey's trial.

In an article titled **'Time has come for Garvey's posthumous exoneration'** that was published in The Sunday Gleaner on January 16, 2022, former Jamaican Prime Minister Percival James 'P.J.' Patterson – now a Statesman in Residence at the P. J. Patterson Centre for Africa-Caribbean Advocacy at The University of the West

Indies that he established on June 26, 2020 - expressed support for Garvey's exoneration:

"As we join in the observation of Martin Luther King Day, on Monday, January 17, the P. J. Patterson Centre for Africa Caribbean Advocacy adds its voice to the call once again for the posthumous exoneration of the Right Excellent Marcus Garvey. No one has devoted more of his life to the fight for freedom from the scourge of racism or written with greater clarity to inspire those who seek no more than the right for the dignity of each and every human being, despite the colour of one's skin, than the Rt. Excellent Marcus Mosiah Garvey. Martin Luther eloquently expressed the significance of Marcus Garvey when he stated, "Marcus Garvey was the first man of colour in the history of the United States to lead and develop a mass movement. He was the first man, on a mass scale, and level, to give millions of Negroes a sense of dignity and destiny, and make the Negro feel that he was somebody .... He gave to the millions of Negroes in the United States a sense of personhood, a sense of manhood and a sense of somebodiness ... that God's black children are just as significant as His white children." The year 2022 marks 100 years since Marcus Garvey was unjustly charged for mail fraud and was later imprisoned and deported from the United States in 1927. The criminal charge of using the mail to defraud was made against four officers of the Universal Negro Improvement Association (UNIA), one of whom had lied about the purchase of a ship when negotiations had broken down. It was in promoting shares for one of the Black Star Line ships, the purchase of which had not yet been finalized, that, in 1922, Garvey alone was charged with mail fraud. He was sentenced to five years in prison in 1925. His sentence was commuted by President Calvin Coolidge in 1927, on the advice of Attorney General John Sargent who was critical of J. Edgar Hoover's investigative tactics, but the goal of getting Marcus Garvey out of the United States was achieved. Legal scholars have analysed the trial and demonstrated the abuse of justice in this case by the judge who was known to be deeply hostile to Garvey; and the principal witness, a 19-year-old temporary employee who committed perjury. The trial by an all-white jury reflected the systemic racial bias of the justice system and followed a pattern of punitive measures against Marcus Garvey. Garvey was the target of an assassination attempt in 1919. In 1921, before his return to the United States, after a successful trip throughout Central America and the Caribbean on a Black Star Line ship, he was denied a visa to re-enter the US. The visa was granted only after protests were made. J. Edgar Hoover employed black secret service agents to build a case to expel Garvey from the United States. A case was made against Garvey for breaking an immorality statute while travelling with his secretary Amy Jacques, to whom he was not yet married. He was also charged, unsuccessfully, with income tax violation. Marcus Garvey was a Jamaica-born activist who had a decisive impact on the struggle for racial equality and civil rights in the United States and Europe, and decolonisation in Africa, Latin America, and the Caribbean. It is for this reason that the Jamaican government chose him as the country's National Hero in 1969. Garvey's work during the first four decades of the 20th century had a global impact. Kwame Nkrumah of Ghana, subsequent leaders of independent African countries and international statesmen of renown, have attested to the value of his imprint on their intellectual emancipation from the perils of mental slavery and social inequity. On the cusp of Black History Month this February, we must not fail to recognise how Garvey kindled the candle of pride in our social heritage. It can be traced to the Convention on the Universal Negro Improvement Association and African Communities League he organised in Madison Square Garden in 1920. Garvey brought together delegates from many parts of the world and they developed the Declaration of Rights of the Negro Peoples, a pioneering document for racial justice and human rights. The organisation sunk roots in 38 states and garnered the support of the black population, especially in the southern states. Garvey's philosophy and teachings continue to inspire in the United States. The red, black, and green flag of the UNIA was to be seen in demonstrations of the Black Lives Matter movement in 2020, particularly after the televised murder of George Floyd. The impact of the Black Lives Matter movement and the mobilisation which followed played an important part in the election of President Joe Biden and Vice President Kamala Harris, who condemned the murder of George Floyd and systemic racism. The

Centre confidently expects that our heads of government will, as they readily did on the previous appeal, reiterate their endorsement for the posthumous exoneration of the Right Excellent Marcus Garvey in a letter now addressed directly to President Joseph Biden. The Centre joins in the global campaign to reverse the travesty of justice against a giant whose only crime was to give legendary leadership in the struggle against racial and economic injustice. Let our voices be heard loud and strong on the continent, across the Caribbean Sea, and throughout our diaspora, as one in the plea, for the tenets of justice demand it."

Patterson – Statesman-in-residence and director of the P.J. Patterson Centre for Africa-Caribbean Advocacy at the UWI - had more to say on the exoneration of Marcus Garvey. Much more. On February 16, 2022, he delivered a speech at the UWI's Vice Chancellor's Forum titled 'Exonerate Marcus Garvey.' The excerpt below from Patterson's speech was published in The Sunday Gleaner on February 27, 2022:

"When Marcus Mosiah Garvey migrated to the United States, the Confederacy revolt and the Civil War had ended; but the stains of slavery and racism had not been erased. Their deleterious effects in the quest for full freedom and equal rights were evident everywhere. Marcus Garvey's outright condemnation of innumerable instances of racial oppression, lynching, and burning as "crimes against the laws of humanity, and ... against the God of all mankind" was gospel to the ears of 370,000 African-Americans who had fought against Nazism and Fascism in Europe. Despite their courage, these men and women returned home to face many instances of violence and racism, e.g. the riots of East St Louis and Chicago in 1919 and the destruction of the black flourishing towns of Rosewood and Tulsa. As his denunciation of these evils intensified, Garvey raised funds to assist the victims of racial violence, publishing the weekly Negro World Newspaper and launching The African-

Communities' League as the business arm of the Universal Negro Improvement Association (UNIA). White supremacists, however, found his message and power of mobilisation repugnant to their designs. To the American establishment, Garvey was regarded as a threat to the very foundation on which their architecture of governance and the practice of racial superiority had been built. Garvey's oratorical skills, his passion for racial justice, his recruitment of black men and women to secure jobs in his Negro Factories Corporation, and the enrolment of six million people worldwide as members of the UNIA were intolerable for white supremacists, and several agencies of the US Federal Government. The Federal Bureau of Investigation feared his power and wanted his expulsion from the USA. Determined to stop Garvey, the powerful J. Edgar Hoover engaged black spies to infiltrate the UNIA and carry out extensive surveillance into Garvey, which was among the most aggressive in his infamous programmes against leaders of the civil rights movement. After many failed attempts to find criminal wrongdoing and reasons to deport Garvey as an undesirable alien, J. Edgar Hoover indicted Garvey and three directors on charges of "conspiracy to use the mail in furtherance of a scheme to defraud". The entire trial process was replete with glaring instances of prosecutorial misconduct, including State attorneys suborning evidence from key witnesses. To this end, in his recommendation for clemency to President Calvin Coolidge, three years after Garvey's wrongful imprisonment, Attorney General Sargent subsequently opined: "the facts as reported to the Department are severely stated and susceptible of modification and explanation". I assert that there was never any evidence against him; and therefore, Garvey had no case to answer. The judge for Garvey's trial should have recused himself. His racist views were notorious, and he falsely denied being a member of a group known to be bitterly opposed to Garvey's mission and the teachings of the UNIA. The judge's frequent outbursts and biased rulings violated every tenet of judicial conduct in the jurisprudence of the common law. He was the 'Persecutor in Chief', and the 12 white jurors acted in compliance with his orders to return a verdict, which was an egregious miscarriage of justice. The principal witness against Garvey was a 19-year-old who was coached by the prosecutors to lie. He admittedly proceeded to commit perjury in his testimony. These travesties should be sufficient to persuade President Biden to order his Justice Department, with the appropriate engagement of the US attorney for the Southern District, to obtain the only legal remedy – exoneration – and clear the blot against Garvey's good name. Egregious though these errors in the proceedings were, there is yet one irrefutable ground why the conviction cannot stand. Perry Mason would have called it 'The Case of the Empty Envelope'. In order to prove that Garvey was guilty of mail fraud, the State had to establish, inter alia, that mail was sent through the postal service from the Southern District of New York by Garvey, or on his orders, soliciting shares in a company which was defunct or bankrupt. But, firstly, the only exhibit offered in support of the mailing of the letter under the indictment count is the front and back of an envelope, marked Black Star Line. The prosecuting attorney, in presenting the letter, simply stated: "I offer the envelope in evidence on the ground it bears on the back a stamp, 'Black Star Line'. It is a reasonable assumption that the envelope contained matter from the Black Star Line". I submit that there is no basis in law to admit the exhibit and to draw any inference as to what were its content. In allowing this evidence, the judge made a serious error of law. Additionally, the witness, Dancy, did not testify that he received the envelope, but that he recognised the envelope, stating further that he could not remember what was in it. No secondary evidence could be adduced with regards to its contents. So how could any judge allow a jury to guess or speculate what its contents might have been? The only evidence submitted was an empty envelope. Where is the proof that it was mailed, or caused to be mailed by Marcus Garvey? What was in the envelope? How can it be assumed that it contained fraudulent matter? How can the jury be asked to speculate on the contents of this empty envelope? There is not a scintilla of evidence that Garvey placed, or caused to be placed in the mail, the circular or letter described or referred to in this count of the indictment. How can any conviction be based on an empty envelope where its contents cannot be assumed or ascertained? The judge must have been unaware of two simple legal tenets or chosen to discard them: a) He who asserts must prove; b) It is for the State to prove beyond reasonable doubt the contents of the envelope and that they were inculpatory. For these compelling reasons, it is clear that Marcus Garvey was not guilty of any offence of moral turpitude. In light of this grave miscarriage of justice against one of the most significant human rights defenders in history, it is my view that the petition for Garvey's posthumous exoneration should not be confined to persons of African ancestry. The appeal for the exoneration of Marcus Garvey deserves the support of every man and woman, on every continent and island who loves justice and equality under the law. It is more than 100 years ago since this manifest act of injustice was perpetrated on Marcus Mosiah Garvey, a man whose only conviction was to Get Up, Stand Up, Stand Up for our Rights."

In addition, on February 3, 2022, the Caribbean Media Corporation reported that St. Vincent Prime Minister Dr. Ralph Gonsalves is urging Caribbean Community (CARICOM) countries and the rest of the world to put pressure on United States President, Joseph Biden, to exonerate Jamaican National Hero Marcus Mosiah Garvey for his "unjust, flawed and dubious" conviction for mail fraud almost a century ago:

> "In a memorandum to the people, mass organizations and civil society in the Caribbean, Africa, the United States and the world, Gonsalves called on them to support the campaign to get the late Black Nationalist and Pan-Africanist exonerated, which was initiated by the PJ Patterson Centre for Africa-Caribbean Advocacy at the University of the West Indies, Mona, Jamaica. Specifically, he encouraged them to sign the online petition that was opened on February 1 and will remain so until February 28, the duration of Black History Month. "The petition will be sent to President Joseph Biden of the USA for his action. Governments are urged to encourage their nationals to sign.... Assuming that President Biden accedes to this just and fair petition, he may find it of great convenience and moment to announce the exoneration of Marcus Garvey at the next Summit of the Americas to be held in June 2022 in California, USA," the Vincentian leader said. Gonsalves urged Heads of State and governments of countries, especially from the Caribbean Community and Africa, to send letters to President Biden. He said leaders of the Organisation of Eastern Caribbean States (OECS) last month agreed to send a joint letter or individual letters, and the CARICOM Secretary-General was also actively working on that. Prime Minister Gonsalves said that these actions are especially important because there have been concerted attempts, in the United States and some other western countries, to roll back the hard-won rights of people of African descent and other historically marginalized groups."

Additionally, on February 19, 2022, The Gleaner, in an editorial, **'Doing Right by Garvey'**, said:

> "In retrospect, this newspaper was wrong in 2016 when it supported an online petition for the then United States (US) President Barack Obama to pardon Marcus Garvey and

expressed our deep disappointment that the document fell woefully short of the 100,000 signatures required to force Mr. Obama to give the matter serious thought. We felt, at the time, that, if Garvey's ancestors were in support of the effort, then it deserved our backing. It is to Mr. Obama's discredit that he, America's first black president, did nothing, and said less, about the petition. P. J. Patterson, and the people behind the current petition, is right. If the US is to do anything about Garvey's conviction and jailing, it must be total exoneration. From this newspaper's perspective, this complete and unfettered absolution of Marcus Garvey wouldn't primarily be about cleaning his record, or to establish that he wasn't a crook and charlatan. Rather, it is about America's acknowledgement of this particularly pernicious and shameful episode in its history and part of its continued reckoning with the question of race in the US. A country telling the truth to itself. In that sense, there is interconnectedness between the exoneration of Marcus Garvey and the unsettled business of the Black Lives Matter movement. Outside of this admittedly important context, Mr. Garvey, a Jamaican national hero, requires no exoneration. He has long since been absolved by history – and global respect. Marcus Garvey was born in Jamaica in 1887, a mere 49 years after the end of slavery on the island. He, however, couldn't be contained by any system or philosophy that held that Africans and people of African descent were somehow intellectually inferior, or less than others. Indeed, by the 1920s, Marcus Garvey was not only espousing radical new thoughts about the place of black people in the world but had built a global organisation of millions of people in support of Back-to-Africa ideas. Marcus Garvey gave black people assuredness about their capacities, without the need for shorting-up or mentorship by other groups. In that sense, he was the forerunner to, and inspiration for, the leaders of the anti-colonial and imperial struggles in Africa and the Caribbean, many of whom acknowledged his influence. But a Black man of Garvey's intellect, charisma and following was, for the establishment, dangerous in early 20th century America. It is not surprising that there was a concerted effort to cut him down – almost by any means possible. Legal and other scholars, as Mr. Patterson pointed out this week, long ago concluded that Garvey's conviction for mail fraud in 1923 was on trumped-up charges. And the trial deliberately skewed to a guilty verdict. Unlike five years ago when the aim of the 100,000 signatures was to get President Obama to consider a pardon for Garvey, this request is for exoneration. "Exoneration is for the innocent, those who should have been acquitted at trial because there was no wrongdoing," Mr. Patterson explained. Even as we hope that the requisite numbers of signatures are collected and President Joe Biden ultimately does right by history, Jamaica, too, has unfinished business with respect to Garvey and others of its heroes. In 2016, in the aftermath of the failure to gather signatures in support of the Garvey pardon, the Holness administration promised legislation to erase and, ultimately, absolve the country's "freedom fighters" of supposed crimes. In 1929, Garvey was criminally convicted in Jamaica for contempt of court. In 1865, Paul Bogle and George William Gordon, were hanged by Governor Eyre for the 1865 Morant Bay Rebellion in St Thomas, in eastern Jamaica. Thirty-three years earlier, in the west, in Montego Bay, Sam Sharpe was hanged in the town square as the leader of a slave uprising. We wonder if the Government still intends to pass that law. The legislation, as would be America's acceptance of its wrong against Garvey, would be a powerful intervention in the argument for reparatory justice for the victims of slavery."

Furthermore, Stephen Vasciannie (Rhodes Scholar and Professor of International Law at The University of the West Indies) in the essay 'Race and Jamaican Society: Three Propositions' in his 2020 book **'Essays on**

Caribbean Law and Policy' that was published by the University of Technology, Jamaica Press, dilated on the question of exoneration of Marcus Garvey. Said Professor Vasciannie:

"On occasion, the Jamaican Government has considered whether to seek a pardon for Garvey in relation to his conviction, and on the visit of President Barack Obama to Jamaica in April 2014, Prime Minister Simpson Miller formally raised the question of exoneration with the American authorities. The Jamaican Government's interest in this matter is reinforced by some members of the United States Congress and by efforts among private groups – including the UNIA – which hold Garvey in special regard. The main argument for exoneration turns on Garvey's international impact, the value of his philosophy of racial equality, and the legacy of his political, economic and social activism on behalf of "Africans at home and abroad." The name of such a leader, a Jamaican National Hero, should not be tarnished by a conviction for fraud, so the argument runs. This argument is reinforced by the view that Garvey's conviction was falsely obtained: it is noted, in particular, that the conviction was secured on the basis of "trumped up" charges concocted by the agents of the American power structure, anxious to undermine the political prowess of "the most famous black man . . . in the world." These two arguments, built, respectively, on Garvey's standing and on perceptions of systemic persecution against Garvey, may be presented independently or cumulatively to promote full exoneration. In the discourse concerning Garvey's exoneration, certain political and legal considerations have been raised from time to time. For example, in 2011, the Obama Administration turned down a pardon request for Garvey made by a private citizen. It is reported that the White House Pardon Attorney rejected the request on the basis that, as a general rule, the United States Government does not grant pardons posthumously. In support of this approach, the Pardon Office indicated that, in the context of limited resources, the time and effort of the Office would be better spent working on applications for living persons.195 The Office of the Pardon Attorney has also noted that posthumous pardons would, generally speaking, give rise to problems of proof, for the evidence on which a particular conviction is based may, with the passage of time, become very difficult and time-consuming to assess. The Office of the Pardon Attorney has also argued that the criteria for granting pardons may be more readily applicable to living persons, and that the grant of posthumous pardons would open the door to too many difficult cases at a time when the system of granting pardons for living persons is already overburdened. The Office also maintains that living persons "can truly benefit from a grant of clemency", in contrast, presumably, to persons who have passed away.196 In the case of an application on behalf of Marcus Garvey, these arguments are not convincing. Garvey's influence throughout the world, including his status as a forerunner of the modern American civil rights movement, should entitle him to a relaxation of the general rule against posthumous pardons; opening up a reconsideration of his case would not mean that all applications for posthumous pardons need to be taken. Added to this, it should be noted that the general rule against granting posthumous pardons is not constitutionally mandated;197 nor does it take into account the possibility that Garvey's application for a pardon was turned down on the basis of racial considerations. Also, on the question of old evidence, the transcript of the case against Marcus Garvey remains available: it is, therefore, open to lawyers from the Department of Justice to undertake an assessment of the case as actually brought against Garvey up to 1925. Two additional political considerations in the exoneration debate may be mentioned at this juncture. The first concerns challenges faced by Garvey in the course of his political activism in the United States. Especially in the decade of the 1920s, Garvey became a relentless opponent of W.E.B. DuBois and other established black American leaders, with fiery language crossing the ideological and strategic borders of the UNIA, on one side, and the National Association for the Advancement of Coloured People, on the other. The main differences between Garvey and other black leaders turned on considerations such as self-determination versus integration for black people, class alliances versus racial unity in promoting the advancement of the poor, the role of self-reliance in racial advancement, and the importance of Africa to the lives of persons in the black diaspora. At the personal level, there was also a stream of criticism of Garvey, suggesting that he lacked competence in financial matters, promoted escapism among supporters, presented unjustifiable perspectives on "racial purity", and was willing to compromise with white supremacists. Some critics also alleged that the UNIA was not averse to relying on demagoguery and intimidation for success. In contrast, Garvey accused DuBois and others of constructing the NAACP for the benefit of a minority of light-skinned African-Americans, challenged their support for assimilation among whites, and suggested that they were naïve in their assessment of white supremacists. Thus, there was undoubted bitterness between Garvey and some of his opponents. What bearing should this have on the exoneration effort? In my view, the history of antagonism should be acknowledged, but it should not bar exoneration. The exoneration effort, it is suggested, should turn on the importance of Garvey to the world today, his powerful legacy and on what his ideas of self-reliance and enterprise have meant to persons in many societies. It should also turn on the possibility that the original conviction was unsound. Against this background, it should matter little in the long run that Garvey had ideological, strategic and personal differences with various African-American leaders. Secondly, it is fair to suggest that staunch supporters of Marcus Garvey may hold divergent opinions on the value and significance of exoneration by the United States Government. The discussion in the present section has highlighted the perspective of those who would wish to have Garvey exonerated through formal channels. But, as a counterview, it may be argued that Garvey's standing is already entrenched within the hearts and minds of many persons across the world. This standing will be unaffected by removal of a conviction and sentence imposed ninety years ago. And the argument continues: why should Garvey's supporters want exoneration from a power structure that continues to oppress persons on the basis of race and colour? Why should Garvey, even to this day, need validation from "Babylon"? On this view, exoneration may paradoxically have the effect of lending credibility to an unfair and unjust political order."

Many Jamaicans have argued that before Jamaica petitions the USA to exonerate Garvey, the country must first exonerate him at home! In the second of a two-part article that he published in The Jamaica Observer, Dr. Michael Barnett of the University of the West Indies addressed the question of Garvey's exoneration in Jamaica, in these terms:

"So far as Garvey's past convictions in Jamaica are concerned, he was jailed twice in Jamaica. These were expunged a few years back. In fact, it was in 2018 that the Government passed the National Heroes and Other Freedom Fighters (Absolution from Criminal Liability in Respect of Specified Events) Act, 2018. What this does in effect is to acknowledge that, in the local context, our national heroes, including Marcus Garvey and other freedom fighters, in their fight for equality and self-determination, resisted unjust laws and oppression and for those acts were convicted. The Act essentially absolves them of all criminal liability in recognition of their sacrifice and efforts to win the freedoms we now enjoy in our nation. This move was partly inspired by a series of consultations with the National Council on Reparation, of which I am a part, on the matter of the then existing criminal records of Marcus Garvey and other national heroes, such as Paul Bogle, Sam Sharpe, and George William Gordon, a few months after the Jamaica Labour Party

Administration came back into power on the back of the March 2016 elections." [Source: Michael Barnett, The Jamaica Observer, February 2022]

Other Notable Black Martyrs

History has many examples of Black People being punished for their work that questions and threatens the status quo that is embroidered with injustice and wickedness. Marcus Garvey was not different in this regard.

I will cite below **Sam Sharpe, Paul Bogle, Claudius Henry, Nelson Mandela, Steve Biko, Dr. Walter Rodney, Patrice Lumumba, Brian Flores,** and **Colin Kaepernick** as examples of other Blacks – martyrs - from whom the 'empire' exacted a high price.

Sam Sharpe and Paul Bogle, protesting injustice, were hanged in Jamaica by, and in the name of, the British Monarchy.

Sam Sharpe: Samuel Sharpe, one of Jamaica's seven National Heroes, was born into enslavement and was murdered by hanging, by the cruel colonial authorities in the parish of St. James, in 1832; Sharpe declared that he would "Rather die on yonder gallows than live in slavery!"

As noted by Fred W. Kennedy, "In December 1831, Jamaica underwent the largest, most significant slave rebellion in its history. The leader of this revolt was Samuel Sharpe. Sharpe was executed at high noon on a bright, sunny day, the 23rd of May, 1832. He was the last of over 300 rebels [I say freedom fighters!] to be hanged." [Source: 'A Narrative of the Life and Adventures of Samuel Sharpe, A West Indian Slave Written by Himself, 1832']

Here is the account of Sam Sharpe's actual execution (from the eyewitness account of Reverend Henry Belby, a Methodist Minister): "The crowds gathered along the street of the marketplace in Montego Bay close to where Sam was to be executed. People leaned out of the upper windows and crowded the doorways of the houses which lined his way to the gallows. He set out for his last walk under the guard of the English Regiment, commanded by Lieutenant Crawford. His hands were tied behind his back and he walked erect, holding his head high and looking about the crowd as if he were searching for familiar faces. When he saw those he recognized, he bowed his head in recognition. His eyes were peaceful and calm. He looked handsome in his white suit which the women of the Sharpe household had sewn for him. It gleamed in the midday sun. His face was bright as if he had achieved some glorious victory."

Belby continued: "The guard started the brisk march from the gaol house but Sam requested of the commanding officer that he slow down his pace so that he might walk his last stretch with as much dignity as possible. When he came to the spot where the Sharpe family was standing, he paused, making the guard stop in his tracks. He looked at his owners [owners!] and bowed his last farewell. As Sam approached the gallows, the Anglican rector, Reverend Mr. McIntyre, greeted him. The rector asked him if he wished to pray. Sam knelt at the foot of the gallows and prayed to the Almighty. He praised God and asked for his mercy. He [then] looked up at the gallows and then back to the crowd. He hesitated, then walked quickly and nimbly up the stairs. When he reached the top step, he paused, placing the left foot first upon the scaffold, and pressing it. He then brought the right foot on a line with the left, placing the heels of the feet about twenty inches apart. Before the hangman did his deed, the deputy marshal asked if he had any final words. Sam spoke from atop the platform of the gallows, his voice reaching out to all gathered in the square: "All I wished was to be free. All I wished was to enjoy the liberty which I find in the Bible is the birthright of every man ... I now bid you farewell." In a few moments the executioner had done his work. I could not help feeling deep sorrow and indignation - as I turned from his death-scene, and brushed away the tears which the contemplation of his tragical fate called forth – that such a man as Samuel Sharpe, who possessed a mind which under proper influence and direction was capable of noble things, should be thus immolated at the polluted shrine of slavery. Samuel Sharpe was the most intelligent and remarkable slave I had ever known. The sun disappeared behind the clouds and a darkness came over the land. Saddened by his loss, we all left the town square, which some likened to Golgotha, the place of a skull." [Source: 'A Narrative of the Life and Adventures of Samuel Sharpe, A West Indian Slave Written by Himself, 1832']

Sam Sharpe's murder was not in vain. By June of the following year, 1833, the British Parliament passed the Act to abolish slavery!

Notwithstanding the dignity with which Sam Sharpe faced his death, I was traumatised by just reading the account above. Like the Reverend Henry Belby, I too was moved to tears. And it is for martyrs like Samuel Sharpe that we will not rest until reparations are paid by the descendants of the criminals who presided over the most heinous crime in the history of the world! Here is a timeline concerning Sam Sharpe:

- 1801 – Born into enslavement
- 1832 – Murdered (hanged) for protesting enslavement
- 1975 – Sam Sharpe Teachers' College established
- 1976 – Sam Sharpe Square named in Montego Bay, St. James
- 1982 – Sam Sharpe named a National Hero of Jamaica

Paul Bogle: "Paul Bogle led the last large-scale armed Jamaican rebellion for voting rights and an end to legal discrimination and economic oppression against African Jamaicans. Because of his efforts, Bogle was recognized as a national hero in Jamaica in 1969. Paul Bogle was born free to Cecelia Bogle, a free woman, and an unknown father in the St. Thomas parish in 1822. Bogle's mother soon died and he was raised by his grandmother. As an adult, Bogle owned a home in Stony Gut and had another house in Spring Garden as well as a 500-acre farm at Dunrobin making him one of the few African Jamaicans prosperous enough to pay the fee to vote. In 1845, for example, there were only 104 voters in St. Thomas parish which had an adult population of at least 3,300.

Bogle became a supporter of George William Gordon, an Afro-Jamaican politician, fellow landowner, and Baptist. In 1854 Gordon made the 32-year-old Bogle a deacon. Bogle, in turn, built a chapel in Stony Gut which held religious and political meetings.

Officially Jamaican slavery ended in 1833 after the Sam Sharpe Rebellion a year earlier. Yet from 1834 to 1838 former slaves served post-servitude "apprenticeships" to their former owners. They were also subject to a judicial system controlled by the Colonial government primarily for the benefit of the former slaveholders. They endured unemployment and taxes but low wages. In 1865, Gordon chose Bogle to lead a delegation to present their complaints to British Colonial governor, Edward John Eyre.

In August of that year, Paul Bogle led a 50-mile march of small farmers and former slaves (enslaved) to Spanish Town (the capital at the time) to meet with Governor Eyre to discuss their political grievances. They were denied an audience with the governor.

Two months after that attempted meeting, the Morant Bay Rebellion started, sparked by the arrest of a supporter of Bogle for protesting the conviction of another black Jamaican for trespassing on a long-abandoned plantation. Bogle and his supporters attended the trespassing trial in Spanish Town on October 7. Shortly afterward when colonial officials attempted to arrest the Bogle supporter who had also attended the trial, he was immediately freed by Bogle's other supporters. They then forced Colonial police to release the man convicted of trespassing. Returning to Stony Gut, Bogle and his supporters learned that warrants had been issued for the arrest of 28 men for rioting in Spanish Town. When the Colonial police attempted to arrest Paul Bogle, his followers fought them off.

On October 11, 1865, Bogle and his brother Moses led a protest march of nearly 300 people from Stony Gut to Morant Bay. They were confronted this time by the colonial militia who opened fire on them, killing seven of the protesters. The protesters retaliated by killing a parish official, Baron von Ketelhodt, and fifteen militia members. They then set 51 prisoners free.

Colonial soldiers were sent to Morant Bay to crush the rebellion. Nearly 500 people were killed and a greater number were flogged before "order" was restored. Stony Gut, considered the stronghold of the rebels, was destroyed. Paul and Moses Bogle were captured and hanged on October 24, 1865, at the Morant Bay Court House a day after George William Gordon, who did not participate in the rebellion, was executed. In January 1866, a Royal Commission was sent from London to investigate the Rebellion. Following their investigation, then Governor Eyre was fired as the Governor of Jamaica and recalled to England where he was charged, tried, but not convicted of murder. Jamaica became a Crown Colony governed directly from England as a result of the rebellion." [Sources: Wooten, A. (2013, October 13). Paul Bogle (1822-1865), BlackPast.dot.com; Jamaica Information Service]

Claudius Henry: The Reverend Claudius Henry featured in Jamaica's first treason/felony trial.

"It was the prosecution's case that: Henry and his followers and other persons unknown on December 5, 1959, encompassed, devised, and intended to excite insurrection against the government of this island. The defendants preached a doctrine calculated to intimidate and overawe the government and they sought to do this by overt acts as set out:

- One, that Claudius Henry and 15 of his followers, contrary to Section 3 of the Treason Felony Law, Chapter 390, with other persons unknown as aforesaid did maliciously and advisedly meet, propose, treat, consult, conspire, and agree by themselves with force to subvert, overawe and intimidate the Government of Jamaica;

- Two, that the defendants and other persons unknown as aforesaid did bring or cause to be brought to and have at 78 Rosalie Avenue, a quantity of explosives, firearms and lethal weapons with the intent to use the same in the accomplishment of their said object of subverting, overawing and intimidating the Government of Jamaica;
- Three, that they with other persons unknown, as aforesaid, did cause to be printed and written a document purporting to elicit the aid and advice of a foreign country to overthrow the government of Jamaica;
- Four, that the defendants and other persons unknown as aforesaid, in breach of the Treason Felony Law section 4, Chapter 390, did cause to be written and printed a document calculated to stir up and cause an insurrection in Jamaica with the intention to subvert, overawe and intimidate the Government of Jamaica."

The prosecution relied on several documents exhibited in court as well as evidence from witnesses. Among the documents were one headed: "Standing in the Gap" and another setting up what was called a "Council of Righteous Government". Also, there was the letter written to the Commissioner of Police and members of the government stating: "I may be forced to invade the church." These, the prosecution referred to as publications of overt acts and took note of the cult's reference to Castro as "Fidelissimo Castro".

The defence claimed that 78 Rosalie Avenue was a citadel just like the Salvation Army and referred the court to Psalm 149 V.6 which reads: "Let the high praises of God be in their mouth, and a two-edged sword in their hand;" to which the prosecution responded that the defence should have gone on to verse 7 which reads as follows: " Let the double-edged sword bring vengeance upon them and bring death."

The defence also claimed that some of the weapons found in their possession were used for fishing, and the others were for worship and to be shipped to Africa when the time came. Each accused denied having any intention to overthrow the Government of Jamaica.

Claudius Henry did admit that two of the documents were inflammatory.

At the end of a 19-day trial, the jury retired for 68 minutes and returned a unanimous verdict of guilty against the 57-year-old Rev. Henry, his wife, and twelve of his followers on all three counts of the indictment.

Justice Herbert Duffus before passing sentence noted: "This is the first trial of its kind as far as I know of in the history of this island." He mentioned that from as far back as 1935 he had come in contact with the Rastafarian movement, through a man named Leonard Howell, whom he said, had assumed exactly the same role - as a self-appointed prophet - as Henry was now assuming, to take the people of the country back to Africa.

He continued: "It is my view this doctrine has been allowed to spread. It has been allowed to spread and take hold of the poor, illiterate people of Jamaica. It is wicked. A wicked doctrine and the people that prey on the unfortunate, illiterate persons like a number of you persons here, persons with poor education, I can have no sympathy for them whatever."

Before passing the longest sentence on Henry himself — that of 10 years imprisonment at hard labour on each count, the sentences to run concurrently — Justice Duffus told him: "It is clear and clear beyond any doubt that the persons charged attempted to influence the Government of this country, properly constituted, by highly unlawful means. It is also clear and clear beyond any doubt also in my mind, that the chief instigator and promoter is you, Claudius Henry, a man who called himself an appointed prophet of God, a man who threw scorn on all other religions in Jamaica, who heard his counsel say 'Never scorn any man's religion'." [Source: Sybil Hibbert, 'Jamaica's first treason/felony trial featuring the Rev. Claudius Henry', December 10, 2013, The Jamaica Observer]

The question is, is the foregoing an accurate picture of the Rev. Claudius Henry, or is there another side? To ascertain this, I contacted and interviewed individuals associated with the Rev. Claudius Henry. One of the individuals lives at a massive and ambitious compound Henry established at Green Bottom in Palmers Cross, Clarendon, after he was released from prison. The other individual whom I interviewed her mother was a caregiver for the aging Claudius Henry. This latter individual described an old Claudius Henry as a kind, soft-spoken, and humble person who preached peace and love.

People who have visited Henry's inner sanctum have reported seeing the "most exquisitely adorned altar in black and gold and at the top, looking down majestically, was a carving in wood of the Black Jesus. On a pedestal nearby was a similar carving of the Virgin Mary. Black scented candles glowed dimly as we tiptoed to other rooms where I saw breathtaking pieces of sculpture reminiscent of Africa and African culture."

I have visited the compound that Claudius Henry established in Palmers Cross, Clarendon; it comprises a three-storey 'great house' with living quarters plus a huge conference room; there are also smaller dwelling houses for workers; there is also a church (the African Reform Church), a school, and a bakery (that produced bread, bullas, and patties, under the 'Peacemakers' label). The entire compound was powered by a massive generator.

Like Marcus Garvey before him, Claudius Henry had a vision of mental (psychological) liberation and economic empowerment for Africans (Black people) primarily through self-reliance and subversion of the obscene 'Babylon system' in Jamaica run by colonial surrogates that subjugated Black People.

And like Garvey, Claudius Henry paid a high price.

And like Garvey, Claudius Henry's supporters remain steadfast in their loyalty to his philosophy.

Nelson Mandela: Nelson Mandela, his wife Winnie, and others in the African National Congress (ANC), were imprisoned and tortured psychologically and physically by the wicked whites in South Africa for having the temerity and cojones to fight against the cruel system of apartheid (a system of racial segregation that privileged whites).

Of course, through sustained and relentless pressure, including from Jamaican musicians, Mandela was released from prison in 1990 after being incarcerated for 27 years and thereafter was elected the first Black President of South Africa.

In his highly-acclaimed autobiography '**Long Walk to Freedom,**' Mandela detailed the bottomless, unsparing cruelty of colonialism and its spawn, apartheid. He also dilated on his motivation to sacrifice everything in his fight against white domination of his people.

The act of oppressors dictating to the oppressed how to protest oppression is itself oppressive! And offensive. Oppressed people do not get what they do not demand. It is the right of the oppressed to resist their oppression as they see and define it. There are two options: demand change or fight for change!

"I do not deny that I planned sabotage. I did not plan it in a spirit of recklessness nor because I have any love of violence. I planned it because of a calm and sober assessment of the political situation that had arisen after many years of tyranny, exploitation, and oppression of my people by the whites" ~ Nelson Mandela

Mandela, at his trial in 1964 (the "Rivonia Trial'), delivered a three-hour speech and in the final paragraph declared, "I have fought against white domination, and I have fought against black domination. I have cherished the ideal of a democratic and free society in which all persons will live together in harmony and with equal opportunities. It is an ideal which I hope to live for and to see realised. But if it needs be, it is an ideal for which I am prepared to die." Mandela's speech is considered one of the "great speeches of the 20th century," and a key moment in the history of South African democracy!

("Better to die fighting for freedom than to be a prisoner all the days of your life." ~ Bob Marley)

Like Garvey, Mandela has since gained international acclaim for his activism. "Widely regarded as an icon of democracy and social justice, he received more than 250 honours, including the Nobel Peace Prize. He is held in deep respect within South Africa, where he is often referred to by his Thembu clan name, Madiba, and described as the "Father of the Nation". [Source: Wikipedia]

"In 1998 Harvard held a special convocation to award Nelson Mandela an honorary degree. At the time, Harvard had held only two other special convocations, one for George Washington and another for Winston Churchill. Mandela's journey from lawyer to revolutionary to prisoner to president was glorious, and also deeply fraught with international pressure about the terms of what a free South Africa would be. Those pressures are still evident in how unequal South Africa remains, despite the fact that it had the most globally significant late-20th-century freedom movement and has arguably the most progressive constitution in the world. At any rate, what I most remember from that day is Mandela noting that this was only the third such event: "George Washington, Winston Churchill, and an African." That category of distinction, "an African," was heavily weighted. An African, in the history of Western global domination, was a being of general dishonor. But not there. And not in these works of art. Though all specific, they also register as generally and collectively Black, a subversion of general dishonor into collective homage." [Imani Perry, 'The Power of the Black Portrait', Unsettled Territory, The Atlantic, August 5, 2022]

"Despite his seemingly progressive actions," Mr. Mandela wrote, "Mr. de Klerk (South Africa's last President under apartheid) was by no means the great emancipator. He was a gradualist, a careful pragmatist. He did not make any of his reforms with the intention of putting himself out of power. He made them for precisely the opposite reason: to ensure power for the Afrikaner in a new dispensation."

The Economist magazine reported that Robin Renwick, Britain's ambassador to South Africa when Mandela was released, admired Mr. de Klerk "as a clear-sighted, pragmatic and principled person who took his religion seriously," yet noted that "he understood that the status quo could only be maintained by ever-greater violence by the state."

When F.W. de Klerk, 85, died on November 11, 2021, The New Times noted that, "As a new generation of Black South Africans found their voice, Mr. de Klerk's legacy faced increasing criticism. In a final message — a video released by his foundation hours after his death — the former president clarified his stance on apartheid. In particular, Mr. de Klerk spoke to those who he said did not believe his apology for the pain and indignity caused by the racist policies, apologizing once again "without qualification." "Allow me in this last message to share with you the fact that since the early '80s, my views changed completely," the former president said, looking visibly frail, his voice shaking. "It was as if I had a conversion and in my heart of hearts, realized that apartheid was wrong." The rogue waited until he was on his deathbed to apologize.

"A son of the conservative establishment, which created and nurtured the racist, fascist system of Apartheid, Mr. de Klerk evolved to partner with the late, legendary Mr. Nelson Mandela in dismantling that evil system and igniting democracy in South Africa. Younger Jamaicans should appreciate that Apartheid wasn't just about racial separation and discrimination as it is often mistaken to mean. It was, in fact, a system of laws which elevated whites above and separate from all other races — who were also separated — with blacks at the bottom, as menial workers and labourers, 'hewers of wood and drawers of water'. South African whites were comforted by religious affirmation of Apartheid. The largest white establishment church in South Africa, the Dutch

Reformed Church, provided ideological sanction for racial segregation. That view upheld whites as the dominant race as part of a natural order. Under Apartheid, whites who were a small minority relative to the Black and coloured population, owned the bulk of arable land Blacks were officially relegated to so-called homelands, though the need for cheap labour meant they were facilitated in shanty towns close to major cities and industrial centres. Blacks were not allowed to vote in South African parliamentary elections." [Source: The Jamaica Observer, November 12, 2021]. In sum, apartheid was a vile and evil system.

Still thrumming with the ongoingness of the legacy of apartheid, South Africa remains one of the most divided and unequal countries in the world. Structural transformation has not occurred. Let us be clear: The abominable system of white (minority) racial rule in South Africa - apartheid - was the creation of white people. Thousands of Blacks (majority) were killed and dehumanised under the cruel system - a system that made it illegal for people of different races to marry, have sex or even socialize, and that denied Black South Africans the right to own property or to live and work without permission across most of the country.

Steve Biko: Like Marcus Garvey, Steve Biko (1946-1977), South African anti-apartheid activist, believed that Black people needed to be psychologically liberated and empowered and rid themselves of any sense of racial inferiority, an idea he expressed by popularising the slogan **"Black is Beautiful."** This is because, as Biko insightfully noted, "The most potent weapon of the oppressor is the mind of the oppressed." Mental capture! Enslavement of the cognitivesphere! In 1972, Biko founded the Black People's Convention (BPC) to "promote Black consciousness ideas among the wider population."

However, the wicked, racist, white apartheid South African government branded Biko a 'subversive threat' and slapped a banning order on him in 1973, severely restricting his activities. Following his arrest in August 1977, Biko was beaten to death by state security officers. He became a political martyr - more than 20,000 people (about the seating capacity of Madison Square Garden, New York, USA) attended his funeral. To read about the horrible treatment of Biko during his incarceration is to take a trip into the bowels of the dank and dark abyss of barbarity of the 'civilised,' white South African apartheid government.

Walter Rodney: Dr. Walter Rodney was killed in Guyana on June 13, 1980, when a portable two-way radio (a 'walkie-talkie') detonated in his car. The radio was given to him by Mr. Gregory Smith, a member of the Guyanese army who, after the murder, fled to French Guiana, where he eventually died in 2002. Rodney's killing was ruled "death by misadventure" by the Guyanese authorities and the Government record stated that he was unemployed at the time of his death. On June 17, 2021, the Attorney General and Minister of Legal Affairs of Guyana, Anil Nandlall, announced that key details on Dr. Rodney's death certificate would be changed and his grave site made a national monument. Mr. Nandlall, in his statement said the cause of death would be changed to "assassination" and the records would be amended to state that Dr. Rodney was a professor. He also announced that the Government will revive the Walter Rodney Chair at the University of Guyana. Mr. Nandlall, in a statement to the National Assembly, said the actions follow a request by Dr. Rodney's family, his widow, children and brother, to bring a level of closure to his brutal slaying. [Source: The Daily Observer, June 18, 2021]) This development calls to mind this aphorism from Dr. Martin Luther King: "The arc of the moral universe is long, but it bends towards justice."

(By labelling Rodney's death "misadventure," prevented the family from gaining the proceeds of his life insurance policy.)

"Walter Rodney was deemed dangerous because of his work with Rupert Roopnarine and the Working People's Alliance (WPA), which was going to ensure an interethnic alliance, and those politicians who appealed to ethnic proclivities would have a shrinking base. He threatened the appeal to ethnic polarisation." [Source: Professor Jermaine McCalpin (Jersey City University), The Sunday Gleaner, July 11, 2021]

"Rodney was not a typical academic. His concerns were not purely theoretical. He was (the archetype of) an academic activist who was determined to expose and change the legacy of European enslavement of Africans – from Africa to the Caribbean – through political activism and education. Like Marcus Garvey before him, Rodney was stirred into taking action to effect change at the psychological level of Black people and in their material circumstances."

Then Prime Minister of Jamaica Hugh Shearer – a colonial stooge and conscript to maintain the status quo – also banned Walter Rodney from reentering Jamaica, in 1968, after Rodney participated in a Black Writers Conference in Canada. He thought Rodney was expressing "diverse, new, and dangerous opinions."

"A JLP Government at that time, mired in political backwardness, had somehow convinced itself that Guyanese lecturer, historian par excellence, political activist, and author Walter Rodney was a danger to the minds of our people." [Source: Mark Wignall, The Gleaner, June 28, 2020]

In his book, **The Groundings with My Bothers**, which was published the following year, Rodney explained why he was banned: "The Government of Jamaica, which is Garvey's homeland, has seen it fit to ban me, a Guyanese, a Black man, and an African. But this is not very surprising because though the composition of that Government - of its prime minister, the head of state, and several leading personalities - though that composition happens to be predominantly Black, as the brothers at home say, they are all white-hearted." I say 'colonial-hearted' and colonial-minded!

(Sidebar: Dr. Rodney's widow, Dr. Patricia Rodney, wants the Jamaican Government to right the wrong it committed against her husband: "I think the party that forms the government in Jamaica now is the same one that declared him persona non grata. I think that government has a responsibility to do what's just and right. He is not alive, but still, he was declared persona non grata under false premises. I think any decent government would want to correct history - history is about telling the truth." [Source: The Sunday Gleaner, July 11, 2021] In addition, when she delivered the 23rd Walter Rodney Memorial Lecture, hosted by the Institute of Caribbean Studies (ICS), at The UWI in partnership with the CRR, on October 15, 2021, Dr. Patricia Rodney painfully outlined the hardships she and the rest of their family faced after her husband was banned from returning to Jamaica; she is demanding reparations from the Jamaican government).

Professor McCalpin posits that "Rodney was feared by the Jamaican authorities because he was teaching the people about themselves and a positive identification with both Black liberation and Africa. He did not pose a physical threat, but emancipation of the mind was far more powerful for political independence than physical threats."

Walter Rodney was one of the Caribbean's best and brightest. Graduating in 1963 with first-class honours in history from the University of the West Indies, the went on to London University to pursue a PhD in African history, which he completed, at age 24; his dissertation, which he completed in record time, was on the slave trade on the Upper Guinea Coast (which included Senegal, Gambia, Guinea-Bissau, Guinea, Sierra Leone, parts of Mauritania to the north, and Liberia to the south) and was published by Oxford University Press in 1970, and praised for its originality. Rodney's reputation as an activist scholar grew immensely on a global scale, and by the time he returned to Mona as a lecturer, his commitment to the popular struggle for grass-roots justice had matured. Taking African history to the African community in Jamaica, the Caribbean, and the wider Diaspora resulted in a political crisis within the immediate post-colonial Caribbean. [Source: The Gleaner, August 30, 2018]

In Dr. Rodney's highly acclaimed book **'How Europe Underdeveloped Africa,'** he posits that the transatlantic trade in enslaved Africans decimated the labour force of many African societies, as only the fittest and the best persons were enslaved. It is not accidental, then, that large deficits currently exist between countries that were colonized and their former colonial powers of Europe.

What is remarkable is that Africa is still being underdeveloped by European (and other countries). At the TEDxBerlinSalon conference in January 2015, Mallence Bart-Williams delivered what was later described by Sissi Johnson as the "boldest TED Talk." Sissi Johnson stated that "It took my IFA Paris MBA students at least two minutes to recover from her hypnotizing deep voice, regalness, and unapologetic delivery of rather unpopular facts. Why? It forces viewers to see abundance where we have been conditioned to see lack. The class was able to connect to the German-Sierra-Leonean's essence, merely dressed in her actual words. A student from Australia said: "It's almost like we have been collectively lied to. I feel bad because Africa is always presented in a negative light and I too had these preconceived notions of others needing our help which is actually quite egotistical."

Here is what Mallence Bart-Williams said in her bold TED Talk: "Good afternoon, I am Mallence. I come from Sierra-Leone - the richest country in the world, located in the richest continent in the world. Of course, the West needs Africa's resources, most desperately. To power airplanes, cellphones, computers, and engines. And the gold and diamonds of course. A status symbol to determine their powers by decor and to give value to their currencies. One thing that keeps me puzzled, despite having studied finance and economics at the world's best universities, the following question remains unanswered. Why is it that 5,000 units of our currency is worth 1 unit of your currency, where we are the ones with actual gold reserves? It is quite evident that the aid is in fact not coming from the West to Africa, but from Africa to the Western world. The Western world depends on Africa in every conceivable way since alternative resources are scarce out here. So how does the West ensure that the free aid keeps coming? By systematically destabilising the wealthiest African nations and their systems, and all that backed by huge PR campaigns, leaving the entire world under the impression that Africa is poor and dying and merely surviving on the mercy of the West. Well done, Oxfam, UNICEF, Red Cross, Live Aid and all the other organisations that continuously run multimillion-dollar advertising campaigns depicting charity porn to sustain that image of Africa globally."

Sissi Johnson interviewed Mallence sometime after her speech and asked her how she felt delivering it and what was the audience's reaction and online? To this question, Mallence replied: "I delivered something bigger than my own personal truth, because at the time I was being instructed to. The quintessence just "came" to me and I volunteered as the "messenger." I refuse to take complete credit for the content."

I return now to Walter Rodney. The decision by then-prime minister Hugh Shearer to declare Rodney persona non grata and ban him from entering Jamaica triggered protest among students at the University of the West Indies, Mona campus and beyond, including large sections of the working-class communities. Yes, Jamaican university youths were 'militant' at the time when the campus was a veritable hotbed of radicalism! It was a kind of 'youths aroused' situation that, sadly, has waned over the years. The pathetic colonial stooge and sympathiser Hugh Shearer also banned all books [including the autobiography of Malcolm X] about the Black Power Movement.)

Rodney was feared, not because he was a criminal or was unemployed, as Guyana labelled him, but because he was a threat to the political status quo of Guyana and the region, and was rewriting the colonisers' narrative of Caribbean and African history. He was a Black Power proponent; a leading voice of Pan-Africanism and his magnetic mobilisation prowess made him a threat to the vestiges of colonial social, economic, and political dominance in the region.

The parallels between Marcus Mosiah Garvey's and Walter Rodney's missions and the price they paid – one with his liberty and the other with his life – are there for all to see. Revolutionaries are always targetted by the powers that be.

Rodney's assassination reverberated throughout and beyond the Caribbean. Undoubtedly, this was a part of the broader aims of his killers. Don Rojas, former press secretary to assassinated Grenadian Prime Minister Maurice Bishop, said the Rodney family has been vindicated for their insistence that he was assassinated by the Forbes Burnham government. "Rodney's murder was a major setback to the WPA, the progressive, multiracial political party that he led. His murder reverberated across the Caribbean and the broader pan-African world. Three years later, PM Maurice Bishop of Grenada was also assassinated by his political adversaries. The death of these two young Caribbean revolutionaries before they reached age 40 was a major blow to the entire progressive movement in the Caribbean and around the world." [Source: The Sunday Gleaner, July 11, 2021]

But Rodney's murder was also a catalyst for the UWI to begin shedding its colonial character. "The transition of the University of the West Indies (UWI) from its colonial footing to nationalist rooting took place within the context of the crisis known as the 'Rodney Affair'. The time had come for the region to find intellectual confidence to decolonise its academic culture. The

Rodney Rebellion constituted a watershed in the development of the university's sense of self and sensibility. The decolonisation of its programmes and policies accelerated. The UWI was forced away from its colonial infrastructure. The modern university, to a large extent, was forged within the bosom of the eruption. Rodney gave of his best - a legacy of brilliant scholarship and an unparalleled commitment to marginalised communities. His vision was clear: The UWI should be both an excellent and ethical University." [Source, The Gleaner, August 30, 2018]

Patrice Lumumba: "[On June 20, 2022], the Belgian government returned a gold-capped tooth to the family of Patrice Lumumba, an independence leader and the first prime minister of the Democratic Republic of Congo. The Belgian government is also in the process of returning looted art. But the tooth is an especially gruesome and heart-wrenching artifact. On January 17, 1961, Lumumba was murdered by a firing squad backed by Belgium and the CIA, and his body was later desecrated: hacked apart, and thrown in acid. Pieces of his burned flesh were kept as souvenirs. Gerard Soete, then the Belgian police commissioner, kept the tooth. In the United States, it took nearly a month for newspapers to report that Lumumba, a leader for Black activists who was admired around the globe, had been killed. The response was immediate. Protests were mounted in major cities. James Baldwin contextualized the event this way in an essay for The New York Times: "My immediate reaction to the news of Lumumba's death was curiosity about the impact of this political assassination on Negroes in Harlem, for he had – has - captured the popular imagination there. Lumumba's tooth was a macabre souvenir not unlike the fingers that were preserved as artifacts after lynchings in America. The violence of racial domination was evidenced by dismemberment the world over." [Source: Imani Perry, 'A Grisly Souvenir of Global Oppression', The Atlantic, June 27, 2022].

Gerard Soete's impulse to pocket the body parts echoed the vile and ghoulish behaviour of European colonial officials down the decades who took remains back home as macabre mementos. But it also served as a final humiliation of a man that Belgium considered an enemy. Soete, appearing in a documentary in 1999, described the tooth and fingers he took as "a type of hunting trophy". The language suggests that for the Belgian policeman, Lumumba - who was revered across the continent as a leading voice of African liberation - was less than human. For Lumumba's daughter, Juliana, the question is whether the perpetrators were human (a very pertinent question!). "What amount of hatred must you have to do that?" she asks. "This is a reminder of what happened with the Nazis, taking pieces of people - and that's a crime against humanity," she told the BBC. Lumumba had risen to become prime minister at the age of 34. Elected in the final days of colonial rule, he headed the cabinet of the newly independent nation. In June 1960, at the handover of power, Belgian King Baudouin praised the colonial administration and spoke about his ancestor, Léopold II, as the "civiliser" of the country. There was no mention of the millions who died or were brutalised under his reign when he ruled what was then known as the Congo Free State as his personal property. This failure to acknowledge the past foreshadowed years of denial in Belgium, which it has only now begun to come to terms with. Lumumba was not so reticent. In an address that was not scheduled on the official programme, the prime minister spoke about the violence and degradation that the Congolese had suffered. In devastating rhetoric, interrupted by rounds of applause and a standing ovation when he concluded, he described "the humiliating slavery that was imposed on us by force". The Belgians were stunned, according to academic Ludo De Witte, who wrote a ground-breaking account of the assassination. Never before had a black African dared to speak like this in front of Europeans. The prime minister, who De Witte says had been described as an illiterate thief in the Belgian press, was seen as having humiliated the king and other Belgian officials. Lumumba's journey from prime minister to a victim of assassination took less than seven months." [Source: The BBC, June 20, 2022]. Just consider the vileness of what you just read. The Belgians and other colonisers must know that, despite their determined efforts, their wickedness will not remain hidden. When Malcolm X described white people, as a collective, as devils was he wrong?

Brian Flores: "This is bigger than me. This is bigger than football. This is bigger than coaching. Persons have stepped up in the past to fight for what is right for our people, and I feel this is my turn to step up ... and be an agent of change. The National Football League (NFL) is rife with racism and run like a plantation. I have two sons, they're 8 and 7. I've got a 5-year-old daughter. When I look at them, I don't want them to go through some of the things I've had to go through." Flores, the former Miami Dolphins team Coach, was speaking about his lawsuit for racial discrimination against the NFL, the New York Giants, the Denver Broncos, and the Miami Dolphins football teams. The 40-year-old Flores, who is Black, says in his lawsuit that the owners of the New York Giants interviewed him for their vacant head coaching job under disingenuous circumstances, as Flores had found out three days before his interview that the Giants had already decided to hire another person! But why might the Giants have wanted to interview Flores after having decided to hire another? Here's the answer: The NFL requires every team to interview at least one nonwhite candidate for any head coaching job. By conducting a pro forma (sham) interview with Flores, the Giants would have been technically following the rule.

According to Shaun R. Harper, "The paucity of Black coaches in the NFL speaks to a colossal policy failure. The Rooney rule, a policy the NFL introduced in 2003, requires teams to interview at least one person of color for head coaching and general managing and equivalent front office leadership jobs." [Source: Inside Higher Ed, February 14, 2022]

Consider this: In a 32-team league where most players are Black — and that has long been the case — only one current head coach is Black. He is Mike Tomlin, who has one of the highest winning percentages of any active coach. [Sources: CNN; The New York Times, February 2, 2022]

In his aforementioned article in Inside Higher Ed, Shaun R. Harper noted that "The [Flores] lawsuit, parallels between this situation and what happens to Black men in head coaching roles at colleges and universities in the United States —especially those with powerhouse revenue-generating football and men's basketball teams. While the National Collegiate Athletic Association (NCAA) and athletics conferences in higher education have not adopted the Rooney rule in policy, many institutions engage in an often-unspoken version of it in practice. That is, they interview one or a few obligatory Black candidates for head coaching positions, knowing full well they have no serious intent to hire them. White decision makers in professional sports, as well as those at higher education institutions, must stop wasting Black coaches' time."

I like Flores' declaration that "This is bigger than me. Persons have stepped up in the past to fight for what is right for our people, and I feel this is my turn to step up ... and be an agent of change."

Flores is clearly aware that, like Colin Kaepernick, his action may spell the end of his career in the NFL, but he is willing to pay the price for the benefit of others in the future, including his children!

Colin Kaepernick: "Is an American civil rights activist and former football quarterback. He played six seasons for the San Francisco 49ers in the National Football League (NFL). In the 49ers' third preseason game in 2016, Kaepernick sat during the playing of the U.S. national anthem before the game, rather than stand as is customary, as a protest against racial injustice, police brutality, and systematic oppression in the country. The following week, and throughout the regular season, Kaepernick kneeled during the anthem. The protests received highly polarized reactions, with some praising him and his stand against racism and others denouncing the protests. The actions resulted in a wider protest movement, which intensified in September 2017 after (then) President Donald Trump said that NFL owners should "fire" players who protest during the national anthem. (Kaepernick explained his protest in these terms: "I am not going to stand up to show pride in a flag for a country that oppresses black people and people of color. To me, this is bigger than football and it would be selfish on my part to look the other way. There are bodies in the street and people getting paid leave and getting away with murder", referencing a series of African-American deaths caused by law enforcement that led to the Black Lives Matter movement and adding that he would continue to protest until he feels like "the American flag] represents what it's supposed to represent.") Kaepernick became a free agent after the season and remained unsigned, which numerous analysts and observers have attributed to political reasons. In November 2017, he filed a grievance against the NFL and its owners, accusing them of colluding to keep him out of the league.

Kaepernick withdrew the grievance in February 2019 after reaching a confidential settlement with the NFL. His protests received renewed attention in 2020 amid the George Floyd protests against police brutality and racism, but he remains unsigned by any professional football team." [Source: Wikipedia]

As tends to happen in these cases, Kaepernick was being punished as a cautionary tale to stop other players in the future from doing what he did. Then-president of the United States Donald Trump bragged in the third person that "NFL owners don't want to pick [Kaepernick] up because they don't want to get a nasty tweet from Donald Trump."

Josh Levin of Slate Magazine noted that "In a different league, with different fans and different owners, Kaepernick might have been hailed as a hero. In the NFL, he strayed from the narrow path that players are allowed to walk, and he lost his job as a result. Kaepernick's race clearly played a massive role in the way his words and deeds were received. The NFL is a white-run league in which the players are 70 percent black. Kaepernick plays the most important position on the field, one of the few that's still mostly occupied by white men. It was telling how quickly the conversation about Kaepernick's protest turned into one about his ability and claims that he was desperate for the attention given that he'd allegedly lost his physical gifts. (No matter that he hadn't been the one to call attention to his silent demonstration.)"

Having regard to the parallels in which they endured social punishment and impairment of their careers because of their activism, Kaepernick has been described as "the Muhammad Ali of his generation." Time Magazine put Kaepernick on its September 2016 cover, kneeling next to the words "The Perilous Fight."

Kaepernick received death threats for being "disrespectful" to the anthem. But demonstrating remarkable courage, Kaepernick said he had anticipated the backlash before he embarked on his protest. "I knew there were other things that came along with this ... It's not something I haven't thought about."

Rather than neutralising him, the 'career lynching' of Colin Kaepernick had the opposite effect - it made him a martyr.

Garvey and the KKK

Garvey made contacts and met with the notorious Klu Klux Klan in the USA. This association has been weaponized against him by his enemies in the NAACP, some members of the UNIA, and even today by contemporary detractors in Jamaica. Therefore, Garvey's 'relationship' with the KKK is a matter impatient of consideration and commentary.

From Professor Rupert Lewis: "Garvey was not anti-white, as he knew he had to dialogue with, engage, involve as well as struggle with white people. He corresponded with a wide spectrum of white leaders, including university presidents such as Nicholas Murray Butler, of Columbia University, whom he asked to address a meeting on the implications of the war for domestic justice in America (MGP, 1:284). He also invited Irish nationalists, socialists and unabashed imperialists such as

Theodore Roosevelt." Source: Rupert Lewis: Marcus Garvey, The University of the West Indies, 2018]

With specific reference to the KKK, Professor Lewis wrote "On 25 June 1922, Garvey had a two-hour meeting with Edgar Young Clark, acting imperial wizard of the KKK in Atlanta. This was a controversial meeting. W.E.B. Du Bois and William Pickens of the National Association for the Advancement of Colored People were critical of Garvey's meeting with the Klan. So were some members of the UNIA, especially James Eason, who had been designated the leader of Black Americans in the UNIA. Apparently, the meeting had been requested by the Klan."

Lewis continued: "But this meeting was not as surprising as it appears on the surface. Garvey was aware that there was no other Black leader in the United States who had such strong support as he had in the American South. In 1920, there were 1,487,000 African Americans in the northern and western United States as against 8,894,000 in the South (MGP, 6:7n1, cited in Lewis 2018). Garvey was also aware that the Klan was not a fringe movement in the United States but an organisation with mainstream influence at the federal level in Congress, the White House and the Supreme Court; at the local and state levels of government; and in the predominantly white business community. Martin Lipset, an American political scientist, has pointed out that in the 1920s the KKK was a mass movement embracing millions of Americans, and that there were many more white

Americans who accepted white superiority as normal but were not members of the Klan."

In a speech to the UNIA at Liberty Hall, New York, on July 9, 1922, Garvey reported on his meeting with the KKK, highlighting that it was "the invisible government of the United States of America. The Ku Klux Klan expresses to a great extent the feeling of every real white American. The attitude of the Ku Klux Klan is that America shall be a white man's country at all hazards, at all costs. The attitude of the Universal Negro Improvement Association is in a way similar to the Ku Klux Klan. Whilst the Ku Klux Klan desires to make America absolutely a white man's country, the Universal Negro Improvement Association wants to make Africa absolutely a Black man's country" (MGP, 4:709, cited in Lewis, 2018).

More: "The Klan had been making inroads in the North between 1922 and 1924 in response to Black migration and they were intent that white supremacy would be maintained. At the UNIA convention, efforts were made by communists to put the UNIA into confrontation with the Klan, which would simply endanger the lives of Garveyites in the southern states (Jacques Garvey, 1970; cited in Lewis, 2018). The politics of dealing with the KKK in localities where the UNIA had strong Black support was an issue that had to be handled carefully. One of the flashpoints for white violence was interracial couples. Nothing was more inflammatory in parts of the United States than a Black having social relations with a white woman. Race riots were ignited as a result and many Blacks lost their lives even when there were only rumours or lies about these relationships. Coupled with this, it was argued by some Blacks and light-skinned [the result of the rape of a Black ancestor by her slave-owning master] individuals that, for Black People to raise themselves up, interracial unions would enhance the prospects of mixed-race children. This was the doctrine of miscegenation as a panacea for the solution to Black People's oppression. It was in response to those who supported miscegenation that Garvey inveighed against racial mixing and advocated ideas of racial purity. His was affirmation of pride in being Black and accepting one's African heritage without apology." [Source: Rupert Lewis, 2018]. On this score, Garvey was defamed and labelled a Black racist.

So, given the above, was Garvey's meeting with the KKK a mistake? Well, I will answer this question by identifying the kind of person who makes no mistake and therefore does not deserve our time or attention: "It is not the critic who counts; not the man who points out how the strong man stumbles, or where the doer of deeds could have done them better. The credit belongs to the man who is actually in the arena, whose face is marred by dust and sweat and blood; who strives valiantly; who errs, who comes short again and again, because there is no effort without error and shortcoming; but who does actually strive to do the deeds; who knows great enthusiasms, the great devotions; who spends himself in a worthy cause; who at the best knows in the end the triumph of high achievement, and who at the worst, if he fails, at least fails while daring greatly, so that his place shall never be with those cold and timid souls who neither know victory nor defeat." ~Theodore Roosevelt

It is a verity that prevailing context and circumstances often impose pragmatism on a leader.

****

Marcus Garvey's Two Wives

=====================####====================

It has been said that behind (beside) every successful man is a good woman. It would be remiss of me, then, not to mention the women in Garvey's life. Interestingly, Marcus Garvey's two wives had the same first name – Amy.

Amy Ashwood Garvey

"Amy Ashwood Garvey was born in Port Antonio, Jamaica, but spent most of her childhood in Panama where her father supported the family as a businessman. She returned to Jamaica as a teen and attended Westwood High School in Trelawney, where she met her future husband, Marcus Garvey, in 1914.

Ashwood and Garvey both held strong beliefs in African American activism and were involved in political activities and soon they began to collaborate on ideas and strategies for the liberation of Jamaica, then a British colony. In 1916 they became secretly engaged. Ashwood's parents did not approve and arranged for her to return to Panama that year. Garvey headed for the United States in the spring of that year.

However, Garvey and Ashwood were reunited in September of 1918 in New York City, New York. This marked the beginning of Ashwood's important role in the development of the Universal Negro Improvement Association (UNIA) branches. She became Garvey's chief aide and the general secretary of the UNIA in 1919.

On Christmas Day 1919, the long engagement between Garvey and Ashwood culminated in an enormous wedding celebration with several thousand friends and associates at Liberty Hall, the UNIA building in New York City. After the marriage, Ashwood took on more prominent roles in the UNIA. She became director of the Black Star Line Shipping Co. and established a ladies auxiliary of the UNIA. She also helped plan an industrial school and helped establish the UNIA's newspaper The Negro World.

In October 1919 at the UNIA offices in Harlem, Ashwood risked her life to shield Garvey from the bullets of attempted killer George Tyler. Despite her heroism, the marriage began to deteriorate after that incident. They divorced in 1922." [Source: Allison Espiritu, Blackpast.org]

Amy Jacques Garvey

"Amy Jacques, editor, feminist, and race activist, was Marcus Garvey's second wife and his principal lieutenant during his incarceration in an Atlanta penitentiary from 1925 to 1927. Born in Jamaica, Jacques attended Wolmers' Girls School; she moved to the United States in 1917 and became involved in the Universal Negro Improvement Association the following year, after hearing Garvey speak. She became Garvey's secretary and traveling companion, as well as the office manager at U.N.I.A. headquarters and secretary of the Negro Factories Corporation, in 1920.

Jacques and Garvey married in July 1922, shortly after his divorce from his first wife, Amy Ashwood. During the period of Garvey's trial, conviction, and imprisonment on mail fraud charges (1923-1927), Jacques emerged as a major propagandist for him. To improve Garvey's reputation and raise funds to pay for his defense, Jacques published two volumes of his speeches and writings as **'Garvey's Philosophy and Opinions'**. She acted as his representative while he was in prison, traveling to speak at local U.N.I.A. divisions throughout the country, meeting with public officials and U.N.I.A. officers to carry out his directions, and organizing U.N.I.A. conferences and affairs.

She became the associate editor of The Negro World (1924-1927) and introduced a new page, called "Our Women and What They Think," which carried international news about the status of women, poetry, profiles of leading Black women and black female historical figures, and columns by and about members of the women's auxiliaries. After Garvey's deportation, Amy Jacques Garvey returned with him to Jamaica and continued as a contributing editor of the U.N.I.A. paper from 1927-1928. She and Garvey toured England, France, and Germany in the spring and summer of 1928, and she wrote articles for The Negro World about her impressions.

Amy Jacques Garvey was the mother of Garvey's two sons, Marcus Mosiah Garvey Jr., and Julius Winston Garvey, born in 1930 and 1933 respectively. When Garvey moved to England in 1934, she and the children stayed behind in Jamaica. The family was united only briefly after that time.

After Garvey died in 1940 at age 53, Jacques became a contributing editor to a Black Nationalist journal, **'The African'**, published in Harlem in the 1940s, and established the African Study Circle of the World in Jamaica in the late 1940s. She published '**Garvey & Garveyism'** in 1963."[http://www.marcusgarveypppja.org/]

Professor Carolyn Cooper, in her inimitable style, gave the following account of Garvey's marriages: "Amy Jacques, the second Mrs. Garvey, gives an intriguing account of Marcus Garvey's first marriage to Amy Ashwood in her book Garvey and Garveyism. "While [Garvey was] in Harlem hospital, Amy Ashwood, a Jamaican friend from Panama, then secretary of the New York local, removed his belongings from his furnished room to her flat. At the end of December, they were married."

Quite a lot is left out of this abbreviated story. There is a big gap between the moving of the belongings and the marriage. What is not said is just as important as what is. It seems as if Amy Jacques is accusing Amy Ashwood of using underhand means to forcefully rush Garvey into marriage while he was in a vulnerable state.

Amy Jacques' description of the divorce is quite elaborate, by contrast. She even recalls, word for word, Garvey's explanation of why the marriage broke down after only three months: "I have to travel up and down the country. I can't drag my wife with me. I can't pay her the personal attention as the average husband. In fact, I have no time to look after myself. My life can either be wrecked because of her conduct or embellished by her deportment."

Garvey's next move seems quite calculated. Amy Jacques reports that "He moved into a flat at 129th Street with an elderly coloured member as a housekeeper. He offered Miss Davis [assistant president general] and me a room to share there; we accepted because we would be better protected at nights coming home from meetings."

Prim and proper Miss Jacques is careful to confirm the elderliness of Garvey's housekeeper. And her acceptance of Garvey's hospitality is purely a matter of chivalrous protection. But I do wonder. Did Amy Jacques have 'feelings' for Garvey? In her judgmental account of the collapsed marriage, Amy Jacques does not immediately mention the fact that Amy Ashwood was her friend. Nor does she reveal that she was a bridesmaid at the wedding and accompanied the couple on their honeymoon!

It was a working honeymoon and Amy Jacques attended in a professional capacity as Garvey's secretary. There's only one kind of work that should be done on a honeymoon. And if you can't do the work, you are going to lose the work.

As is to be expected, Amy Ashwood gives a quite different version of the story of her marriage. Her needs and Marcus Garvey's ambitions clearly clashed. Embellishing her husband's life was not her priority. She was a woman ahead of her time, and who could not be contained by her husband's expectations.

Amy Ashwood was, apparently, a hot-blooded woman who needed a partner who could and would pay her sexual attention. Garvey should have taken her on a proper honeymoon. However, much he admired Amy

Ashwood's mind, spirit and, presumably, body, Garvey soon concluded that his wife was going to wreck his life. His peace of mind required defensive action.

Garvey admitted that his visionary work for the advancement of Black people "came first in his life". This was his big romance. And in Amy Jacques he found a perfect second wife. She was a devoted, morally upright companion who certainly did not cause any anxiety in Garvey about what she might possibly be doing behind his back while he was travelling up and down the country.

Garvey's second wife decidedly embellished his life. But even she had cause to complain about Garvey's commitment to his first love, The UNIA. In Garvey and Garveyism, Amy Jacques paints a picture of Garvey as a taskmaster, pushing her relentlessly to publish the second volume of his philosophy and opinions.

This is how she puts it: "I thought I had done almost the impossible when I was able to rush the first copy of Volume II to him, but he callously said, 'Now I want you to send free copies to senators, congressmen and prominent men who might become interested in my case, as I want to make another application for a pardon.'"

Amy Jacques confesses: "When I completed this task, I weighed 98 lbs., had low blood pressure, and one eye was badly strained. Two doctors advised complete rest." Having sacrificed her health for Garvey's cause, she fleetingly rebels against the callous regime of domestic servitude she had willingly embraced.

"Perhaps, Amy Jacques should have followed Amy Ashwood's example and made a lucky escape. But who would have ensured the completion of **The Philosophy and Opinions of Marcus Garvey** and so consolidated the great man's reputation?" [Source: 'Marcus Garvey's Love Life,' The Gleaner, August 17, 2014]

We Garveyites - and the rest of humanity - owe Amy Jacques Garvey an eternal debt of gratitude for compiling and rendering permanent the philosophy and opinions of Marcus Garvey. Interestingly, there is an 'Amy Jacques Garvey Hall of Residence' for female students at the University of Technology, Jamaica.

Here is the preface to the **Philosophy and Opinions of Marcus Garvey** compiled, published, and distributed by Amy Jacques Garvey: "This Volume is compiled from the speeches and articles delivered and written by Marcus Garvey from time to time. My purpose for compiling it primarily, was not for publication, but rather to keep as a personal record of the opinions and sayings of my husband during his career as the Leader of that portion of the human family known as the Negro Race. However, on second thought, I decided to publish this volume to give the public an opportunity of studying and forming an opinion of him, not from inflated and misleading newspaper and magazine articles, but from expressions of thoughts enunciated by him in defense of his oppressed and struggling race; so that by his own words he may be judged and Negroes the world over may be informed and inspired, for truth, brought to light, forces conviction, and a state of conviction inspires action.

The history of contact between the white and black races for the last three hundred years or more, records only a series of pillages, wholesale murders, atrocious brutalities, industrial exploitation, disfranchisement of the one on the other; the strong against the weak; but the sun of evolution is gradually rising, shedding its light between the clouds of misery and oppression, and quickening and animating to racial consciousness and eventual national independence black men and women the world over.

It is human, therefore, that few of us within the Negro race can comprehend this transcendent period. We all suffer to a more or less degree; we all feel this awakened spirit of true manhood and womanhood, but it is given to few the vision of leadership – it is an inspiration – it is a quality born in man. Therefore, in the course of leadership, it is natural that one should meet opposition because of ignorance, lack of knowledge, and sympathy of the opposition in understanding fully the spirit of leadership.

With the dawn of this new era, which precedes the Day of National Independence for Negroes, it is well for all members of the race to understand their leadership; know what its essentials, its principles are, and help it to attain its goal and liberate a race in the truest sense of the word.

In Chapter 1 of this volume, I have endeavored to place before my readers, gems of expression convincing in their truths. Chapter 2 deals with definitions and expositions of various interesting themes. Chapters 3 and 4 contain a collection of brief essays on subjects affecting world conditions generally and Negroes in particular. In Chapter 5 I have reproduced what I consider two of the best speeches of my husband.

It is my sincere hope and desire that this small volume will help to disseminate among the members of my race everywhere the true knowledge of their history, the struggles, and strivings of the present leadership, and the glorious future of national independence in a free and redeemed Africa, achieved through organized purpose and organized action." [Amy Jacques Garvey, New York City, February 23, 1923]

Oftentimes, the important role the women in the lives of famous men is effaced. But there is no doubt that, were it not for Amy Jacques Garvey, humanity would not have the immense benefit of Marcus Garvey's philosophy and opinions in published form. This book is one of the most important publications for the empowerment of Black People!

Barbara Blake-Hannah, in the 'Liv-ication' section of her book **'Growing Out: Black Hair & Black Pride in the Swinging Sixties',** showers Amy Jacques Garvey with encomiums: "By her almost single-handed publishing efforts, she brought about a new awareness of the prophetic philosophy of her husband, Marcus Mosiah Garvey, and fought to overcome the derision and criticism with which people regarded this great man. The world's upsurge of attention given to Garvey in the late

60s and early 70s caused a re-examination of his work and greater respect. Mrs. Garvey perpetuated the Universal Negro Improvement Association through her books **'Garvey and Garveyism'** and **'Power in America and the Impact of Garvey in Africa and Jamaica.'** She compiled the writings and speeches of Garvey into a volume: **'The Philosophy and Opinions of Marcus Garvey,'** the most comprehensive collection that exists today."

I think the **Philosophy and Opinions of Marcus Garvey** is one of the most important books ever published in the history of humanity. Every Black person should read this book! Every Black parent should introduce their children to this book and read and discuss it with them! And our high schools and universities should be using this book as a stable text in the general education component of their curricula! This book should be Black People's 'Bible.'

Blake-Hannah continued her gracious salute of Amy Jacques Garvey in these terms: "She was an indefatigable speaker who held her audience spellbound with her fiery explanations of the meaning of Garvey's teachings always maintaining the theme that freedom would come to the countries of the Third World only when those countries truly and totally controlled their economic resources. In 1969 Jamaica awarded Garvey its highest honour – National Hero – and Mrs. Garvey was subsequently offered a National Hero's pension of Three Thousand Pounds a year, but she refused the offer, saying that to accept it would not change the way of life of the poor people for whom she had worked all her life. One can think of only a few widows of famous men who have dedicated their lives to the furtherance of the beliefs of their husband, as did Mrs. Garvey, and because of her efforts, Garvey lives on. The Black race still searches for a particular "ism" that will be appropriate to its own particular situation. We search through Marxism, Communism, Socialism, Castro-ism, and Capitalism, taking from each something which is relevant, but never finding a complete whole. The life work of Mrs. Garvey re-awakened the interest in the indigenous Jamaican "ism" - Garveyism, and the possibility that it may prove to be the most successful and lasting philosophy for the Jamaican and Black people."

It is remarkable, yet not fully appreciated by many Jamaicans – except perhaps by former prime minister Michael Manley – that a Jamaican has developed a homegrown template for Jamaica's socio-economic development.

That Jamaican is Marcus Mosiah Garvey.

At its core, this template is scaffolded on the philosophy of self-reliance – knowing our history, empowering ourselves through education, fiercely deploying our creative imagination, and strategically using the assets nature has provided.

****

'Interviewing' Garvey

==================####==================

In this section, I have taken artistic license to conduct an 'interview' with Marcus Garvey on various topics that I think would be of interest to him and others on which he had expressed views, or taken positions.

Paul W. Ivey (PWI): In a report launched on July 9, 2021, the Caribbean Policy Research Institute (CaPRI), a Think Tank located at the University of the West Indies, found that "The social and economic situation of the lives of Jamaicans in poor communities is marked by unemployment, low incomes, and violence." What do you think about this reality in which many Black Jamaicans live?

Marcus Mosiah Garvey (MMG): You know, my mission was to help my people to not only think empowerment, but to orchestrate their empowerment primarily through their own efforts, but also through institutions established by the State to assist them. That is why I established the UNIA and its various affiliated businesses to demonstrate to my fellow Blacks that their imaginations should not be limited by possibilities, not of their own choosing, but that they should create their own possibilities. Just looking at how my people comported themselves, I realised their disablement was largely at the level of their psychitecture ... their psychologicalscape was distorted by the obscene colonial ideology that fabricated the 'barbaric Negro' through deliberate conditioning to leach their self-esteem and supplant it with an intractable inferiority complex and learned helplessness. So, I am beyond disappointed by the fact that "The social and economic situation of the lives of Jamaicans in poor communities is marked by unemployment, low incomes, and violence."

PWI: What books do you suggest for us to read?

MMG: Well, forgive me for a fleeting moment of immodesty by allowing me to suggest that every Black person should read 'The Philosophy and Opinions of Marcus Garvey' so competently compiled by my wife Amy Jacques Garvey. From this book, they will not only learn what motivated me to act, but they will get my template ... my blueprint, if you will, for empowerment. One of the things that please me is that there are several of my people who have authored books that I would recommend to the rest of my people; these include:

- **Josef Ben Jochannan** - 'Africa: Mother of Western Civilization'.
- **Ivan Van Sertima** - 'They Came Before Columbus'.
- **Walter Rodney** - 'How Europe Underdeveloped Africa'.
- **Orlando Patterson** - 'Slavery and Social Death'; 'The Children of Sisyphus'; 'The Cultural Matrix: Understanding Black Youth'; 'The Sociology of Slavery'; 'Freedom in the Making of Western Culture'
- **Cyril Lionel Robert 'CLR' James** - 'Black Jacobins: Toussaint L'Ouverture and the San Domingo Revolution'.
- **Joy DeGruy** - 'Post-Traumatic Slave Syndrome'

- **Frances Luella Cres-Welsing** - 'The Isis Papers: The Keys to the Colors'.
- **Barbara Blake-Hannah** - 'Growing Out: Black Hair & Black Pride in the Swinging Sixties'.
- **Charles W. Mills** - 'The Racial Contract'.
- **Neely Fuller Jr** - 'A Compensatory Counter Racist Code'.
- **Toni Morrison** - 'Beloved'; 'Jazz'; 'Sula'; 'The Bluest Eye'; 'Paradise'.
- **Michael Manley** - 'The Politics of Change: A Jamaican Testament'.
- **Joel A. Rogers** - 'From 'Superman' to Man'; 'Nature Knows No Color-Line'; 'World's Greatest Men and Women of African Descent'; 'The West Indies: Their Political, Social, and Economic Condition'; 'The Negro's Experience of Christianity and Islam'; 'The Suppression of Negro History'.
- **Phillip Sherlock and Hazel Bennett** - 'The Story of the Jamaican People'.
- **Frederick Douglass** – 'The Narrative of the Life of Frederick Douglass, An American Slave'.
- **Harriett Jacobs** – 'Incidents in the Life of a Slave Girl'.
- **Booker T. Washington** - 'Up from Slavery'.
- **Douglas Hall** - 'In Miserable Slavery: Thomas Thistlewood in Jamaica, 1750-86'.
- **Amos N. Wilson** – 'The Developmental Psychology of the Black Child'.
- **Frantz Fanon** - 'Black Skin, White Masks'.

- **Olaudah Equiano** - 'The Autobiography of Olaudah Equiano or Gustavus Vassa, The African (published 1789)'.

PWI: What do you think of other Black Leaders such as Obama, Haile Selassie, Booker T. Washington, Malcolm X., Martin Luther King, Jnr., and Louis Farrakhan?

MMG: I find it remarkable that Barack Hussein Obama was given to America through a father from Africa! I like when he said he "chose Black." (The young Obama's formative years were spent in Hawaii. He inhabited two worlds. But he found Black culture attractive). Writing in his highly-acclaimed autobiography **'Dreams From My Father,'** Obama declared: "I would watch the University of Hawaii players laughing at some inside joke, winking at the girls on the sidelines, or casually flipping lay-ups. By the time I reached high school, I was playing on Punahou's teams, and could take my game to the university courts, where a handful of black men, mostly gym rats, and has-beens, would teach me an attitude that didn't just have to do with the sport. That respect came from what you did and not who your daddy was. That you could talk stuff to rattle an opponent, but that you should shut the hell up if you couldn't back it up. That you didn't let anyone sneak up behind you to see emotions—like hurt or fear—you didn't want them to see. I decided to become part of that world."

The Black world!

Because of his 'hybridity', Obama had a choice.

And he chose the Black world.

I have noted with much sadness, though, how his election has led to the resurgence of white supremacy in the USA. Alas, seeing a Black man and his Black family in the White House is too much for the white racists to bear.

Regarding Haile Selassie, I had some harsh words for him because, instead of staying with his people when Italy invaded his country in 1935, he chose to go into exile. One should be prepared to pay whatever price it takes to fight for one's people.

These are some of the things I said about Haile Selassie:

- "Haile Selassie ... kept his country unprepared for modern civilisation. He resorted to prayer, feasting, and fasting, whilst other nations were building up armaments ...
- When Haile Selassie departed from the policy of the great Menelik and surrounded himself with European advisers, he had taken the first step to the destruction of the country.
- If Haile Selassie had only the vision, inspired with negro integrity, he would have still been the resident emperor in Addis Ababa, with not only a country of twelve million Abyssinian citizens, but with an admiring world of hundreds of millions of negroes [around the world].
- Why he kept the majority of his countrymen in serfdom and almost slavery is difficult to tell. Why he refused to educate the youth of his country to help him to carry on the government

and lead the masses in a defensive war against Italy cannot be understood.

- When the facts of history are written Haile Selassie of Abyssinia will go down as a great coward who ran away from his country to save his skin and left the millions of his countrymen to struggle through a terrible war that he brought upon them because of his political ignorance and his racial disloyalty. It is a pity that a man of limited intellectual caliber and weak political character like Haile Selassie became Emperor of Abyssinia at so crucial a time in the political history of the world. Unfortunately, Abyssinia lost the controlling influence of a political personality of patriotic racial character like the late Menelik, whose loyalty to his race and devotion to his country excelled all his other qualities, to the extent that he was able to use that very strength to continuously safeguard the interests of the Ethiopian Empire."

I was strongly criticized for my criticism of Selassie.

Concerning Booker T. Washington, I admired what did at Tuskegee University and I wanted to replicate that model in Jamaica. So, I wanted to meet with him to forge a partnership to bring this to reality. Malcolm X was the real deal after his mind was transformed. I am proud to have influenced him! Concerning the abominable treatment of Black people in the USA, that brother called a spade a spade! Martin Luther King, Jr. shamed America into acknowledging and advancing the civil rights of

Black people in that country. I am proud to have influenced him! Louis Farrakhan speaks unvarnished and uncomfortable truths."

PWI: If you could talk to the little white girl who was once your friend when you were a child what would you say to her now?

MMG: I would prefer to talk with her parents. The little girl was a victim; her mind was poisoned and polluted with the toxin of racism by her parents, so it is they whom I would want to talk. Not to shame them, mind you, but to enlighten them out of their cave of ignorance.

PWI: Would you wish to be exonerated for your "crimes" or do you consider it a badge of honour to be a so-called "criminal" in the eyes of, evil men such as J. Edgar Hoover, oppressive regimes, and those who lack vision? Should you be pardoned, especially by Barack Obama?

MMG: Yes, I must be exonerated! Not pardoned! Exonerated! The charges against me were trumped up by those wicked bastards. All false! I am not a criminal! So, I must be exonerated. I don't want any pardon, as that would suggest that I'm being forgiven for something for which I was guilty.

PWI: Which Jamaican Prime Ministers understood or was closest to implementing your philosophy?

MMG: Michael Manley.

PWI: What do you make of Black-on-Black violence?

MMG: It is sad. It breaks my heart. It is learned behaviour, starting with the epithet "nothing Black nuh good." Our people have internalized self-hate and are projecting it onto each other. I think that if they were taught their true history there would be comity and communal solidarity. And that is why I declared that a people without knowledge of their history, is like a tree without roots. And it is also for this reason that I sought to reprogram their minds toward self-love and racial pride! And I will repeat 'UP, up, ye mighty race you can accomplish what you will."

PWI: What do you think of social media?

MMG: Like all technologies, it may be used for good, or bad. My advice to my people is to be vigilant and use it strategically and constructively - be alert to how the great powers may use it as a new variant of colonialisation; use it to keep in touch with family members and friends, especially those who are overseas; use it to mobilise yourselves in the battle against discrimination and marginalization; use it for education and enlightenment; I also say to my people, leverage social media for entrepreneurial opportunities!

PWI: Are you a racist?

MMG: No, I am not! Absolutely not! My primary concern is for my people; my race; my fellow Africans! Other races demonstrate fierce communal solidarity. Black People should do likewise!

PWI: What's your greatest contribution?

MMG: Awakening the consciousness of my race - Black People of African origin – and instilling in them self-respect, pride, dignity, and confidence to empower themselves socially and economically! This, of course, was at a great personal sacrifice to me, but I would unhesitatingly do it again. I thank all the Garveyites who supported me, the mission, and the movement.

****

Marcus Garvey's Death

==================####==================

Reader, consider the uncommon courage Marcus Garvey demonstrated to launch and implement his mission for the upliftment and empowerment of his race .... his fellow Black People. And consider the tremendous personal sacrifices he made ("I am prepared to face the arrows of hell for the principles of the UNA"). And then consider the circumstances of his death, as set out below.

"At the end of May 1940, Marcus Garvey sat cold and forgotten in a tall draughty rented house at 53 Talgarth Road in West Kensington, London. Recovering from a stroke which had left him partially paralyzed, he was sorting through the newspapers that his secretary, Daisy Whyte, had placed beside his bed when he came across a headline which he knew could not be true: 'Marcus Garvey Dies in London.' He scanned the other papers, some of which also carried notices of his death. They were not kind obituaries. It took almost a week for many of the papers to issue corrections. By then, wakes and memorials had been held for Marcus Garvey in the Caribbean and the United States. Garvey found himself eulogized by a number of people whom he'd considered enemies and vilified by others who had not forgiven him for his alleged exploitation of black people. Miss Whyte tried to shield her boss from some of the more uncharitable news more stories but he insisted on seeing them all. Garvey was still weak from the stroke, but more than the distress and embarrassment of his disability, he was deeply upset by his public and private impotence, by his inability to arrest the decline of his mass movement, and by his estrangement from his family: two years previously, his wife had left him and returned to Jamaica with their children; he hadn't seen them since. Marcus Garvey was now 'faced with clippings of his obituary [and] pictures of himself with deep black borders,' wrote Daisy Whyte, '[and] after the second day of this pile of shocking correspondence, he collapsed in his chair.' Reading through the damning accounts, written by former friends and enemies, Garvey had suffered another massive stroke: he died two weeks later, on 10 June 1940." [Source: Colin Grant, **'Negro With a Hat: The Rise and Fall of Marcus Garvey'**, Oxford University Press, 2008]

The account above reveals the massive price Garvey paid for being the father of Black Lives Matter. For what Garvey achieved, and for what he endured, he personified all the criteria of a hero, to wit: a person who, despite clear danger demonstrates uncommon courage and makes extraordinary personal sacrifices to achieve goals that produce intergenerational benefits for many people.

******

Marcus Garvey's Enduring Relevance
=============####===========

If Jesus is 'King of the Jews', Marcus Garvey is Black People's Messiah!

Before Martin Luther King, Jr., before Malcolm X, and before Nelson Mandela there was Marcus Garvey, a Jamaican-born Black multi-faceted philosopher and empowerment leader who produced the most comprehensive blueprint for psychological liberation (freedom from mental enslavement and disablement) and economic empowerment of his people!

Marcus Mosiah Garvey is peerless!

An ordinary man made extraordinary by circumstances!

In December 2020, UNESCO proclaimed August 31 as **'The International Day for People of African Descent.'** Thanks to Marcus Garvey! That was the date in 1920 on which Garvey's month-long International Convention of the Negro Peoples of the World drew to a close.

From Prof. Rupert Lewis: "What the Garvey movement stood for and why it is relevant today is its demand for a radical redistribution of power in the world, which involved not only the end of colonial rule, but the development of the capabilities and resources of Africans and those in the diaspora to realise the social, economic, and cultural goals we set ourselves. Garvey's philosophy and teachings continue to inspire in the United States and elsewhere. The red, black, and green flag of the UNIA was to be seen in demonstrations of the Black Lives Matter movement in 2020, particularly after the televised murder of George Floyd." [Source: 'Life, times, and legacies of Marcus Garvey', The Sunday Gleaner, May 22, 2022]

Without the metanoia (mindset) of independence, unity, self-determination, and self-reliance Marcus Garvey advocated, Black People will never achieve true freedom, empowerment, and prosperity. Renowned philosopher Alain Locke, author of **'The New Negro'** declared that the path to Black progress was self-determination and regard for and embrace of our homeland heritage; he also encouraged Black artists to look to Africa for inspiration.

Influence is "the capacity to have effect on people or situations" whereas relevance means "appropriate to a given context." I am positing that the effect (influence) of Garveyism (Garvey's philosophy) was tremendous.

And is ongoing.

And remains relevant (applicable).

Garveyism has no shelf-life.

It is alive!

Marcus Garvey's philosophy and opinions have influenced ... and continue to influence ... many people and progressive movements globally! And in this regard, Marcus Garvey has achieved cognitive immortality. This is a stupendous feat for a Blackman from St. Ann, Jamaica.

Kwame Nkrumah, the first president of Ghana, wrote in his autobiography that of all the literature he had studied, the book that did more than any other to inspire him was **'The Philosophy and Opinions of Marcus Garvey or Africa for the Africans.'** As president, Nkrumah named Ghana's national shipping line the

"Black Star Line"; there is a Black Star Square in Accra, and a Black star on the Ghanaian flag. In addition, Ghana's national football team is also nicknamed the Black Stars.

Below is another example – from Ta-Nehisi Coates - of the depth and breadth of Marcus Garvey's influence [on the Black Panthers in the USA for whom his writings were required reading].

"The Black Panthers, also known as the Black Panther Party, was a political organization founded in 1966 by Huey Newton and Bobby Seale to challenge police brutality against the African American community. Dressed in black berets and black leather jackets, the Black Panthers organized armed citizen patrols of Oakland and other U.S. cities. At its peak in 1968, the Black Panther Party had roughly 2,000 members. The organization later declined as a result of internal tensions, deadly shootouts and FBI counterintelligence activities aimed at weakening the organization." [Source: History.dot.com].

(Sidebar: Reading the case of Panther member Albert Woodfox (who spent was held in solitary confinement for more than forty years - longer than any prisoner in American history. He and two other Black Panthers, who were in solitary confinement for a total of more than a hundred years, became known as the Angola 3) will make your hair stand on end. And if you are not a stone masquerading as a human, you will cry. What these Black men endured was psychological torture – at the hands of the white racist establishment run by 'civilised, God-fearing Christians'. A psychologist who studies the effects of solitary confinement, wrote, "I have never encountered any situation nearly as profound or extreme as that of the Angola 3." In a deposition, one of the 'Angola 3' said being in solitary confinement for forty-one years had reduced him to a "state of being where I can barely collect my own thoughts" and that "It's like a killing machine." And before this particular 'Angolan' died, he asked that his funeral program begin with a quote by Frantz Fanon: "If death is the realm of freedom, then through death I escape to freedom." [Source: Rachel Aviv, 'How Albert Woodfox Survived Solitary', The New Yorker, January 8, 2017]. In his autobiography **'Long Walk to Freedom'** Nelson Mandela also recounted the debilitating psychological effects solitary confinement had on him. Prisoners of War (P.O.W.s) have reported that the simple experience of isolation is as much of an ordeal as any physical abuse they have suffered. Atul Gawande in an article in The New Yorker on March 23, 2008, noted that "Human beings are social creatures. We are social not just in the trivial sense that we like company, and not just in the obvious sense that we each depend on others. We are social in a more elemental way: simply to exist as a normal human being requires interaction with other people."

Scholar and writer Ta-Nehisi Coates, concerning his father, who was a member of the Black Panther Party, states:

> "My father was Conscious Man. He stood a solid six feet, was handsome, mostly serious, rarely angry. Week days, he scooted out at six and drove an hour to the Mecca, where

he guarded the books and curated the history in the exalted hall of the Moorland Spingarn Research Center. He was modest - brown slacks, pale yellow shirt, beige Clarks - and hair cut by his own hand. He collected out-of-print texts, obscure lectures, and self-published monographs by writers like **J.A. Rogers** (a Jamaican from Westmoreland) Dr. Ben, and Drusilla Dunjee Houston, great seers who returned Egypt to Africa and recorded our history, when all the world said we had none. These were words that they did not want us to see, the lost archives, secret collections, folders worn yellow by water and years. But brought them back. From the day we touched these stolen shores, he'd explain to anyone who'd listen, they infected our minds. They deployed their phrenologists, their backward Darwinists, and forged a false Knowledge to keep us down. But against this demonology, there were those who battled back, universities scorned them, compromised professors scoffed at their names. So, they published themselves and hawked their knowledge at street fairs, churches, and bazaars. For their efforts, they were forgotten. Their great works languished out of print, while those they sought to save grew fat on integration and amnesia. Dad tracked the autodidacts and relatives of the ones who'd passed. Over tea in their living, he unfurled his ambition. Dad proposed restoring these lost geniuses to their esteemed chairs in the university without walls, through a publishing operation he built from saddle-stitch staplers, a table-top press, and a Commodore 64. Never had republishing been so radical. He called this basement operation Black Classic Press, and for the Coates family there was no escape. He covered the house with Knowledge, until rooms overflowed with books whose titles promised militant action and the return to glory. 'Wonderful Ethiopians' and 'Black Egypt and Her Negro Pharaohs.' He found others like him, formed collectives, held festivals in honor of Malcolm X and **Marcus Garvey** and the taking of arms. Brother and sisters would drum and dance the unearthed rhythms, poets revealed words with teeth. Even the food was conscious. Dad just played the back, peering from behind his table covered with African cloth and the awesome spread of books brought back from the dead. This bounty drew the survivors, the ones who outlasted J. Edgar Hoover and COINTELPRO." [Source: Ta-Nehisi Coates, The Beautiful Struggle, A Memoir]

Ta-Nehisi Coates himself described Garvey as the "patron saint" of the Black Nationalist movement.

In October 2021, I bought Professor Amos N. Wilson's book **'The Developmental Psychology of the Black Child'** and this is stated in the 'About the Author' section: "Colleagues, lay and professional, acclaimed him the ultimate Garveyite."

Former Governor General of Jamaica and former principal of the University of the West Indies (UWI), Mona, and historian, Sir Kenneth Hall, delivered the annual Marcus Garvey lecture on June 11, 2015, 75 years after the death of Garvey. Public relations consultant and writer Lance Neita, writing in **The Daily Observer** on June 14, 2015, noted that Sir Kenneth Hall's thesis was that:

"In assessing Garvey's relevance to Jamaica and to the Black world, it is the impact of his ideas that stands out. In Africa, many of the leaders who led their respective countries into independence refer to Garvey's philosophy as having great influence on their thinking, among them Kwame Nkrumah of Ghana and Jomo Kenyatta of Kenya. And in the United States, the leaders of the civil rights and black power movements, such as Malcolm X and Martin Luther King Jr, drew on Garvey's philosophy in the organisation of their own movements."

A young Barack Obama during the formative years of his worldviews and political philosophy was also exposed to the philosophy and opinions of Marcus Garvey! Obama, in his book '**Dreams from my Father**, mentioned how he was exposed to and became enamored of the philosophy of Marcus Garvey. (And yet when Obama became the 44th President of the USA he did not consider granting Garvey a pardon. I think in this regard Obama was a hostage fearing the backlash from white America such an action would unleash.

Some people have opined that Garveyites should "stop begging the USA to pardon Garvey because he did nothing wrong! Rather, his records should be expunged."

This is what Malcolm X had to say about the potency of Garvey's message: "Every time you see another nation on the African continent become independent you know that Marcus Garvey is alive. Had it not been for Marcus Garvey and the foundations laid by him, you would find no independent nations in the Caribbean today. All of the freedom movement that is taking place right here in America today was initiated by the work and teachings of Marcus Garvey."

It is a fact that Garvey and his philosophies were revered by many leaders in their independence bids in mid-19th-century Africa. This is instructive: On April 20, 2022, Paul Kagame, president of Rwanda, visited Jamaica. "Moments after disembarking an aircraft at the Norman Manley International Airport on Wednesday, Kagame laid a floral tribute at the shrine of Marcus Garvey as his first order of business on his three-day visit to Jamaica." [Source: The Gleaner, April 14, 2022]

Professor Clinton Hutton posits these views: "During the heights of the Garvey movement, the Universal Negro Improvement Association (UNIA) and Garvey's philosophy had a very important impact on the development of the liberation struggles in Africa. The first cohort of independent leaders, especially led by Kwame Nkrumah, a prominent pan-African organiser who helped Ghana to achieve independence in 1957, felt that Garveyist doctrine of Black self-rule and pride was the key to development. In the period of European dominance in Africa in the 1920s and even before that, where genocide was committed against the people of Namibia and in Congo where 10 million Congolese were killed by the Belgians, the major organised force globally against colonialism then was led by Garvey. It is one thing that was not spoken about as much. In the 1920s when Europe really consolidated their power in Africa, it was the UNIA and Marcus Garvey's leadership that was at the centre of African liberation." [Source: The Gleaner, April 14, 2022]

Like powerful waves, Garvey's influence has been tremendous! He sent out powerfully impactful signals. He was a powerfully impactful signal.

- "Garvey has invariably been described as the Black Moses of his race, a group psychologist and idealist planner, an iconoclast, an egotist, a zealot, charlatan and buffoon. He has also been portrayed as flamboyant, dynamic, bombastic, defiant, ruthless, a dreamer and a fool. Regardless of what history will write about him, and his personal shortcomings notwithstanding, Marcus Garvey was undoubtedly the peerless champion of his race. He was a bulwark for the world-wide organization of people of African descent. [Source: Milfred C. Fierce in The Black Scholar, 1972]

- "Doubtless, Marcus Mosiah Garvey opened the minds of Black People in America and the rest of the world. With his Universal Negro Improvement Association (UNIA), founded in 1914, he inspired a myriad of people, including the legendary Martin Luther King and the Civil Rights Movement, the Black Panthers and the Black Power Party. My colleague Ras Dr. Michael Barnett has produced a copious body of work, demonstrating how the Nation of Islam has deep roots in Garveyism. We might be even surprised that many of the modern-day successful economic policies, including that followed by Singapore, and the American economists of the post-World War II era, were influenced by Jamaica-based St Lucian, Sir Arthur Lewis. His ideas, nurtured while at the fledgling University of the West Indies (UWI), ultimately made him the first black person to receive the Nobel Prize in any other category than peace. Lewis' father was a strong Garveyite, who took him to many UNIA meetings in his boyhood. America's popular economic perspective, modernisation theory, developed by W.W. Rostow, therefore has some of its roots in Garveyism." [Source: Orville Taylor, The Gleaner, February 7, 2021]

Marcus Mosiah Garvey was, like all humans, imperfect. But he is an icon, a giant among men, and a true hero, who is deserving of respect, adulation, and emulation because he left a template that may be adopted or adapted by an individual, a community, or a nation aiming for transformation and empowerment.

Marcus Garvey raised and dilated on questions of race and identity, issues with which Jamaicans still have to come to terms, in 2021! I don't think as an independent and predominantly Black (92%) country, Jamaica has satisfactorily dealt with the issues he raised.

Marcus Garvey urged Blacks to assume a greater role in the larger scheme of things. He had a vision of united Black nations governed by Black leaders. Was he over-ambitious or naive in this regard?

Garvey combined his scholarship and intuitively radical genius with charisma. Charisma is that most desired, yet elusive personality trait (Charisma: noun. 1. personal magnetism: the ability to inspire enthusiasm, interest, or affection in others by means of personal charm or influence. 2. Divine gift: a gift or power believed to be divinely bestowed).

Marcus Garvey intuitively understood that the affirmation or consciousness of the value of Black or African culture, heritage, and identity was a potent weapon to overthrow and vanquish the obscene ideology that invented the 'barbaric Negro.'

Every time I reflect on Garvey, I rediscover anew the depth of his genius.

This is true: **"Garvey was so far ahead of his time, particularly concerning his promotion of entrepreneurship among Blacks" [Owen James, Business Journalist, on Twitter, November 30, 2018].**

I am sorely disappointed that Garvey's philosophy has not been mainstreamed in the minds of our people. I agree with economist, author, and lecturer Mark Ricketts when he said: "We can't forever cloak ourselves in an excuse-driven thought process which allows us as individuals, government, and the private sector, to make bad decisions, and then tie everything to disadvantages arising from slavery, imperialism, and colonialism." [Source: The Gleaner, January 27, 2019]

It deeply saddens, worries, and animates me when I traverse Jamaica and see Black Jamaicans setting up unsightly 'stalls' on the sides of roads or 'cotching' adjacent to established businesses, or dodging traffic with their wares, to 'hustle' to make a living. This is not what Garvey envisaged.

I've often wondered how people from China can come to Jamaica, barely able to speak the English Language, if at all, but set up businesses, while many Jamaicans erect what I have just described. I think these two vastly different ethnic scenarios arise from two different culturally-derived mindsets and a lack of empowerment of our people.

On September 23, 2019, I observed a man setting up a rickety stall on the side of the main road in eastern Jamaica. Because I knew that this was not what Garvey envisaged, I took a photograph of the scene and posted it on my Facebook page with the caption 'One photograph, many words.' Several of my friends commented on it. Here is a sample of their comments: "The struggle is real"; "Money haffi mek"; "Hustle on!"; "Better than go thief, hustle hard"; "Hustling, creativity, survival, industrious, hard work, sole trader." Only one of my friends cautiously (from fear of being cursed) commented that the man was breaking the law. This is instructive: in the absence of opportunities or other types of personal enablement, survival and law-breaking converge in Jamaica!

Each year for the last decade, researchers at the University of Technology, Jamaica have published the Global Entrepreneurship Monitor (GEM) which is a barometer of entrepreneurial activity in Jamaica. Over the years, the findings of the GEM reports have been insightful and revealing. The reports are available online and thus easily accessible to persons wishing to peruse them.

I am arguing that Marcus Garvey sought to instill wealth creation through entrepreneurship in Jamaicans, and we should embrace and mainstream entrepreneurial education in our educational institutions.

Education systems have been implicated in the maintenance of structures of domination by being vehicles for the reproduction of classism, racism, sexism, and hierarchical historical privilege. Progressive thinkers such as Marcus Garvey, Michael Manley, Amartya Sen, and Paulo Freire all posit that the moral purpose of education must be for peoples' liberation!

Liberated people are empowered people!

Also, Frederick Douglass – American social reformer, abolitionist, orator, writer, and statesman - clearly understood the value of enlightenment and empowerment through education, when he averred that: "Knowledge makes a man unfit to be a slave."

A colonized mind is a terrible kind of tragedy. I also think Garvey's realization that 'consciousness-raising' had to be his starting point is further irrefutable evidence of the elegance and depth of his intuitive genius!

When Barbados removed the statue of Horatio Nelson from its National Heroes' Square to the Barbados Museum and Historical Society on November 16, 2020, Prime Minister Mia Mottley chanelled Marcus Garvey as an inspiring force! The removal of Horatio Nelson's statue from its prominent position reflects a move away from vestiges of colonial rule, and acknowledgment that Nelson was a strong defender of the British Colonial system that included slavery. During the removal ceremony Prime Minister Mottley stated: "While we accept that the statute of Vice-Admiral Lord Horatio Nelson is an important historical relic, it is not a relic to be placed in the National Heroes Square of a nation that has to fight for too long to shape its destiny." [Source: Barbados.com]

Anyone who says Marcus Garvey's philosophy does not have contemporary relevance is an idiot.

This brings me to an interesting convergence of methodology by an impressive trio of change agents: **Garvey platformed his mission on 'consciousness-raising'; Michael Manley predicated his mission on 'politics of change,' and Paulo Freire, similar to Garvey, and perhaps inspired by him, predicated his mission on 'conscientization.' And all three enlightened men were on a mission aimed at empowerment and liberation of historically underprivileged people!**

"Each conscious one must teach a not-yet-conscious-one" and "when you learn, teach" are approaches I strongly endorse and unreservedly recommend.

These approaches are analogous to the approach taken by Harriet Tubman, who, having escaped the wretched cotton fields of America where she was held in enslavement, did not turn her back on those left behind. Instead, Tubman covertly returned multiple times to the south to free 70 others, during which she gave them this advice: "If you hear the dogs, keep going. If you see the torches in the woods, keep going. If there's shouting after you, keep going. Don't ever stop. Keep going. If you want a taste of freedom, keep going."

My fellow Jamaican, we must say enough, already! with the high per capita levels of collective unconsciousness and dysconsciousness among our people, and act to fix the worrisome situation.

Alas, most Black People I know, including family members, friends, co-workers, professional colleagues, and acquaintances, are frighteningly 'unconscious' and 'dysconscious.' I think this results from two factors:

- The psychological burden and effect of the accumulated scar tissue from colonialism they epigenetically inherited from our formerly enslaved ancestors, and
- Their inattentiveness.

Perhaps it is the former that has led to the latter, or other factors are at play, such as willful ignorance or an education system designed to produce such an outcome. I think, though, that with so much information available at our fingertips, ignorance is not a superpower. Nevertheless, those who know must teach others.

A colonized mind is truly an awful tragedy to behold because the mental bondages are the toughest to unravel. They are embedded deep in the psyche.

The colonizers knew this and expended considerable effort to condition and pollute the mind of enslaved persons!

In a Facebook post on July 1, 2020, 'AB' put it this way: "A significant percentage of Jamaica's population is gripped in a daze, transfixed in a Stockholm Syndrome-like state of being."

The sad reality of cultural and identity schizophrenia is real.

Indeed, W.E.B. DuBois lamented the "double-consciousness" (the cognitive 'two-ness') of the Black man, "always looking at oneself through the eyes ... measuring oneself by the means of a nation that looked back in contempt."

"I had always sensed, even among the most confident Black people, that their fear was right there at the top, ready to overwhelm them." ~ Albert Woodfox

Black People's reality is straddling and toggling between the contrasting cognitive states of being required to inhabit Black and white worlds. The allostatic load of the constant code-switching is exhausting.

Additionally, Frantz Fanon puts it this way in his epic book **'Black Skins, White Masks'**: "The Black man possesses two dimensions: one with his fellow Blacks, the other with the Whites. A Black man behaves differently with a white man than he does with another Black man. There is no doubt whatsoever that this fissiparousness is a direct consequence of the colonial undertaking. Nobody dreams of challenging the fact that its principal inspiration is nurtured by the core of theories which represent the Black man as the missing link in the slow evolution from ape to man. These are objective facts that state reality. The divided self-perception of a Black Subject who has lost his native cultural origin, and embraced the culture of the Mother Country, produces an inferior sense of self in the "Black Man." They will try to appropriate and imitate the culture of the colonizer where such behavior is more readily evident in upwardly mobile and educated Black people who can afford to acquire status symbols within the world of the colonial ecumene, such as an education abroad and mastery of the language of the colonizer, the white masks."

Colonization fashioned a self-image of Black People for Black People and imposed it on Black People. An image that prescribes notions of "beauty", "intelligence", "normal," "acceptable," and "worthy," among others. And it was continuously reinforced with remarkable success through multiple means, including, religion, the education system, television, movies, comics, and other overt and covert technologies. For example, even highly successful Black women, are ashamed of their natural hair. And many successful Black men think their greatest achievement is to 'bed' a white woman.

Therefore, I'm arguing that Garvey's actions collectively represent a **template** – a blueprint - that still has relevance and utility for us as individuals, communities, and a nation to adopt or adapt for transformation and empowerment. Yes, Garveyism is a philosophy to be **actioned and lived** and not just regarded and treated as an excursion in intellectual masturbation or romanticism.

Fittingly, at the 27th annual staging of IRIE FM's Marcus Garvey Celebration, held on August 19, 2018, the Guest speaker was Haitian historian, teacher, and writer Professor Bayyinah Bello who, in her passion-filled speech, declared that **"As a people, we must not just repeat Garvey quotes, but incorporate the principles of his teaching in our lives!"**

Professor Bello's exhortation and challenge to avowed or nascent Garveyites is spot on. I agree with her because this is how, I think, as a people, we will truly honour Garvey, and benefit in tangible ways from his philosophy of Black empowerment and Black self-reliance anchored in and scaffolded upon education and racial pride!

And in an article titled **'Why won't we listen to Marcus Garvey?'** that was published in The Sunday Gleaner on August 16, 2020 – one day before the 133rd anniversary of Garvey's birth - Professor Carolyn Cooper declared that "Marcus Garvey's philosophy and its application are certainly relevant in Jamaica today. But who is listening? All secondary and tertiary students should read Professor Rupert Lewis' definitive biography of Garvey. A national hero whose words are neither heard nor heeded cannot inspire a society that is still struggling to define its identity."

In addition, on August 17, 2020, 'SA' posted the following on his Facebook Page "Marcus Garvey in my opinion is the greatest hero produced by the Black race to date, unlike most other great leaders, he backed up his rhetoric with practical displays of what the Black man had to do, to command respect, dignity, and economic independence. The massive conglomerate that he created at a time when Black People were disenfranchised from creating wealth of any kind is a testament to his remarkable vision, bravery, and confidence that Black People can defeat the forces of evil, when he said "Up, you mighty race, you can accomplish what you will." On this anniversary of his birth, I celebrate this great Icon, and hope that more Black people will read about his exploits, and imagine where we could have been today if we followed the blueprint he left us eighty years ago. The fact that Marcus Garvey's birthday is not celebrated in a manner befitting his contribution to the upliftment of the Black race around the world is testimony to our timidity in offending the white establishment and realizing our full potential. Happy birthday Marcus Garvey, may your spirit continue to guide us."

I am pleased to say I have incorporated Garveyism in my andragogy (teaching of adults). You see, I teach topics in innovation and entrepreneurship from time to time to students pursuing masters' and doctoral degrees, and I always start with the question: "What lessons can nascent innovators and entrepreneurs draw from Marcus Mosiah Garvey?"

On these occasions, I find that only a few of the students are familiar with Garvey's life and work while others, at this advanced level of education, are only aware of his name. The latter situation is an indictment of the Jamaican education system. Anyway, in my discussion with the students, I seek to get them to 'connect dots' between the mindset nascent innovators need to have and the corresponding philosophical and tangible aspects of Garvey's life and work.

For example, Garvey declared "without confidence one is twice defeated in the race of life." Clearly, nascent innovators and entrepreneurs need to be doggedly confident to reap success in their endeavours. I also recommend to my students, for further reading, my paper **'Illuminating the Andragogical Dimension of Marcus Garvey's Legacy'** which was published in the Journal of Arts Science and Technology (Volume 7, 2014, pp. 1-11). Reader, I recommend my paper to you too.

So, as a learning facilitator, my objective is to get my students to appreciate and understand that, as espoused and articulated by Garvey, their mindset, their self-confidence, their embrace of scholarship, and their systematic approach to doing things, are critical to their success - especially against the background of our education system training students to seek '9-to-5 jobs' rather than leveraging their talents, training, skills, and passions, to create wealth for themselves as innovators and entrepreneurs!

Interestingly, some of the students openly admitted their lack of knowledge of the potency and contemporary relevance to Black people of Garvey's philosophy and message!

My 'take-home-point' here is that, those of us educators who understand the value of Garvey's philosophy and message, have a responsibility to expose our students to them ... without waiting for any 'official approval.'

In an article published in The Daily Observer newspaper on August 9, 2020, Stephen Vasciannie, Professor of International Law at The University of the West Indies, recalled how, for him and his peers as 'BSc Economics students' at the UWI circa 1978,' "Question 1 on the tutorial sheet for the course 'Introduction to Politics' was about Marcus Garvey: "Garvey preached racial pride but the main point of his work was anti-imperialism. Discuss." (I like this question, and I would love to read what a young Vasciannie wrote in response!)

One day in 2020, I posted on Facebook that I routinely introduced my post-graduate level students to Marcus Garvey's philosophy; my post elicited a veritable flood of comments (more than 100!) – both for and against Garvey. The 'against-Garvey' comments came thick and fast. But the 'pro-Garvey' brigade quickly mobilized itself to defend their man!

It was a remarkable intellectual 'war' that played out on my Facebook page revealing Garvey's capacity to animate people 80 years after his death. Clearly, he has achieved immortality and has ascended to the pantheon of those persons who have made it impossible for history to forget them.

Here's a sampling of the 'anti-Garvey' comments:

"For innovations and entrepreneurship, I'd prefer the teachings of Steve Jobs, Mark Zuckerberg, Bill Gates, Elon Musk, Warren Buffett; Jeff Bezos; Dan Lok, etc." I think an electric car from Elon Musk; technological possibilities from Mark Zuckerberg and a digital marketplace from Jeff Bezos (e.g.) are more pertinent to the future than the philosophical quotes of Garvey. Not to discount Garvey, don't get me wrong." Someone who agreed with these comments said, "iPhones and Mac computers are more common among Black people than knowledge of Africa or Garvey."

"I'd say, take leadership examples from great leaders, despite race. Jack Ma and Donald Trump added to my previous list." [This comment, though, made one of the commenters cringe: "I could not go with Trump ... I have been reading that guy for over 20 years ... he is a world-class asshole ... Not Trump ... he is a lucky dunce ... you will never find too many like him."]

"Garvey's teachings are a little outdated for me. Maybe we need to look for a new hero. I understand what Paul Ivey is saying and I know that he means good but this is not going to happen and for good reasons... Garvey was over 100 hundred years ago and even though he was ahead of his time .... that time has run out... We must look to someone who is going to carry us for the next 100 - 200 hundred years."

"There are many women in this country who can give us a lot more guidance than Garvey at this time...

'One God, One Destiny' is not a pragmatic mission because too many factors are up against that possibility."

"Garvey's problem was that he did not take his own quote as seriously as he should have educated himself on world matters... he was no match in education to his wife, Amy Jacques Garvey... not even close."

"We have to look at his errors and try NOT to make those... His philosophies are not new or unique... just that he had the platform to preach his... Garvey did not know about Africa, although it was his ambition to become the President of Africa... Not many Garveyites talk about this... Garvey was largely uneducated and basically learned a few things as he went along ... Malcolm X was way above Garvey ... just as the current leader of the Nation of Islam."

"Garvey is simply outdated ... We are now in a far newer dispensation with new paradigms ... no one needs Garvey's philosophies because it is not that they are unique ... His philosophies are what I call common sense philosophies that anyone with sense will use and it so happens that many who have never studied his philosophies have been practicing those same common-sense philosophies ... This is like saying that we should all learn mathematics ... or technology or a second language ... The main vehicle that he developed to carry his center-piece philosophy failed ... Garvey's biggest neglect and oversight are how he treated women in the philosophy of how Black people should rise ... If anyone today were to run the UNIA the way Garvey ran it, they too would fail miserably."

"Garveyites tend to be as arrogant as Garvey was ... they entertain nothing but what they would like to hear ... How is that a healthy approach to the consideration of a man who has clearly erred in several ways? Why are Garveyites so intolerant of questions about 'God Garvey'?"

"Garvey's philosophy and what he stood for is not only outdated, it's dangerous. Every time I read posts like this one, I ask myself if these people really took the time to learn about Marcus Garvey, or are they only about style? Garvey was downright disrespectful of mixed-race people and as a consequence did not allow any to hold positions in the UNIA. How many children at school age now can claim to be of Garvey's pure African stock? Garvey was no doubt a brave man back in the 1920s and would have been admired for that back then by millions of oppressed blacks around the world, but he was far from being the visionary that would make him relevant 100 years hence. To embrace Garvey's philosophy today, one would have to embrace his push for the segregation of races. Who among us would select racial segregation over racial integration? Garvey is outdated, plain and simple."

"There are so many things about Garvey that make him a waste man, I have to wonder what is the objective for a post such as this ... If only Garvey was able to meet with Booker T. Washington, he might have approached things differently ... might have.

Garveyism is as dead as Manley's democratic socialism."

And here's a sampling of the 'pro-Garvey' comments:

"GARVEY Must Be Placed at The Foundation of ALL TEACHERS COLLEGES in JAH MEKYA."

"Pro-activism is the lightning rod of Garvey's relevance, in this time and forever."

"Garvey subscribed to creating our own and created many institutions that were serviced by and served Blacks. He is a man for all our seasons."

"We take inspiration from him because his aim was for Black People to raise their standards by taking their own economics into their own hands. While his principles may be universal, we cannot deny his ability to move a base ... we have several successful individuals from our community but he was leading a movement to bring widespread improvement. Generally speaking, our people have been lost ... Garvey energized people to go beyond thinking, wondering doubting, and perhaps never doing to actually doing. He died long before my birth and still holds such a thrust ... do not underestimate his greatness."

"For a man to have inspired leaders and nations across the globe. Many successful individuals have been inspired by him. That man is not just successful; that man is great!"

"It is interesting that some Black people will say Garvey's philosophy and opinions are outdated and irrelevant today, but they will readily quote Shakespeare, Plato, Aristotle, Henry Ford, Seneca, Marcus Aurelius, Niccolò Machiavelli, and others, without batting an eyelid."

"In 2003, Ian Adams, honorary fellow of the University of Durham, UK, and his co-author R. W. Dyson, Director of the Centre for the History of Political Thought, jointly published a book titled **'50 Major Political Thinkers.'** This publication included Marcus Garvey among giant thinkers and well-known philosophers over 2,000 years, beginning with Plato, and Aristotle, and including others such as St. Thomas Aquinas, Niccolò Machiavelli, and Karl Marx.

And Joel A. Rogers included Garvey in his incomparable book **'World's Great Men of Color'**.

Yet, some of our people say Garvey's philosophy and opinions are irrelevant!"

"Garvey's philosophy is grounded in a state of mind, that is to say, actions toward constructive ends must begin with the right frame of mind. For example, to wit: "Without confidence, you are twice defeated in the race of life!" I guess if Richard Bronson or Steve Jobs said this, it would be okay to quote them and run wid it."

"New interpretation of his courage and bravery is necessary." Fear is a reaction; courage is a decision.

"One of the gravest mistakes we make as a people is to constantly and consistently elevate the Caucasian as lords over us in all things. So, we consistently look to him to teach us, to validate us and to be the standard by which we strive for all things. There are so many innovators and innovative successful entrepreneurs among us, that we need not look anywhere greater than within for inspiration. People such as Daymond John, Richard and Sheila Johnson. Mansa Musa, Madam CJ Walker, Aliko Dangote, Mike Adenuga, Robert Smith, Oprah Winfrey, Byaruhanga Kimberly, Femi Otedola, and Strive Masiyiwa, to name a few. When there is greatness within, greatness without fades in comparison. Sankofa - greatness is our DNA! The great daddy Marcus is as relevant today as he was 100 years ago. It's good for us to teach our children about him and to look to his philosophies for many solutions, entrepreneurial, philosophical, and otherwise. Greatness begets greatness. Sankofa!"

"When I saw that list of white entrepreneurs, I was taken aback. Not one Blackpreneur?! I was shaking my head in sadness. As for Garvey's relevance in these contemporary times, with this generation, we do have to find some relatable heroes to add to Garvey. He is an important part of our past. If we don't know where we are from, we will have no clue where we are headed. Garvey is an important link."

"Many have not failed having never tried ... no shame in trying and continuing to try to be successful ... success is not guaranteed to anyone."

"Our brother Paul Ivey is shining a light on some facts about Garvey's leadership, and I think it is healthy for the whole family. No one is demoting our first national hero!"

"Very balanced discourse on the topic of Garvey as an innovator/philosopher/entrepreneur and its relevance to nation building and the sharpening of our minds collectively. I am thankful to Paul Ivey for being forthright in driving the discussion and for providing useful comparisons. I am grateful for the privilege to be a part of history in the making. Continue to keep this space interesting"

There still is much work to be done concerning the psychological rehabilitation and liberation needed by many Black people (perhaps the majority) in Jamaica.

The psychological harm inflicted by colonialization is a difficult 'internal parasite' to get rid of. It is kind of like how the Human Immunodeficiency Virus (HIV) works in high-jacking the body's DNA-replicating apparatus and using it to produce more viruses! Or how malware takes over the operating system of computers!

Here is an example of what I'm talking about: On Friday, October 18, 2019, American rapper Kanye West was approved by the Minister of Entertainment, Culture, and Gender Affairs, Olivia Grange, to perform a 'Pop-up Sunday Service' in Emancipation Park in Kingston.

Now, this is the same feckless and craven Kanye West who has not only expressed his admiration for Donald Trump (who Andrew Sullivan of the New York Magazine labelled a "monstrous and ridiculous fool"), but in an interview with the entertainment television station TMZ on May 1, 2018 said: "When you hear about slavery for 400 years ... for 400 years! That sounds like a choice." A choice, he says. Black people chose to enslave themselves for 400 years!

The fact that Kanye West (a vacuous buffoon, in my opinion) could have been allowed to perform in Emancipation Park – a place built in honour of our ancestors who endured the bottomless barbarity of enslavement - is, in my opinion, unacceptable. It's the equivalent of giving the 'middle finger' to our ancestors and their extant descendants! One commentator likened Kanye's presence to a 'one-night stand' and that Jamaica was, as Bob Marley sung, truly a 'Pimpers' Paradise.'

Persistent Hunger for Positivity

Black people's persistent hunger for positive representation and affirmation was seen in the release in the USA of the movie **Black Panther** in February 2018. The movie broke records, becoming the top-grossing film with a Black director and predominantly Black cast. The Marvel blockbuster grossed $235 million in the USA alone.

"Even before the movie's release, it was clear that Black Panther represented much more than an evening's entertainment (although at a 97 percent rating on Rotten Tomatoes, it's certainly an outstanding example of that): This was a movie made by and for Black people" [Source: Chloe Hall and Mariel Tyler, Elle Magazine, February 20, 2018].

Elle Magazine spoke to Black Panther viewers at Washington, D.C.'s Regal Cinema 12 and New York City's

AMC Magic Johnson Harlem theater about what the groundbreaking film means to them. Here is a sampling of the responses:

- "I hope it wins Oscars. For the first time, someone Black could win an Oscar for being a hero and not a crooked cop, a slave. They would win for being articulate, smart, successful and loving. It's just such a positive image for once."

- "It paints Black men, for one, in a positive image. I'm originally from Indiana and they [white people] like to use the word "thug" instead of the N-word, but you know what they really mean. I think the movie is a great way to show we are more than what you say we are. We always have been, we always will be, and you're going to see more of this."

- "With the particular political climate that we're in, especially in the shadows of the comments that have recently been made, I think it recasts Black folks as overcomers, which we are. We have a strong history of overcoming—no matter what we've been given, we rise above and beyond it. We have a strong history of overcoming—no matter what we've been given, we rise above and beyond it. I think it's such a beautiful narrative to have put forth on a global stage, especially in light of what we're dealing with right now."

- "I think it's important that Africa receives what is due. I think in many instances we've overlooked the immense contributions that have come from the African continent: contributions to math, contributions to engineering, contributions to science. And I think this story, seeing how advanced Wakanda is being portrayed as, almost kind of tells us about the ability that we were able to build pyramids when other folks were struggling in caves."

- "I think it's important that Black people see a superhero. When I grew up, all we had was Superman. We had the real-life superhero which was Muhammad Ali but never anybody on screen to see. I'm the first generation of Black women who grew up with dolls; my mother didn't have Black dolls, her mother didn't have any—so every step we're going further and further, and I just think it's beautiful."

- "It's monumental. I just think Black people are the most beautiful thing in the world.... It's a good story, because it's showing what would happen if we were never colonized, if we were never enslaved, where we would've taken it. We can tell just by the super people in our own background—Harriet Tubman, Frederick Douglass, Muhammad Ali, all these people who are real superheroes—that we would've been something else. I think it's great for [Raisah] to see. That's why I made sure to bring my daughter out—she'll remember it and her generation will take it even further."

- "There's so many reasons, but I'm excited to see people that look like me as superheroes on the big screen. I'm excited to see people that look like me as superheroes on the big screen. I think there's a lot of narratives around Blackness that have to do with slavery and history, but this is more like Afrofuturism. I'm just really happy to be here, and it's a prideful moment."

- "This is the thing I want my daughter to see, this kind of representation of Black people."

- "We're in a time where it's almost frowned upon to celebrate your Blackness. People are really conflating pro-Black with anti-white, and that's not what it is. That's why it's so important and so special we give our little ones this type of representation. We're being told we aren't allowed to celebrate at times."

- "It means everything to me, especially in superhero culture you don't see a lot of Black people. Just like we can be doctors and lawyers, we can be magical superheroes too."

- "It's excellent for our kids to see. It's a boost for our community and our culture."

- "I love it. I love that Black people are loving their culture right now. We are in love with our hair, we are in love with everything. I teach my students all the time, you've got to love who you are and stop trying to be other people. Be you, and you are gorgeous."

- "It's great hearing the story told by our own people and not having others tell it for us. It's refreshing."

- "It means everything. Representation, everything. We have our kids out here to see people who look like them reflected on the screen. To be a part of this really big cultural event. I don't think we've been excited about anything like this as a collective since president Obama's inauguration. I don't think we've been excited about anything like this as a collective since president Obama. It's been a long time for us to be excited about something collective."

- "It's allowing us to vision what liberation could be. It's kind of bittersweet too, because it's like if y'all would have left us the hell alone, this is where we would be."

Garvey Public Sector Graduate Scholarship

I was immensely pleased in September 2020 when the following announcement caught my attention: "The Minister of Finance and the Public Service Dr. the Hon. Nigel Clarke officially launched the Marcus Garvey Public Sector Graduate Scholarship Programme which will offer 30 graduate scholarships each year for the next five years for public sector employees, at an estimated cost, over the five years, of J$1 billion.

The first scholarship award ceremony was held on August 17, 2021. The event also commemorated the 134th anniversary of the birth of Marcus Garvey. The scholarships were established to provide Jamaican nationals and citizens employed in the public sector with the opportunity to pursue post-graduate studies in areas that are in alignment with Jamaica's national priorities and strategic objectives.

In his remarks at the scholarship award function, Governor General Sir Patrick Allen said "The Marcus Garvey Public Sector Graduate Scholarship Programme is a bold initiative that will provide an excellent opportunity for the recipients. I was honoured to have been asked to serve as the Chairman of the Scholarship Selection Committee. All the candidates who were interviewed have excelled in their professions and demonstrate a clear vision of how this will contribute to national development."

For his part, Dr. Nigel Clarke, Minister of Finance and the Public Service, stated that "The Marcus Garvey Public Sector Graduate Scholarship Programme is a core element of the Government of Jamaica's (GOJ's) human capital development strategy. Through this scholarship programme, the GOJ is building the human capital and organizational capacity of the public sector. As such, the Marcus Garvey Scholarship Programme has been conceived to ensure that the next generation of leaders in the public service have the best opportunities in the world to improve and add to their skills. As many as 150 public sector leaders will benefit from full graduate scholarships over the next five years in areas aligned with GOJ's policy priorities. We are proud of the fact that the Marcus Garvey Scholarship is the largest and most ambitious scholarship programme in Jamaica's history. It was Marcus Garvey who exhorted us to 'Accomplish what we will.' In the design and implementation of this scholarship programme we are merely following this command."

The benefits of the scholarship are:

- The Marcus Garvey Scholarships will cover 100% of tuition costs for the eligible programmes at the participating universities.
- Scholarship awardees will be provided with a stipend to cover reasonable costs for living expenses including meals and accommodation. These will be standard rates determined by the Technical Secretariat and subject to revision on an annual basis.
- For scholarships tenable in overseas universities, the programme will provide the awardees with transportation, including airfare, from Jamaica to the university and on completion of studies, from the university to Jamaica.

The first set of scholarships will attend the University of the West Indies (UWI) Mona and the University of Technology, Jamaica; Johns Hopkins University and Harvard University in the USA; and King's College London and Oxford University in the United Kingdom.

Marcus Garvey had a reverence for education and scholarship. He would be pleased with these scholarships.

Potent Cognitive Gems from Marcus Garvey

- "The greatest possession of mankind is character."
- "I like honesty and fair play."
- "If we as a people realized the greatness from which we came we would be less likely to disrespect ourselves."

- "The Black skin is not a badge of shame, but rather a glorious symbol of national greatness." Black people are melaninaires!
- "A people without the knowledge of their past history, origin and culture is like a tree without roots."
- "We are going to emancipate ourselves from mental slavery because whilst others might free the body, none but ourselves can free the mind." [This proclamation, uttered in 1937 at UNIA regional conference in Ottawa, Canada, is one of the most profound ever made by a Black Man! Many people 'mouth' these words from Garvey without grasping their profundity and prerequisiteness. This emancipation (the installation of a new cognitive operating system) is a prerequisite - a sine qua non - for true Black liberation and Black empowerment.]
- "Mind is your only ruler, sovereign. The man who is not able to develop and use his mind is bound to be the slave of the other man who uses his mind." [Here Garvey was channelling Buddha who averred that "All that we are is the result of what we have thought'; James Allen's book 'As a Man Thinketh' is his best-known work]
- "Be Black, buy Black, think Black, and all else will take care of itself."
- "Liberate the minds of men and ultimately you will liberate the bodies of men."
- "Do not remove the kinks from your hair … remove them from your brain."

- "If you get up every day and you don't learn, you are a fool.'
- "If you have no confidence in self, you are twice defeated in the race of life."
- "I trust that you will so live today as to realize that you are masters of your own destiny, masters of your fate; if there is anything you want in this world, it is for you to strike out with confidence and faith in self and reach for it."
- "Every man has a right to his own opinion. Every race has a right to its own action; therefore, let no man persuade you against your will, let no other race influence you against your own."
- "There shall be no solution to this race problem until you, yourselves, strike the blow for liberty."
- "Real men laugh at opposition; real men smile when enemies appear."
- "Men who are in earnest are not afraid of consequences."
- "Marcus Garvey does not give a snap for anything human but justice, and that which is based upon righteousness."
- "Glorious shall be the battle when the time comes to fight for our people and our race."
- "If the enemy could only know that Marcus Garvey is but a John the Baptist in the wilderness, that a greater and more dangerous Marcus Garvey is yet to appear, the Garvey with whom you will have to reckon for the injustice of the present generation."
- "Progress is the attraction that moves humanity."

- "Whatsoever things common to man, that man has done, man can do."
- "Intelligence rules the world, ignorance carries the burden."
- "The man who is not able to develop and use his mind is bound to be the slave of the other man who uses his mind."
- "Ambition is the desire to go forward and improve one's condition. It is a burning flame that lights up the life of the individual and makes him see himself in another state. To be ambitious is to be great in mind and soul. To want that which is worthwhile and strive for it. To go on without looking back, reaching to that which gives satisfaction."
- "Take advantage of every opportunity; where there is none, make it for yourself."
- "We must give up the silly idea of folding our hands and waiting on God to do everything for us. If God had intended for that, then he would not have given us a mind. Whatever you want in life, you must make up your mind to do it for yourself."
- "God does not... give people positions or jobs or... good conditions such as they desire; they must do that for themselves ... God does not build cities nor towns nor nations, nor homes, nor factories; men and people do that and all those who want must work for themselves and pray to God to give them strength to do it."
- "There is no force like success, and that is why the individual makes all effort to surround himself

throughout life with the evidence of it; as of the individual, so should it be of the nation."

- "A race that is solely dependent upon another for economic existence sooner or later dies. As we have in the past been living upon the mercies shown by others, and by the chances obtainable, and have suffered there from, so we will in the future suffer if an effort is not made now to adjust our own affairs."
- "A reading man and woman is a ready man and woman, but a writing man and woman is exact."
- "Never forget that intelligence rules the world and ignorance carry the burden. Therefore, remove yourself as far as possible from ignorance and seek as far as possible to be intelligent."
- "Always try to associate with people from whom you can learn something. All the knowledge that you want is in the world, and all you have to do is go and seek it."
- "I have no desire to take all Black people back to Africa; there are Blacks who are no good here and will likewise be no good there."
- "The enemies are not so much from without as from within the race."
- "The greatest weapon used against the negro is disorganization."
- "The thing to do is to get organized; keep separated and you will be exploited, you will be robbed, you will be killed. Get organized and you will compel the world to respect you."

- "Having had the wrong education as a start in his racial career, the Negro has become his own greatest enemy. Most of the trouble I have had in advancing the cause of the race has come from Negroes. Booker Washington aptly described the race in one of his lectures by stating that we were like crabs in a barrel, that none would allow the other to climb over, but on any such attempt all would continue to pull back into the barrel the one crab that would make the effort to climb out. Yet, those of us with vision cannot desert the race, leaving it to suffer and die."
- "Chance has never yet satisfied the hope of a suffering people."
- "Africa for the Africans... at home and abroad!"
- "Africa has become the big game of the nation hunters. Today, Africa looms as the greatest commercial, industrial and political prize in the world."
- "The whole world is run on bluff."
- "You may call me a Klansman if you will, but, potentially, every white man is a Klansman, as far as the Negro in competition with whites socially, economically and politically is concerned, and there is no use lying."
- "The white man has succeeded in subduing the world by forcing everybody to think his way.... The white man's propaganda has made him the master of the world, and all those who have come in

contact with it and accepted it have become his slaves."

- "The history of contact between the white and black races for the last three hundred years or more, records only a series of pillages, wholesale murders, atrocious brutalities, industrial exploitation, disfranchisement of the one on the other; the strong against the weak."

- "The Negro will have to build his own industry, art, sciences, literature, and culture before the world will stop to consider him."

- "The [Black] race needs workers at this time, not plagiarists, sophists and mere imitators; but men and women who are able to create, to originate and improve, and thus make an independent racial contribution to the world and civilisation."

- "Every student of political science, every student of political economy, every student of economics knows that the race can only be saved through a solid industrial foundation; that the race can only be saved through political independence. Take away industry from a race, take away political freedom from a race and you have a slave race."

- "There can be no peace among men and nations, so long as the strong continues to oppress the weak, so long as injustice is done to other peoples, just so long we will have cause for war, and make a lasting peace an impossibility."

- "Hungry men have no respect for law, authority or human life."

- "To see your enemy and know him is a part of the complete education of man."
- "At no time within the last five-hundred years can one point to a single instance of the Negro as a race of haters."
- "A man's bread and butter are only insured when he works for it."

Marcus Garvey has deepened and enriched Black people's knowledge of ourselves, our glorious history, and boundless potential despite deliberate countervailing forces determined to subjugate us. He gave us an ideal.

Marcus Garvey devoted his life to living his message – contending with triumph, disaster, derision, disdain, disapproval, jealousy, oppression, imprisonment, and rejection. In other words, in contemporary parlance, they tried to 'cancel' Garvey.

Marcus Mosiah Garvey has left an indelible mark on the world, most profoundly in the realm of enduring ideas, opinions, and philosophy. He has earned a place among the pantheon of the great philosophers of the 20th Century.

Wikipedia describes Marcus Garvey as "a Jamaican political leader, publisher, journalist, entrepreneur, and orator."

Fittingly, the St. Ann Homecoming and Heritage Foundation, the St. Ann Parish Library, and the St. Ann Municipal Corporation have ensured that Marcus Garvey's memory is honoured at his birthplace with the staging of an annual Marcus Garvey lecture series in his hometown, St. Ann's Bay. The lecture series is timed to coincide with the anniversary of Garvey's death and has drawn motivational and learned speakers each year. Consider presentations from Rex Nettleford, historian Arnold Bertram, The University of the West Indies lecturer Dr. K'Adamawe K'nife, former Governor General Sir Kenneth Hall, and well-known barrister Lord Anthony Gifford, retired educator James Walsh, and director of the Institute of Jamaica Vivian Crawford. Marcus Garvey is also memorialised in several countries in Africa with streets, towns and schools named in his honour. In England there is the Marcus Garvey Library in North London, and statues and various other shrines at centres across the country. The USA has parks, streets, and a culture centre bearing his name, and honour of honours, a bust of Garvey is housed in the Organisation of American States' Hall of Heroes in Washington, DC. [Source: Lance Neita, May 14, 2016]

"It was the first time that a national figure from the English-speaking Caribbean was selected for inclusion in this distinguished gallery. It was an honour to Jamaica and to the son of St Ann who earned international fame as the man who lit the torch of Pan-Africanism and raised the banner of Black awareness around the world. Jamaica's then Deputy Prime Minister and Minister of Foreign Affairs, the Hon. P. J. Patterson, flew to Washington to take the leading role at the ceremony. To him was accorded the privilege of unveiling the bust and of making the keynote speech for the occasion."

"The Garvey movement was an historical praxis of anti-imperialist struggle geared towards the freedom of a race. It is with this in mind that we understand Marcus Garvey and his creativity. What he did developed concretely out of the struggle he was involved in and had committed his life to. Garvey was indeed a polymath: he excelled in many different areas of human thought and practice. He exemplified a capacity for creating complex organizations, for extraordinary leadership talent, for extrapolating from the last half-millennium new philosophical insights relevant to the survival and development of Africa and its diasporas; in addition, he demonstrated an appreciation for the arts and was also, as poet, song lyricists and playwright, a practitioner of the arts; he was an entrepreneur, publisher, journalist and visionary. It is therefore not surprising that such a person would have made a number of tactical errors in some of these multiple activities, but on the fundamental goals and pursuits toward African empowerment and economic self-reliance he was consistent. And this is why he remains relevant in the twenty-first century." [Source: Rupert Lewis, Marcus Garvey, 2018]

Marcus Mosiah Garvey was indeed a polymath, the foundation of which was his early exposure to books in his father's library and the reverence for scholarship that they cemented into him. A person of wide-ranging knowledge and learning. Another famous Black polymath was Imhotep.

"No other Jamaican has had such a profound international impact as Marcus Garvey has. In an era that treated the idea of black inferiority almost as a given fact, Garvey shouted "No!" in a voice heard across the planet."

[Source: Kevin O'Brien Chang, 'Marcus Garvey: Black Champion of Vision and Destiny,' The Gleaner, August 3. 2012]

According to the Jamaica Information Service (JIS) "Garvey's legacy can be summed up in the philosophy he taught – racial pride, the need for African unity; self-reliance; the need for black people to be organised and for rulers to govern on behalf of the working classes."

Robert Hill, a research professor of history at UCLA and a Garvey scholar posits that "the UNIA created a societal model of Black nationalism and Pan-Africanism through political, economic and social means!"

(Steven Golding – son of former Prime Minister Bruce Golding – is the president of the UNIA in Jamaica)

Here is my take on Garveyism: Garvey's actions collectively represent a template .... a blueprint .... a roadmap .... that still has relevance and utility for Black individuals, Black communities, and Black nations to adopt or adapt (given new realities with the passage of time and the advent of new technologies) for transformation and empowerment. Key elements of Garvey's metanoia-scaffolded template are: racial pride, self-confidence, education, creative self-reliance, creative innovation, creative entrepreneurship, and creative wealth creation.

Yes, Garveyism is a philosophy to be internalised and incorporated into their psychitecture and actioned and lived by Black People and not just to be regarded and treated as an excursion in intellectual masturbation or romanticism by them.

The desired alternative to romanticism is powerfully expressed in these brain drops from Barbara Blake Hannah: "The Black race still searches for a particular "ism" that will be appropriate to its own particular situation. We search through Marxism, Communism, Socialism, Castro-ism and Capitalism, taking from each something which is relevant, but never finding a complete whole. The life work of Mrs. Garvey [in compiling and publishing her husband's work, thus rendering it permanently available) re-awakened the interest in the indigenous Jamaican "ism" - Garveyism, and the possibility that it may prove to be the most successful and lasting philosophy for the Jamaican and Black people."

I think Garvey would be pleased by this example of what his vision has spawned: On December 16, 2020, the United Nations General Assembly adopted, by Resolution 75/170, **'The International Day for People of African Descent'**, celebrated for the first time yesterday, August 31, 2021. The day was chosen in recognition of August 31, 1920, when the first 'International Convention of the Negro Peoples of the World' ended in New York; and as a result of the discussions led by The Rt. Excellent Marcus Mosiah Garvey, the 'Declaration of Rights of the Negro Peoples of the World' was promulgated. Typically, international days reflect the values that society shares (or ought to share). Through this observance, the United Nations aims to promote greater recognition and respect for the diverse heritage, culture and contribution of people of African ancestry to the development of societies, and to promote respect for human rights and fundamental freedoms, especially for women and girls who experience multiple forms of discrimination. Africans and people of African ancestry have suffered for centuries from a doctrine of racial superiority, which has caused us to experience slavery and other violent practices, excessive use of force by law-enforcement agencies and structural racism in criminal justice systems around the world. Yet, the doctrine of racial superiority, in particular white supremacy, is scientifically false, morally condemnable, socially unjust, and dangerous and must be rejected. As we continue to mark the International Day for People of African Descent; and as we approach the 20th anniversary of the 'World Conference Against Racism, Racial Discrimination, Xenophobia and Related Intolerance' held in Durban, South Africa, from August 31 to September 8, 2001, let us commit, not just to the elimination of all forms of racial discrimination and proclaim the rights of African people, but also intensify our fight for reparatory justice from states that committed crimes against humanity that have caused historical and contemporary harm to Africans and persons of African ancestry." [Source: The International Day for People of African Descent, The Centre for Reparation Research, The Gleaner – Letter of the Day - September 1, 2021]

Marcus Mosiah Garvey, the radically courageous Africa-descended genius from St. Ann, Jamaica, through the ongoingness of the cachet and influence of his philosophy, has earned immortality ... he has transcended being more than a man .... he has become a symbol – a symbol for upliftment and empowerment of African people at home and in the diaspora.

Garveyism - Marcus Mosiah Garvey's philosophy - is immortal and retains its relevance and resonance. Garveyism is timeless. There is Garvey the man, and there is the movement that he founded. Garvey the man died in 1940. Garveyism – the movement that the founded - lives on as a template for Black liberation and empowerment!

"In death, I shall be a terror to the foes of Negro liberty. Look for me in the whirlwind or the song of the storm. Look for me all around you."~ Marcus Garvey, Atlanta Penitentiary, 1925.

******

About the Author
============####=============
"I have cast my lot with the intellectual resistance, deploying my intellect in service of upliftment of my race, my country ... and ultimately humanity" ~ Paul W. Ivey

----

Paul W. Ivey was born the year after Jamaica received political independence from Britain in 1962. Except for brief periods spent abroad studying, he has lived in Jamaica all his life.

He is an unassuming, confident, and contented Introvert. After an unpromising start when he was perceived to be a 'dunce' child and relegated to the back of his class in kindergarten, he has since earned five College/University degrees – ASc., BSc., MSc., M.Ed., and Ph.D. - in agricultural and biological sciences and andragogy (adult education). Some persons have declared that he scans luminously as a scholarly, readerly, writerly, and thinkerly person - a Polymath.

Dr. Ivey has been an Adult Learning Scientist (Educator), Higher Education Administrator, and Applied Scientist at the secondary, college, and university levels since 1983. And from 2004-2009, he was President of Jamaica's premier multi-disciplinary college, one of his alma maters. He is an associate professor and senior academic manager at Jamaica's leading public University, since 2010.

Dr. Ivey is a prodigious and voracious reader. He has evolved into a passionate Cerebral Activist and Griot-Scholar (socio-cultural historian, town crier, observer, commentator, and influencer), who is now deploying writing as a powerful cognitive instrument to craft books and novels that will enhance readers' minds by inspiring, motivating, educating, enlightening, enthralling, empowering, and entertaining them. His aptitude for writing emerged as early as primary school, where he wrote creatively interesting 'compositions'. So far, Dr. Ivey has written and published 15 books that are all available online in e-book and paperback formats.

His first book was his highly-acclaimed 4-volume autobiography – **'It All Began With The May Rains: An Introvert's Remarkable Journey'** – that was published in August 2015, as a tribute to his parents and a tool for inspiring and motivating others, especially young persons, to triumph, as he did, over challenging life circumstances. In writing his autobiography, Dr. Ivey also captures and blends into the narrative of his life story historical tie-ins (notable events) that reflect the zeitgeist (spirit and mood) of the time he grew up in Jamaica. The deployment of this innovative and creative approach to writing gives readers a captivating and educative reading experience. "Engrossing"; "Unputdownable"; "Never-put-downable"; "A page-turner"; "A vocabulary-enhancer"; "Captivating"; "Frank", and 'Relatable' are some of the terms and phrases readers have used to describe his autobiography.

In May 2016, Dr. Ivey published his second book – **'My Daughter & Me: Parenting a Polymath'** – in which he shares his initial trepidation on learning he was going to be a father, and how an 'open education philosophy' plus other strategic parenting actions contributed to his daughter's academic and social success.

Dr. Ivey then published his third book – **'The Golden Boy'** - in December 2016, in which the main character shares with readers the creative adaptations and critical mental competencies required to overcome adversity, forgive one's adversaries, and thus experience post-traumatic growth. Several readers have said this is Dr. Ivey's "most creatively written book!"

And in July 2017, Dr. Ivey published his fourth book – **'Silent River'** – which is a novel that blends erotic excitation and education in exploring the anthropological, biological, cultural, evolutionary, psychological, and sociological forces that drive and mediate amorous desires and behaviours in humans.

Later in 2017, December, Dr. Ivey published his fifth book – **'The Matriarch: Life & Legacy of Edith 'Pearl' Ivey'** – a paean (tribute) to his paternal grandmother, the 'mighty little giant'-who, by eliminating 'land poverty' and bequeathing positive values, established a solid and enduring foundation for the family. In this book, Dr. Ivey not only traced his oldest paternal ancestors in Jamaica back to the year 1822, but he also includes – through an unapologetic Black African-Jamaican-centric lens and positionality – significant slices of Jamaica's history and cultural heritage.

Continuing his writing binge, in June 2018, Dr. Ivey published his sixth book – **'Dog-Hearted: My Life Has Gone to the Dogs'** – in which he offers readers (in particular persons who love Dogs) an intellectually-rich account of the physical and emotional dimensions of one of the strongest bonds on earth between two different species of organisms – that between humans and dogs!

Dr. Ivey's writing spree continued in 2018 and in August of that year he published his seventh book - **'Jamaica: Paradise and Paradox, Volume 1'** - in which he reports the results of a 'scholarly multidimensional scan' he performed on Jamaica - the ups and downs, the beauty and ashes, the problems and possibilities, the failures and triumphs .... and includes a suite of 'crowd-sourced' prescriptions for addressing the socio-economic illnesses afflicting Jamaica. He also calls on his fellow Jamaicans to deploy passionate patriotism to rescue and bequeath a better Jamaica to future generations.

In 2020, demonstrating amazing literary innovation, Dr. Ivey started writing 'pop-up books' – relatively short books crafted for quick reading by busy readers. So, in January 2020, motivated by his civic consciousness and role as a public adult educator, Dr. Ivey wrote and published his first 'pop-up' book **'Active Citizenship: Overcoming Political Apathy in Jamaica'** in which, noting that the time was 'rescue-Jamaica o'clock,' made a cri de coeur (cry from the heart) to his fellow Jamaicans to set and keep their 'civic antenna' at the 'on' position, enabling them to be able to perceive, process, comment, and act on matters of national interest.

Showing no signs of letting up, in February 2020, Dr. Ivey published another 'pop-up' book - **'Toxic Masculinity: Disordered Models of Manhood in Jamaica'** - his 9th book, in which he declared that, "when it comes to how they view and relate to women, many Jamaican men are 'dinosaurs' with outdated schemas (ways of thinking and acting), which need to be updated to be in alignment with contemporary realities." He then discussed the problematic of toxic masculinity, including its historical antecedents, as well as some of its horrible manifestations in Jamaican society. And, acknowledging that toxic masculinity is based on hegemonic patriarchy, which is derived from culture, he posited that the reform of Jamaican men, starting with new models of socialization of boys, was dependent on, and bound up in, cultural change.

'Dog-Hearted: My Life Has Gone to The Dogs': In his usual scholarly, but engaging writing style that is common to all his books, Dr. Ivey offers readers – and in particular dog lovers - an intellectually rich account of the physical and emotional dimensions of one of the strongest bonds between two different species on earth – that between humans and dogs. Don't think, though, that this book is just about dogs – it's much, much deeper!

'Jamaica: Paradise and Paradox, Volume 2': Additional reporting of the results of the 'scholarly multidimensional scan' Dr. Ivey performed on Jamaica - the ups and downs, the beauty and ashes, the problems and possibilities, the failures and triumphs .... and includes a suite of 'crowd-sourced' prescriptions for addressing the socio-economic illnesses afflicting Jamaica. He also calls on his fellow Jamaicans to deploy passionate patriotism to rescue and bequeath a better Jamaica to future generations.

'Fostering a Culture of Lawfulness: Fixing Jamaica's Normalised Abnormalities': In this book, Dr. Ivey reminds that, under the 'social contract' that Thomas Hobbes articulated in 'Leviathan' in the mid-1600s, the maintenance of law and order is the first responsibility of a government. In this well-researched and cogently argued publication, he calls on the Jamaican Government to foster a culture of lawfulness through consistent and fair enforcement of the corpus of laws enacted to regulate the conduct of citizens and the overall public administration of the country.

In November 2021, Dr. Ivey published **'Jamaica: Likkle But Tallawah, Cultural Superpowers & Other Successes'**. This book is about Jamaica's 'Tallawahness.' In it, Dr. Ivey posits that Jamaica's massive reservoir of cultural capital makes it a 'cultural superpower' that has projected its cultural influence and impact globally - a reality that is encapsulated in the expression 'Wi likkle but wi tallawah' – making Jamaica the biggest little country on Earth!

In May 2022, Dr. Ivey published **'The Case for Reparations for Chattel Slavery: An Overdue Debt for The Worst Crime in The History of The World.'**

And in July 2022, he published his 14th book, **'Jamaica: Paradise & Paradox, Volume 3'**.

Dr. Ivey immensely enjoys the intellectual liberation of his cerebralist lifestyle ('life of the mind') and the psychological and physiological consolations and gifts of nature; he is eager to retire to continue his writing life on the bucolic, unspoiled, and exquisite beaches of Jamaica - his country of birth and where he currently lives.

****

Selected Bibliography
===================####=================

Altbach, P. G., & Kelly, G. P. 1992. Education and colonialism (2nd ed.), Piscataway, NJ: Transaction Publishers, cited by Hope Mayne & Raymond Dixon, The Epistemological Dilemma: Student Teachers Shared Experiences of Jamaica's National Standards Curriculum (NSC),' Journal of Curriculum and Teaching, Vol 9, No 4, 2020]

Blake Hannah, B. 2010. Growing Out: Black Hair & Black Pride in the Swinging Sixties. Hansib Publications. London.

Cesaire, A. 1972. Discourse on Colonisation: A Poetics of Anticolonialism.

Cookson, P. S. 1998. (Ed.), Program planning for the training and continuing education of adults: North American perspectives. Krieger Publishing Company. Florida, USA.

Curtin, M., Hamilton, B., & Patterson, P. 1987. Marcus Garvey. JAMAL Foundation, Kingston, Jamaica.

Edwards, W. 1988. Garveyism: Organizing the masses or mass organization? In Lewis, R., & Bryan, P. (Eds.), Garvey: His work and Impact (pp. 215 – 226). Institute of Social and Economic Research and Department of Extra-Mural Studies, The University of the West Indies, Mona, Kingston, Jamaica.

Espiritu, A. Amy Ashford Garvey. www.blackpast.org; accessed July 4, 2021.

Frantz Fanon. Black Skin, White Masks. Grove Press, New York. 1952, 2008.

Freire, P. 1970. Pedagogy of the Oppressed. Continuum New York, USA.

Grant, C. 2008. Negro With a Hat: The Rise and Fall of Marcus Garvey. Oxford University Press

Girvan, N. 1988. The political economy of race in the Americas: The historical context of Garveyism. In Lewis R., & Bryan, P. (Eds.), Garvey: His work and impact (pp. 11-21). Institute of Social and Economic Research and Department of Extra-Mural Studies, The University of the West Indies, Mona, Kingston, Jamaica.

Hill, R. 1987. Marcus Garvey: Life and Lessons. University of California Press. Berkeley, California, USA.

Ivey, P. 2014. 'Illuminating the Andragogical Dimension of Marcus Garvey's Legacy, Jamaica's First National Hero'. Journal of Arts Science and Technology (Volume 7, pp. 1-11).

Jacques-Garvey, A. 1969. Philosophy and Opinions of Marcus Garvey. Vols. 1 & 2. Arno Press, New York.

Jacques-Garvey, A. 1970. Garvey and Garveyism. London: Collier Books.

Jones, K. 1993. Marcus Garvey Said.

Knowles, M.S. 1998. The Andragogical Model: The Evolution of a Model of Learning. In Cookson, P.S. (Ed.), Program planning for the training and continuing education of adults: North American perspectives (pp. 46-56). Krieger Publishing Company. Florida, USA.

Lewis, R. 2018. Marcus Garvey. The University of the West Indies Press. Jamaica.

Lewis, R. 1988. Garvey's Perspective on Jamaica. In Lewis, R., & Bryan, P. (Eds.), Garvey: His work and impact (pp. 229-242). Institute of Social and Economic Research and Department of Extra-Mural Studies, The University of the West Indies, Mona, Kingston, Jamaica.

Lewis, R. 1987. Marcus Garvey: Anti-Colonial Champion. Karla Publishing, London.

Mandela, N. 1994. Long walk to freedom: The autobiography of Nelson Mandela. Little, Brown and Company. New York, USA.

Manley, M. 1974. The Politics of Change: A Jamaican Testament. Andre Deutsch Ltd., UK.

McCarthy, P. R., & McCarthy, H. M. 2006. When case studies are not enough: Integrating experiential learning into business curricula. Journal of Education for Business, 81(4), 201-204.

Neita. L. 2016. Garvey and today's generation. The Daily Observer, May 14, 2016.

Patsides, N. 2005. Marcus Garvey, Race Idealism and his Vision of Jamaican Self-government. Caribbean Quarterly, 51(1), 37-52. Retrieved July 10, 2021, from http://www.jstor.org/stable/40654492.

Rodney, W. 1974. How Europe Underdeveloped Africa. Howard University Press.

Sherlock, P., & Bennett, H. 1998. The Story of the Jamaican People. Ian Randle Publishers. Kingston, Jamaica.

Wilson, A.N. 2014. The Developmental Psychology of the Black Child. 2nd Edition. Afrikan World InfoSystems.

****

Made in the USA
Columbia, SC
09 July 2023

19932368R00239